HIGH-PERFORMANCE CHEVY Small-Block Cylinder Heads

GRAHAM HANSEN

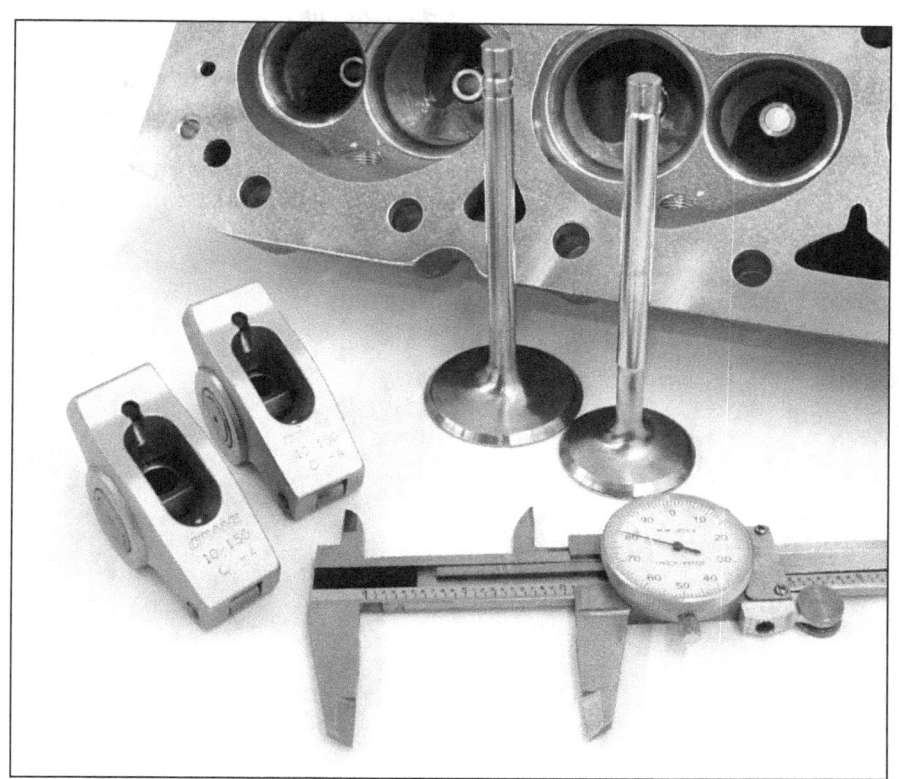

CarTech®

Copyright © 2007 by Graham Hansen

All rights reserved. All text and photographs in this publication are the property of the author, unless otherwise noted or credited. It is unlawful to reproduce – or copy in any way – resell, or redistribute this information without the express written permission of the publisher.

All text, photographs, drawings, and other artwork (hereafter referred to as information) contained in this publication is sold without any warranty as to its usability or performance. In all cases, original manufacturer's recommendations, procedures, and instructions supersede and take precedence over descriptions herein. Specific component design and mechanical procedures – and the qualifications of individual readers – are beyond the control of the publisher, therefore the publisher disclaims all liability, either expressed or implied, for use of the information in this publication. All risk for its use is entirely assumed by the purchaser/user. In no event will CarTech®, Inc., or the author, be liable for any indirect, special, or consequential damages, including but not limited to personal injury or any other damages, arising out of the use or misuse of any information in this publication.

This book is an independent publication, and the author(s) and/or publisher thereof are not in any way associated with, and are not authorized to act on behalf of, any of the manufacturers included in this book. All registered trademarks are the property of their owners. The publisher reserves the right to revise this publication or change its content from time to time without obligation to notify any persons of such revisions or changes.

Edited by: Josh Brown

ISBN-13 978-1-61325-063-1
Item # SA125P

Printed in USA

CarTech®
39966 Grand Avenue
North Branch, MN 55056
Telephone (651) 277-1200 • (800) 551-4754 • Fax: (651) 277-1203
www.cartechbooks.com

Back cover top: One of the best ways to evaluate the performance potential of a cylinder head is by testing the ports on a flow bench. The SuperFlow 600-cfm flow bench has become an industry standard because of its excellent repeatability and ease of use.

Back cover middle: Most of the conservative cylinder heads can really benefit from slight port work within the port throat area, just underneath the valve job. Always go easy here and concentrate your attention on the exhaust side of the head.

Back cover bottom: Flowing an intake manifold on the head to measure flow reduction is a good way to judge the effectiveness of the intake. A single plane style intake will always test better than a dual plane, so the best test is to see which style intake among dual planes or single planes is the best.

TABLE OF CONTENTS

Chapter 1: Introduction 4

Chapter 2: Flow Bench..........................9
   Test Drop 9
   Inclinations 11
   Testing 12
   Evaluation 14
   Conclusion..........................17

Chapter 3: Airflow Basics 20
   Intake Flow 22
   Exhaust Flow 27
   Conclusion 35

Chapter 4: Production Heads 37
   Head History 37
   Iron Maidens 38
   Aluminum Upgrade 40
   Vortec Heads 42
   Conclusion..........................47
Heads in Review 48

Chapter 5: Small Aftermarket Heads..50
   S/R Torquer 50
   Dart Iron Eagle SS..........................51
   Edelbrock Performer 52
   Edelbrock E-Tec 53
   Edelbrock Performer RPM 55
   RHS Vortec Iron 56
   Conclusion 58
   Heads in Review 58

Chapter 6: Medium Aftermarket
   Heads 60
   AFR 180 (Version 1) 61
   AFR 180 Eliminator..........................62
   Brodix Race-Rite 180 64
   Brodix –8 Pro 64
   Dart 180 Pro 1..........................65
   AFR 195 (Version 1) 66
   AFR 195 Eliminator..........................66
   TFS 195 68

Canfield 195..........................68
Conclusion..........................69
Heads in Review 69

Chapter 7: Large Port Heads..........................71
   Edelbrock E-Tec 200..........................74
   Dart Iron Eagle 200..........................75
   Dart Platinum 200 76
   Dart Pro 1 200 Aluminum 76
   World Products Sportsman II..........................76
   Brodix Race-Rite 200 77
   AFR 210 (Version 1) 78
   AFR 210 Eliminator 78
   Dart Iron Eagle 215 79
   Dart Platinum 215 Iron 79
   Dart Pro 1 215 Aluminum 80
   Edelbrock Victor Jr. 215
      Aluminum 80
   TFS 215 81
   Brodix Track 1 215 81
   Motown 220 Aluminum 82
   Canfield 220..........................83
   AFR 220 (Version 1) 84
   AFR 220 Eliminator 84
   Dart CNC 227 84
   AFR 227 Eliminator 85
   Dart Pro 1 230..........................86
   Conclusion 87
   Heads in Review 87

Chapter 8: Small-Block Race Heads...89
   Valve Angle..........................89
   Canted Valves 90
   Head Changes 91
   Advantages..........................92
   Conclusion 93
   Race Head Flow Charts 94

Chapter 9: Cylinder Head Rebuilding
   and Assembly..........................95
   Valve Guides..........................95
   Valves..........................96

Valve Seat Angles..........................97
Springs, Seats and Retainers 99
Installed Height 102
Retainer-To-Seal Clearance 103
Coil Bind 104
Conclusion 104

Chapter 10: Basic Porting
   Techniques..........................106
   Tools of the Trade..........................107
   Getting Started 110
   Chamber Mods..........................113
   Conclusion 113

Chapter 11: Combustion Chamber .115
   Chamber Shape and Wet Flow ..117
   Clues to Combustion..........................118
   Conclusion 120

Chapter 12: Matching Cams and
   Cylinder Heads..........................126
   Heads and Cams..........................128
   A Matter of Timing..........................133
   Conclusion 135

Chapter 13: Power Packages..........................136
   Engine 1: 355-ci Mild Street
      Package 138
   Engine 2: Mild 355 Street
      Package II..........................139
   Engine 3: The 383 Power Deal..140
   Engine 4: The 406 Burner..........................141
   Engine 5: 434-ci Small-Block Street
      Heater 142
   Engine 6: Monster 454 143
   Simulated 402-ci GEN III
      Engine..........................143

Appendix A: Sources 144

CHAPTER 1

INTRODUCTION

One of the best reasons to decide to build a small-block Chevy is that this engine family enjoys the largest selection of aftermarket cylinder heads of any domestic performance engine. Aluminum heads represent the majority of these selections and the selection is vast.

Ask any professional performance engine builder about the most powerful and important component in an engine and he will invariably answer with "cylinder heads." The simple fact is that if you can afford to invest serious money in one component for a street engine, in most cases it should be a set of cylinder heads. Sure, you need decent induction and exhaust systems, a good cam, and respectable compression, but all of those things support and are supported by a good set of cylinder heads.

For those performance enthusiasts who pledge allegiance to the Bow Tie flag, this is one of those times when it's good to be a small-block Chevy guy. No other internal combustion engine made has more parts available and more information written about it. Chevy's little Mouse motor has a flood of cylinder heads available. From production iron pieces through the most exotic race-bred drag race or NASCAR-derived powerplant, the small-block Chevy stands alone as the most prolific performance engine on the planet. Let the Mopar and Ford guys wallow in their own self-pity—it's good to be a Mouse motor guy.

Of course, this incredibly broad selection swath brings its own set of responsibilities. How do you choose the best cylinder head for your application? That's what this book is dedicated to uncover. But you'll have to work for it. Not to say that we're going to make things hard on you, but in order to really understand all the mysteries that surround cylinder heads, you must put forth a certain amount of effort. Most of what you will have to invest is just a little bit of your time in reading these chapters. We've designed this book exactly like its predecessor, *High-Performance Chevy Small-Block Cams & Valvetrains*, in that we start with the basics and work our way into more in-depth concepts and variables in an attempt to uncover all those subtle nuances that make up the internal combustion engine. It never ceases to amaze this author that a man-made invention could be so confusing and have led to as much discussion and wonderment.

This book taps into some of the best small-block Chevy cylinder head resources this country has to offer with a combination of insight and best guesstimates because much

INTRODUCTION

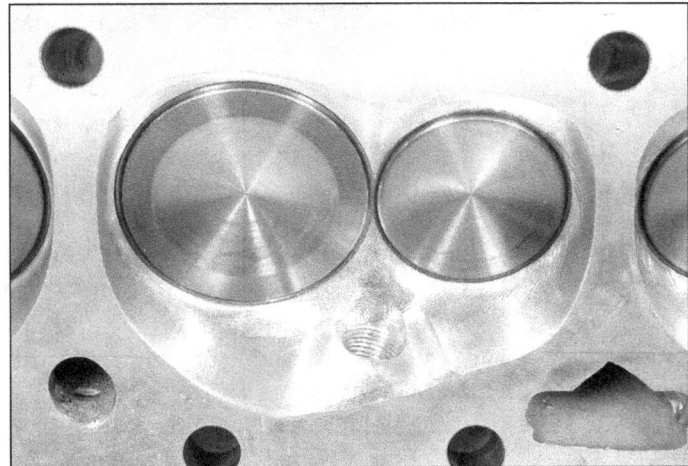

Besides intake port flow, one of the more important features of a cylinder head is the combustion chamber shape. Not only does the chamber affect port flow, but the shape of the chamber also has a direct impact on combustion efficiency.

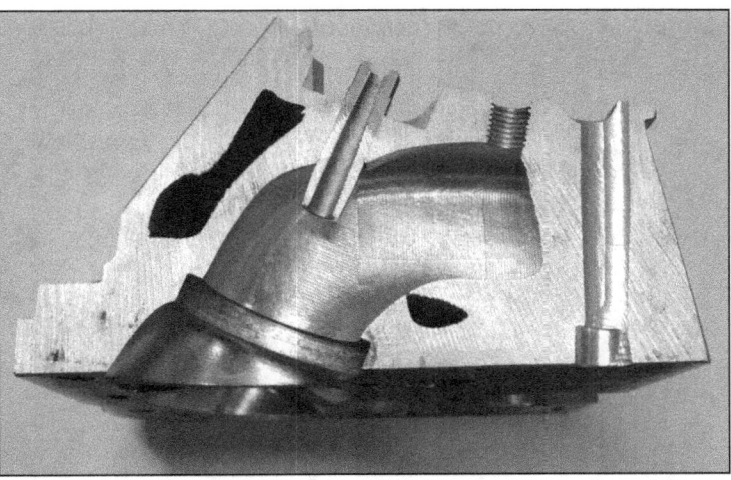

The shape of the intake port directly affects port flow. One of the things you will notice with a properly configured intake port is the gentle radii and no abrupt, sharp turns that can not only cause flow deficiencies but also create air-fuel separation.

of what we know about port design and airflow management falls under the category of art rather than science. The science part is well documented with computers now playing an ever-increasing role in port design and prototype development as well as cylinder head production. Increasingly more complex programs are just now becoming available to small aftermarket companies with another tool for the development process. These programs, most often referred to as CFD or computational fluid dynamics programs, can predict with increasing accuracy the type of flow that a given port will produce long before the first prototype model is produced. These programs were originally designed to assist aerodynamicists in developing wing designs for aircrafts to maximize lift while minimizing drag. The programs eventually filtered down into the automotive field to be used to predict air movement through a port.

This is the high-tech side of the business. On a more realistic note, the majority of performance cylinder heads for the small-block Chevy are still developed the old fashioned way: with a flow bench and a grinder. But even standard applications like the small-block's production 23-degree intake and exhaust valve angles are subject to revision in the search for more power. This is part of the small-block Chevy's heritage that is perhaps the most frustrating, since this valve angle is most restrictive. This dimension refers to the angle of the valves in relationship to the block deck surface with the top of the valve angled in toward the engine centerline. In order to produce a compact engine design, the original small-block Chevy engine designers also "bent" the ports inboard to accommodate this valve angle.

It's no secret that air has inertia and that at speed, much like a racecar, air doesn't like to turn corners. When it does, it loses a certain amount of speed in the process. This energy loss (and that's really what it is) reduces the total flow produced by the port, and the direct result of that is less power. What we intend to discover with this book is how best to recover that energy without sacrificing power in other areas to make more at higher engine speeds.

This is perhaps the greatest lesson that any performance enthusiast can learn in the process of building a performance street engine. The concept is really very simple, and it actually applies to almost all aspects of life. It's easy to make power with almost any internal combustion engine within a very narrow power band. Formula 1 engines that spin all the way up to 19 000 rpm make phenomenal horsepower per cubic inch, around 750 hp from 146 cubic inches—creating an outrageous 5 hp/ci. But these engines do so at stratospheric engine speeds and all within a 1,000 to 1,500 rpm power band. Let's define this as the power created between peak torque and peak horsepower. A street engine may also only have a 1,500 to 1,700 rpm power band (between 4,000 and 5,700 rpm, for example). However, that engine must still deliver decent throttle response and torque all the way from its 850-rpm idle to its

CHAPTER 1

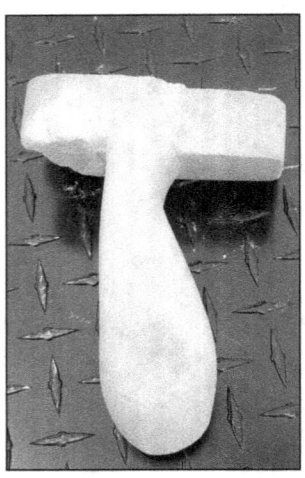

Although rarely employed by the average enthusiasts, a rubber plug or duplicate of the intake and exhaust ports is a great way to allow the port designer to closely evaluate the entire port and to more accurately measure cross-sectional area throughout the entire port. This is actually a sand core for the first version AFR 210 head.

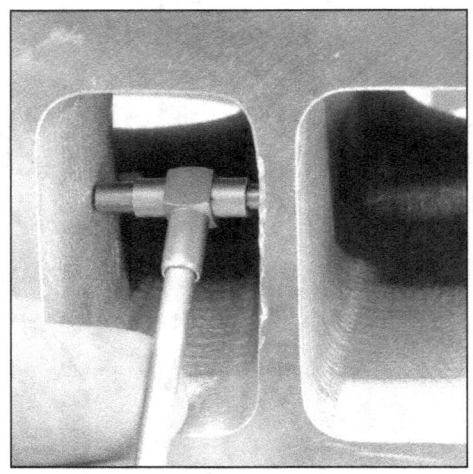

Another critical element in port flow evaluation is something called port cross-sectional area. Measuring this area should be a prerequisite for any serious cylinder head evaluation effort.

6,000-rpm redline, and must do so for years of reliable service. Ponder that for a few moments and you begin to see the incredible range of compromises that a street engine must endure. This is also dealt with in this book.

The chapters that follow this introduction deal mainly with what has become known as the GEN I small-block Chevy. To clarify these classifications, GEN I is defined as the original small-block Chevy produced between 1955 and 1991. This constitutes the overwhelming majority of the production-run small-block. This engine went through some minor revisions that had more to do with solving nagging little problems (like rear main seal oil leaks and the like) and only established a few minor tweaks to the cylinder heads, that we get into in Chapter 4, on production pieces like the iron Vortec head.

The GEN II small-block is defined as the 1992 and later engines identified as the LT1 and LT4 versions. They retained the majority of the GEN I architecture, but with a few significant changes. The most drastic alteration for the GEN II small-block was the engine's "reverse cooling" system. The GEN II engine moved coolant through the cylinder heads first and then through the block, which is the opposite of the GEN I engine.

On occasion we may touch on the GEN III and GEN IV production versions of the small-block that, if you are part of the small-block *cognoscenti*, you no doubt know is the new production engine used in the Camaro, Corvette, and new trucks. We use these new engines and their cylinder heads as reference points mainly to evaluate how good a job GM has done with these new engines, especially with the performance variants like the LS6 and LS7 powerplants. When Chevy produces a production engine that makes an honest-to-God 505 hp, we must all sit up and take notice. We may all pay homage to the performance engines of the past, but frankly this new LS7 engine makes them all pale in comparison. It's that good.

You have no doubt already breezed through this book and perused its pages and perhaps noticed that we have expended one whole chapter exclusively on flow benches with a focus on the Super-Flow 600 bench. This flow bench has become the standard in the performance industry, despite its significant $8,000 investment. The beauty of a flow bench is its ability to deliver quick and concise concrete results to questions of airflow. Perhaps you've also heard the statement, as we have, "the flow bench will lie to you." While far be it for us to discount or trivialize these statements, they are probably true within the realm of a few focused and hardcore race-only instances. For the street-engine crowd, our experience in front of the flow bench has been nothing less than completely consistent with engine testing. In other words, if the flow bench shows a significant improvement in flow, you can be certain of a power increase. The details, as you will see, are worth knowing.

The remaining chapters in this book take a very detailed look at all the individual areas of the cylinder head. The major focus is on both intake and exhaust port design, shape, flow, revisions, selection, cross-sectional area, and the like. But we also delve into combustion chamber design and shape in addition to valve size and shape along with even some more esoteric areas such as the head's water jackets. One cylinder head manufacturer called this area a place of "golden opportunity," which sounds promising.

We also talk about the flow potential for many different cylinder heads and look at areas where the backyard porter can extract power at a very reasonable cost. This is an area

INTRODUCTION

One of the best ways to evaluate the performance potential of a cylinder head is by testing the ports on a flow bench. The SuperFlow 600-cfm flow bench has become an industry standard because of its excellent repeatability and ease of use.

The next evolution of the flow bench is something called a wet flow bench that evaluates both the air and fuel flow characteristics as both substances transition the port and enter the cylinder. This is Dart's very expensive wet flow bench developed by Joe Mondello for Dick Maskin and crew.

that is shrouded in urban legend, folk tales, and outright misinformation. Our goal is not to transform you into a "book-learned" porting magician. Instead, we point you in the direction of areas where your focused attention and judicial use of the porting tool will be most justly rewarded—and also where it can just as easily be punished!

We also spend a good deal of space on the process of selecting the right cylinder head for your street or mild race application. It borders on the repetitive to bash on the old "bigger is better" wheeze, but the sheer number of enthusiasts who are easily swayed by the siren song of big horsepower are also the ones who most often fall into that trap. Thankfully, going excessively overboard on port size is not as big a problem with the small-block as it is with its steroid-infested big-block cousin. It's incredibly easy to dive off the deep end with respect to Rat motor cylinder heads, and frankly the cylinder head companies will sell you whatever you want to buy, regardless of

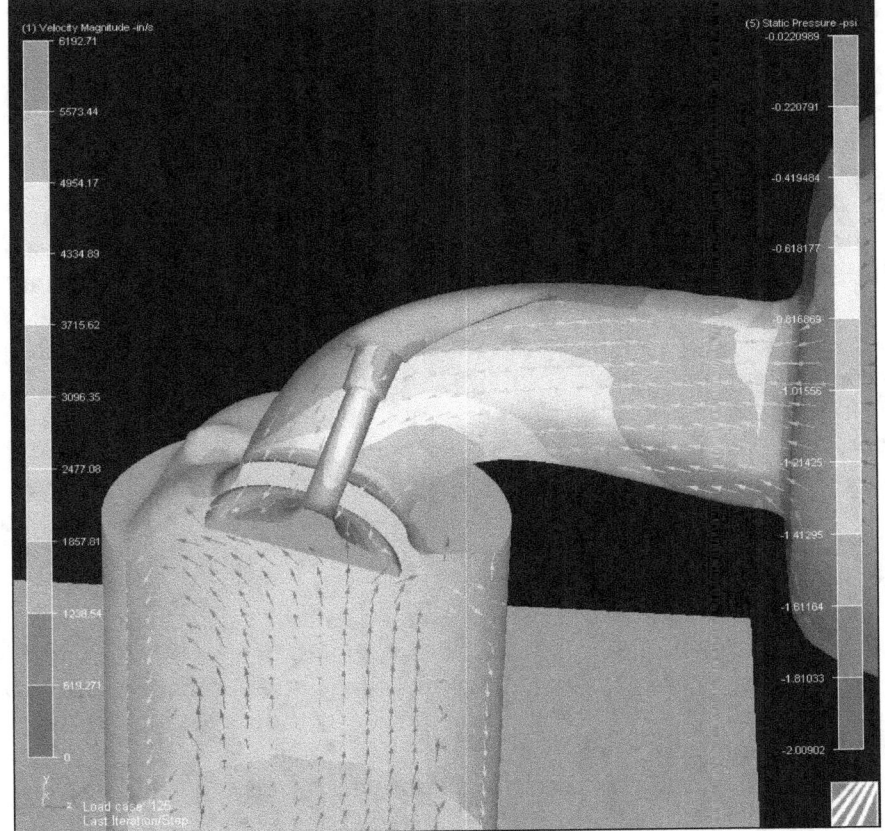

It was only a matter of time before aerospace and aviation aerodynamic advancements trickled down to the automotive high-performance arena. This is a screen capture of a computation fluid dynamics (CFD) program used by Edelbrock to create and evaluate intake and exhaust ports.

HIGH-PERFORMANCE CHEVY SMALL-BLOCK CYLINDER HEADS

CHAPTER 1

Even with all the excellent computer simulation and evaluation programs available, it still comes down to the established engine dyno method to evaluate a cylinder head's true potential. The dyno rarely lies.

Eventually, all this technology ends up in your engine compartment. The selection process and the right cylinder heads for your application depend mainly on how you intend to use the vehicle and engine. If you have an application, chances are there's a head that is a perfect match.

whether it's the best head for what you need.

The small-block does not suffer as greatly from the debilitating effects of oversized port cross-section (unless you get into thumper race heads), mainly because the engine's original architecture prevents the aftermarket from creating cavernous intake ports. Nevertheless, it is still rather easy to choose a somewhat oversized intake port in search of big-time horsepower, which is why we devote space in several chapters to matching cylinder heads with somewhat specific street applications in terms of power and driveability to ease your decision-making process as much as possible.

We also devote a fair amount of space in Chapter 12 to matching camshafts and cylinder heads. The focus is on using certain concepts to help you decide on the best cam that will optimize the power potential of your engine without overly sacrificing street manners. Ideally, this is the context around which this entire book is created. Given a choice on camshaft or cylinder head, it's important you know that this book most often errs on the conservative side of the decision line. We have imposed this basic concept on this effort mainly because we feel that the majority of the enthusiasts reading this are looking for answers that go beyond the combination that the hero down the street has created through trial and error. We often see hot rodders more than willing to accept poor driveability, less-than-optimal part-throttle performance, and abysmal fuel mileage at the price of strong full-throttle power. This book takes the path less taken and approaches this street effort from the standpoint that you can have both excellent street manners and good power without having to sacrifice either. If that means some of the recommendations in this book are overly conservative, then so be it. We feel it is better to be slightly conservative and have excellent mid-range torque and throttle response than it is to dive into the deep end of the pool only to discover too late that the water is a bit over your head. By design, we intend to set you up to apply what you have learned through these examples, and then to go on and create other engine combinations that will take this whole performance industry to the next level.

So to play the game by the rules, it's best to start with the beginning chapters and work your way from the front to the back in chronological order. Don't worry if you don't completely understand everything that is delivered in each chapter through the first read. Sometimes it takes a second review to really understand the nuances of airflow and how these ideas come together to create horsepower and torque. But if you employ the ideas that are delivered in this book, you will come away with a much better appreciation for both the art and the science of airflow and how it can turn your pedestrian powerplant into a fire-breathing street engine.

CHAPTER 2

FLOW BENCH

The SuperFlow 600 flow bench is easily the most popular and capable flow bench on the market today, so this is the bench that we use as our standard for discussion.

You might wonder why we would be starting a book on small-block Chevy cylinder heads with a chapter on flow benches. The reason is that most of what this book is about concerns intake and exhaust port flow. The best way to accurately measure this air movement is with a flow bench. So, in order to grasp the importance of the numbers that we are flinging about throughout this publication, we must first understand what a flow bench is and what it does. Before we do that, let's first illustrate what a flow bench won't tell you. It won't tell you horsepower or torque. We can infer that from improvements (or losses) that we measure on a flow bench, but there is no direct, irrefutable evidence of a hard and fast horsepower increase with a given airflow improvement, and it would be misleading to make that connection. The flow bench does not always tell you that you're heading down a dead-end path. Racers we know swear that their flow bench lies to them on a regular basis like some kind of evil automotive Ouija board. And a flow bench will probably not make you rich. In fact, if you decide to invest in a quality bench like a SuperFlow 600, it may be a significant financial burden—an $8,000 bench is not something you pick up on your way home from work like a gallon of milk.

All that sounds like a flow bench is some kind of angry automotive beast that must be approached carefully and cautiously—and in a way, it is. While it is a wonderful tool, flow benches are incredibly adept at eating an enormous amount of your time. But if approached with an eye toward using it as a learning tool that teaches you what port flow is all about and what works and what doesn't, then the flow bench is a great invention. But don't expect the flow bench to do everything for you. You will be sorely disappointed.

Test Drop

Testing cylinder heads is all about measuring airflow and evaluating changes made to port flow in search of more flow. The bench is also a wonderful comparison tool, assuming that your testing is done properly. This requires air movement. In your engine, the rapid downward motion of the piston creates low pressure. With the intake valve open, there is a direct path from the cylinder to atmospheric pressure (especially when the throttle is wide open) and the higher atmospheric pressure creates air movement toward the cylinder in order to equalize this difference in pressure. This may sound overly simplistic, but for a reason. Enthusiasts talk about how a piston "sucks" or that it "pulls" air into the cylinder. The reality is that atmospheric pressure pushes the air in that direction. Even naturally aspirated engines don't suck—they are pressure fed. That's why all engines run better at sea level than they do at

CHAPTER 2

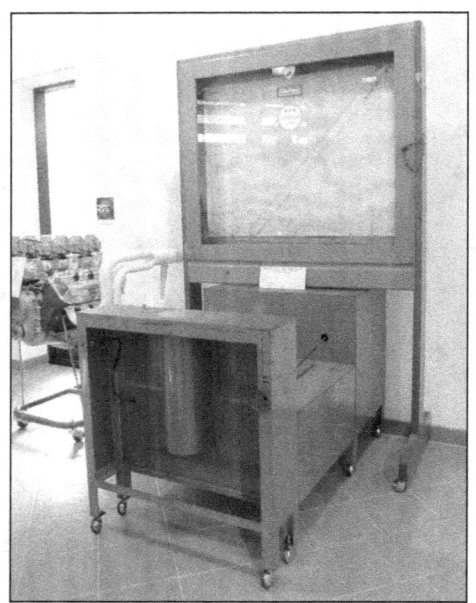

Long before SuperFlow, many dedicated enthusiasts and businesses built their own flow bench in order to evaluate airflow. This bench was built for Edelbrock by Carl Axtell in the late 1950s and currently occupies a place of honor in Edelbrock's museum in Torrance, California.

5,000 feet above sea level. Ask any racer how well his car runs at Bandimere Speedway's mile-high Denver, Colorado, altitude compared to Pomona, California's 900-feet elevation. We're making this point because it's a common misconception, and it's always best to start with the basics before we move on to more complex applications.

A flow bench uses electric devices like vacuum cleaner motors that are designed to move large volumes of air to create low pressure. Generally, large airflow benches employ several smaller electric motors used together to generate the larger test depression necessary for high-performance work. Next, the bench must also be able to move air in both directions so that the user can accurately test intake and exhaust ports. This is accomplished with a simple flow director device that changes the direction of the airflow inside the bench depending upon whether you are testing intake or exhaust ports. Let's assume for a minute that we now have a bench with electric motors and a flow director so that air moves in and out of the bench freely, we have mounted a cylinder head on a cylinder adapter of the proper diameter, and we have a way to open the valves to a precise lift. Now we need some way to measure how much air actually flows through the ports.

Expanding the previous discussion on pressure differential and creating a low-pressure area that creates air movement, the size and number of motors in the flow bench determine the amount of test depression that bench can create. The typical SuperFlow 600 bench uses nine electric vacuum cleaner motors that draw roughly 37 amps of electrical current when running since all the motors run whenever the bench is operating. A test depression is an expression of vacuum or pressure less than atmospheric. The term "depression" probably originated from the fact that when vacuum is applied to a water manometer, the water column is moved, or dropped (depressed), by atmospheric pressure. A manometer is a very simple device beginning with a vented reservoir from which extends a vertical tube calibrated (for our use, in inches) to measure a test depression. One end of the tube is vented to atmosphere and the other end is connected to the tube where the test depression will occur. If

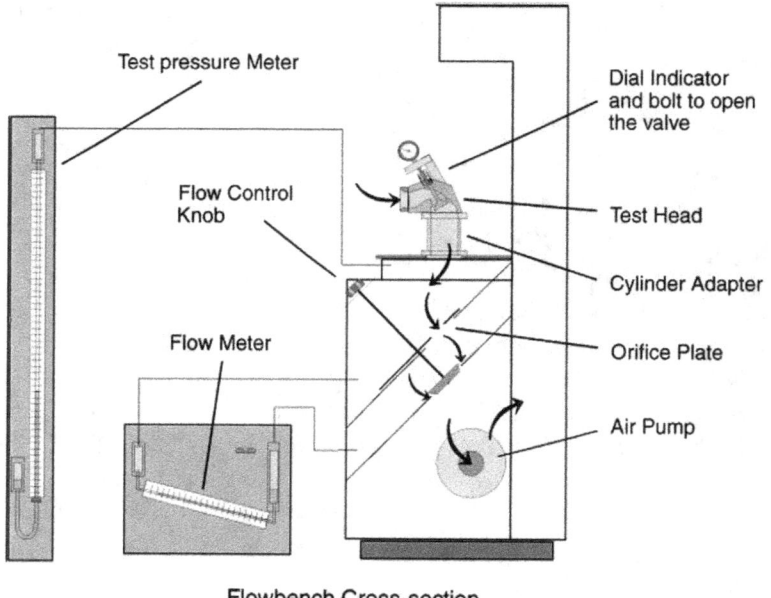

This illustration reveals the basic flow path for a typical SuperFlow bench. For the intake side, the blower motor creates a depression measured by the vertical (test pressure) manometer. Air moves through the head, cylinder adapter, and through the orifice plate. The flow meter (or inclined manometer) measures the pressure differential across the orifice plate and this expressed as a percentage of the calibrated flow orifice is what is used to calculate CFM of airflow.

you've ever seen a vertical barometer, this is a manometer that uses mercury as its working fluid. For flow bench work, the test fluid is water. So if a test depression (again, a vacuum) is created in the flow bench underneath the cylinder head with an intake valve open, for example, then atmospheric pressure will push air from the surrounding area through the intake port and into the bench. We can use a manometer to measure the amount of test depression to establish a standard test pressure by measuring the depression just under the base of the cylinder adapter.

According to S-A Design's *Smokey Yunick's Power Secrets*, written by Yunick with help from author Larry Schreib in 1983, Smokey was a pioneer in the design and implementation of a performance-oriented flow bench in the early 1950s. The bench was designed to accurately measure airflow through a cylinder head. According to Yunick, he did extensive testing to determine an ideal test pressure. Early tests previous to Yunick's work had chosen 10 inches of water as the standard test depression; however, Yunick discovered significant improvements in accuracy of port changes when using test pressures between 26 and 28 inches of water after evaluating pressures at 2-inch increments all the way up to 34 inches. Since 28 inches of water is equivalent to 1 psi, this has become, it appears from Yunick's efforts, the automotive industry standard for cylinder head port testing.

Inclinations

So now that we have established a test depression from which to work, the next thing we need to figure out is how to measure the actual amount of flow through our test port. Using a SuperFlow 600 bench as our standard, we can use a second manometer to

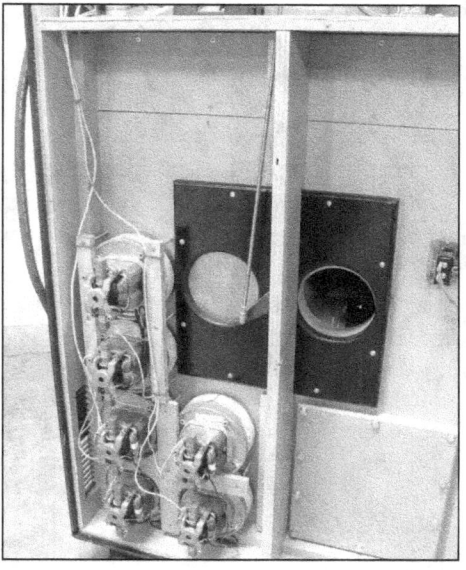

This view is inside the back wall of a SuperFlow 600 bench. In this particular case, this bench has been modified with additional motors to be able to test larger intake ports at 28 inches of water.

establish flow. In this case, the bench employs an inclined manometer set at 45 degrees. This manometer is connected to either side of the orifice plate located inside the flow bench. SuperFlow benches use four orifice plates of varying size in order to improve accuracy. A wide range of airflow can be accurately measured this way by using the same inclined manometer. Here's how it works: If we are measuring flow at 0.050 inch of valve lift, there is very little actual flow. So we need a relatively small flow orifice in order to produce above 50 percent flow efficiency numbers on our inclined manometer. As we increase valve opening, volume increases. This requires a larger flow orifice in the flow bench in order to accurately measure the percentage of flow through the larger orifice. The SuperFlow 600 bench offers six different flow ranges to provide the necessary accuracy up to 600 cfm of flow volume.

Because the inclined manometer is connected to either side of the flow orifice, what we are measuring is the pressure differential across this orifice. If we know the actual maximum flow of this orifice, the pressure differential expressed by the inclined manometer can be used as a percentage of actual flow. For example, if the flow for range 4 is 300 cfm on the intake side, then 75 percent flow of 300 would be 225 cfm. The CFM flow number for each flow range is measured by Super-Flow and stamped on the side of each flow bench for this reason. These flow range numbers are established by SuperFlow after the bench is constructed and tested and vary slightly for each bench. As you can see from the chart (Flow Numbers), we've included that exhaust flow is slightly better than the intake side,

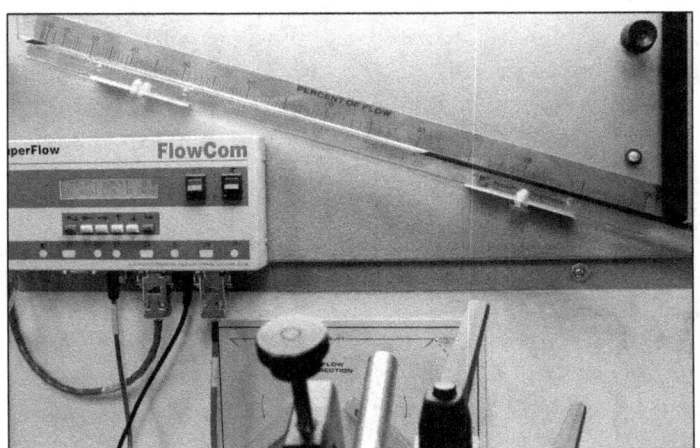

The inclined manometer measures the pressure drop across the flow orifice and delivers this information as a percentage of flow for the orifice being used. This means that a 75 percent flow on a 300 cfm orifice equals 225 cfm.

CHAPTER 2

Manometers

A manometer is defined as a simple device that measures pressures of gases. In terms of flow benches, the most common manometers are simply glass or plastic liquid-filled tubes that are directly affected by pressure at a given location. For the purpose of relating to flow benches, this discussion is narrowed to u-tube and reservoir manometers using water as the test medium. As an example of another medium, atmospheric pressure is most often expressed in terms of inches of mercury, using a reservoir-type manometer filled with mercury.

Water is used for testing pressures in cylinder heads because it is not as dense, which creates a way to more accurately measure small changes in test pressure. A u-shaped manometer is really nothing more than a length of plastic tubing you can buy at your local hardware store that can be affixed to a vertical plate or board. Filled with water treated with a food coloring to make it easer to see, we can apply pressure to one side of this device and watch the column height change based on the strength of this applied pressure. If we calibrate this change in height in terms of inches using nothing more than a simple ruler, we now have a way to accurately measure small changes in pressure. In the case of a u-tube manometer, the total change in height represented by both columns is used to determine the level of pressure differential. So if we apply pressure to one end of the tube, and the water moves two inches down on the pressure side and two inches up on the opposite side of the tube, the pressure differential is expressed as being a test pressure of four inches of water.

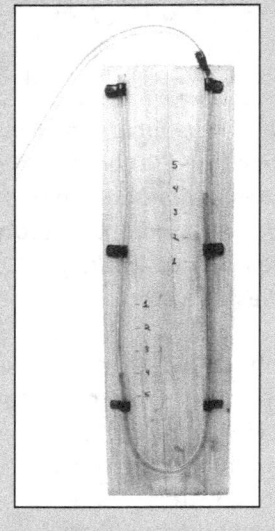

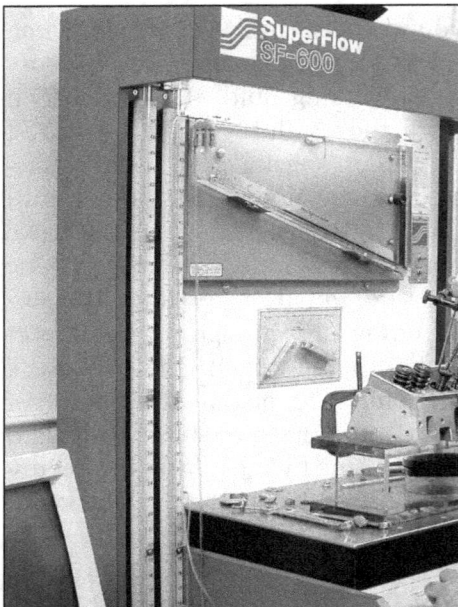

A vertical manometer measures the actual test depression and is referenced just underneath the cylinder adapter. Most performance aftermarket cylinder heads are tested at 28 inches of water. All SuperFlow 600 benches include a second vertical manometer that can be used in several different applications, such as measuring port pressures at various points in the intake port.

but each bench will be slightly different. The six flow ranges are designed to maintain bench accuracy by maintaining sufficient flow velocity through a small enough orifice to push the inclined manometer above 50 percent, which improves accuracy. As a point of reference, because each flow orifice is calibrated, there is no need to "correct" the flow numbers based on atmospheric conditions. This is a common error made by flow bench operators.

Testing

Now that we know how the flow bench operates, we can get into the specifics of how to use the bench properly to obtain maximum benefit. The first step is to choose the proper cylinder adapter. From the photos, you can see that a short length of cylinder attaches the cylinder head to the bench. Different cylinders may be adapted to simulate different bore sizes. For a small-block Chevy, a 4.030 bore size is the most typical, but testing reveals that using larger-bore cylinders such as a 4.155 or even a 4.250-inch bore (for a 454ci small-block for example) will deliver higher flow numbers. This is why you need to closely inspect the entire test process when evaluating flow bench reports. Intake flow numbers improve because the cylinder wall is moved further away from the intake valve, unshrouding the valve and improving flow.

Once the cylinder bore adapter is in place, most flow bench operators employ a head gasket between the cylinder head and the cylinder adapter. Ensuring that the head is centered over the cylinder improves the accuracy of your test procedure: A little trick that works well is to center the gasket and then mark the bolt holes with a Sharpie marker. Then line up the head with the gasket, and the head will be centered on the bore. Some shops drill the horizontal top of the cylinder adapter for bolts, but most merely use piston-grip clamps or C-clamps.

Once the head is firmly affixed to the cylinder adapter, the next step is

Conversion Factors

Not everyone evaluates ports at 28 inches of water test depression. SuperFlow, for example, rates all of its testing at 25 inches of water. The good news is that it is easy to convert different test depressions with this included conversion chart from SuperFlow that allows the user to convert his test data either to 28 inches, or to a different test pressure. Keep in mind that the greater the difference in test pressures away from our standard 28 inches, the greater the chance for error. If you find the need to do this on a regular basis for multiple valve lifts, it would probably be a good idea to create a spreadsheet program that would calculate these values quickly and efficiently. Note that this chart uses 25 inches of water as the standard.

Test Pressure (Inches of water)	Intake Flow	Exhaust Flow
45	0.980	1.016
40	0.985	1.012
35	0.990	1.008
30	0.995	1.004
28	0.997	1.003
25	1.000	1.000
20	1.005	0.996
15	1.010	0.992
10	1.014	0.988
5	1.019	0.984

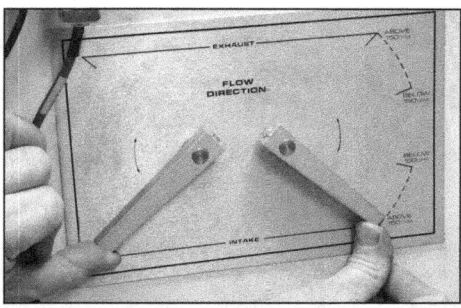

The flow-direction handles open and close a pair of simple valves inside the SuperFlow 600 bench to change the direction of the airflow for testing either intake or exhaust ports. Levers also change the location of the reference point for the inclined manometer so that the readings are always consistent.

The flow bench requires the head be clamped over the cylinder adapter along with some means of accurately creating and measuring valve lift. There are various fixtures available from several companies that make this procedure more efficient, or you can make your own.

to create or buy a fixture that makes quick work of using a threaded screw to open the valve at precise positions. Many shops demand flow numbers every 0.050-inch, so this requires a fine-thread adapter along with a dial indicator. Several shops, such as Brezinski's, offer slick aluminum adapters that bolt to the valve cover holes and allow you to quickly position the dial indicator over the appropriate valvestem. You also don't want to attempt to open the valve against normal valvespring pressure, so this also requires replacing the stock valvesprings with special light-duty test springs. These offer enough pressure to keep the valve closed under low-lift testing while still making it easy to open the valve with the screw adapter.

But before we start testing, we must also place a spark plug in the chamber and test the head for leakage. This is an important step since any leakage erroneously adds flow volume to the test. A leak test is simple enough to execute. With closed valves, turn the machine on and read the flow movement on the percent scale. Often, you may see 3 to 5 cfm. You can attempt to repair the leak that may be coming from the gasket or one of the valves. The easier thing to do is to merely subtract the leakage from the final flow numbers once they are achieved. This way, you don't have to spend time repairing leaks.

Once the leakage test is accomplished, we can now actually begin flow testing. Let's assume we're going to test the intake port. The next step is to make sure the flow direction lever is set to "Intake" and the flow range is set to position 1. This is the lowest flow range on the bench. The SuperFlow bench also has another

Replacing the valvesprings with light-duty test springs makes it much easier to open the valves and measure valve lift. These test springs are available from several sources including Manley and Pioneer. Brezinski is probably the most popular source for valve lift checking fixtures that includes a threaded valve opener and a dial indicator mounted on a solid base.

switch that is positioned for low-lift testing that merely creates a return air path to the electric motors to help cool them during low-lift tests. Once cylinder head flow reaches 150 cfm or greater, this switch can be closed since sufficient airflow is achieved to keep the motor cool. SuperFlow benches are also equipped with thermal limiter switches that cut off power to the electric motors if they begin to overheat. If this occurs during testing, just allow the bench to cool for a half-hour or so before continuing the test. Now we can also turn the threaded valve screw to the first lift point. Generally, this is either 0.050 or 0.100 inch.

Right away we have to establish the proper test pressure. Most, if not all, performance flow bench tests are performed at 28 inches, so opening the right-hand intake flow valve will create airflow, and the test depression vertical manometer on the left side of the bench will begin to rise. If the inclined flow manometer hits or exceeds 100 percent, quickly turn off the machine and reposition the flow knob to the next highest flow position. Restart the machine and adjust the test pressure until you have established a solid 28 inches, and then read the percent of flow on the inclined manometer. Shut off the machine and record this percent number along with the flow range on which that test was performed. Now you can go on to the next valve lift step. Most flow tests are performed at 0.100-inch steps, but that choice is up to you.

At some point along the way, you will have to change to a higher flow range in order to maintain the percentage of flow above 50 percent on the inclined manometer. This is necessary to improve the accuracy of your tests. It's also crucial to always record the flow range used along with the percent of flow. This is because the percentage of flow is based on a specific flow range to calculate the amount of flow. While this information can be written down on any scrap of paper you have available, the best thing to do is to use a copy of Super-Flow's data sheet, or create your own.

Once you have a percentage for each of the valve lifts, it's a simple task to merely multiply the percentage times the established CFM of the flow range. As an example, let's say you were testing an intake port on flow range 3 that is calibrated from SuperFlow at 151 cfm and your test port flowed exactly 75 percent. Multiplying 151 cfm x 0.75 = 113 cfm. Let's also assume that you found 3 cfm leakage when you originally tested the head. Subtracting the leakage figure from the test cfm (113 – 3 = 110), we find the port flowed 110 cfm. It's that simple.

Testing the exhaust side of the head is accomplished in exactly the same manner except that the flow direction lever is set to push air out the port, rather than move air in when testing on the intake side. Also, the intake flow knob is closed and the exhaust flow knob is opened in order to change the direction of the flow of air through the bench. One variable that has become popular when testing exhaust ports is a flow pipe. A flow pipe simulates the use of an exhaust header on the exhaust port and actually improves flow from the exhaust port much like a radiused entry is used to standardize port flow tests on the intake side. Generally, the pipe improves flow numbers above 0.100 inch of valve lift, which is why most porting companies include them in their test results since the pipe makes their work look even better. When reporting exhaust port testing results, it's important to note on the flow sheet whether the port has been tested with or without the pipe. Ideally, the test will be performed in both cases, so that either flow number can be used depending upon the situation.

Evaluation

Once we have performed a complete flow test on a representative intake and exhaust port, the real work of evaluating the results can begin. Most performance enthusiasts immediately begin this process by looking at the peak intake flow numbers, generated usually around 0.600-inch or higher valve lift. The intake port's peak flow numbers are used to quickly judge whether this port and cylinder head is a player. While quick, and simplistic, this is generally a poor way to evaluate an intake port, let alone an overall cylinder head. A more practical approach demands data from the entire valve lift curve and employs this data to create a more practical and useful determination of the head's flow capabilities.

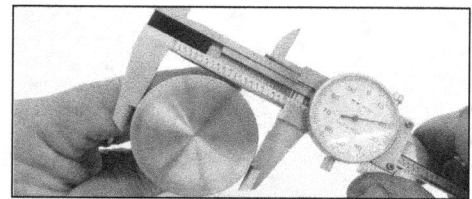

To accurately assess the effect of valve diameter on performance, the best way to evaluate this is by using a lift-to-diameter procedure rather than merely using the same valve lifts with a larger valve.

Since this book is written from the street performance standpoint, the proper approach requires the evaluator to look at the cylinder head's entire flow curve beginning with the low-lift flow all the way through the peak flow numbers. If you talk with racers or race cylinder head builders, you may find that their interpretation of the term "low lift" is far different from the one that is used in this book. When building monster 815-ci IHRA Pro Stock engines that push valve lift up into the 1.250-inch area, low lift to them might be 0.500 inch! But for us mere mortals, low lift begins with 0.100 inch of valve lift.

High peak valve lift flow is certainly important to cylinder filling; however, a simple glance at a camshaft profile indicates that in order to reach max lift, the valve goes through the mid-range lifts both on the way up and on the return trip back to the cam's base circle while the cam achieves peak valve lift only once. This should place more emphasis on the cylinder head's mid-range valve lift flow numbers. Perhaps even more importantly, the mid-lift flow numbers on the closing side are important since this is when the piston is on its way back up toward Top Dead Center (TDC) and pressure is rising in the cylinder. If the port has sufficient velocity and is capable of strong CFM numbers as it approaches the closing side of the valve lift curve, it's possible to achieve additional cylinder filling and therefore more power. These are two excellent reasons why mid-lift flow numbers are as important—or perhaps more important—than the peak valve lift flow achievements.

We get into more detail in Chapter 3, Airflow Basics, but it is important to note that the entire flow curve contributes to filling the cylinder on our way to making more power. We hammer this part home throughout this book: The entire induction system must be taken as a whole when evaluating port flow rather than looking just at the intake port alone. While this may take it farther than necessary for a street enthusiast, race engine builders routinely evaluate the entire induction system by placing the intake manifold on the head to gain a better perspective on induction efficiency. The late Smokey Yunick went so far as to place the cylinder head and intake manifold on a cylinder block and moved air through the cylinder. The rest of the industry has used a portion of that idea by simulating cylinder bore diameter with the bore adapter on the flow bench.

So far, we've been addressing only the intake side of things, but exhaust port flow is equally important. It should be easy to see that a strong intake port will be quickly minimized if shackled with a lame exhaust port. Exhaust gas does not burn a second time, and residual exhaust remaining in the chamber as a result of poor exhaust port flow has the net effect of reducing cylinder pressure and reducing power. While good exhaust port flow is critical, sizing the exhaust to work with the intake port is equally important. Most successful aftermarket cylinder heads for the small-block Chevy tend to utilize an exhaust-to-intake flow relationship in the 70 to 80 percent range. This means that if the intake port flows 250 cfm at 0.500-inch valve lift, for example, then the exhaust port would flow around 187 cfm at 75 percent. This relationship is usually expressed as the exhaust-to-intake, or E/I, relationship and is determined by dividing the exhaust port flow by the intake flow CFM. The E/I is always determined at the same

Flow Numbers

Each SuperFlow bench is clearly marked with the flow numbers for each flow range. In the case of a SuperFlow 600 bench, there are six flow ranges with six matching flow numbers. There are specific numbers for each SuperFlow bench that are only applicable to that bench. The numbers listed here are for example purposes. Also note that the flow numbers change based on intake or exhaust flow.

Flow Range	Intake (cfm)	Exhaust (cfm)
1	36	38
2	72	78
3	151	156
4	300	318
5	449	481
6	598	644

CHAPTER 2

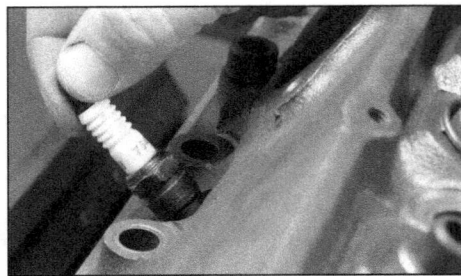

Testing cylinder head intake ports requires consistent test procedures. One of these steps is to always use a radiused flow adapter on the leading edge of the intake port. For oddball ports, a hand-fashioned clay radius will work, but if you plan on testing a large number of heads, Brezinski sells dedicated radius inlets machined into 3/4-inch thick plastic using a 1/2-inch radius. These are matched to specific Fel-Pro gasket sizes or for a specific head.

Always be sure to include a head gasket and spark plug for the cylinder you are testing to minimize leakage during testing. It's also a good idea to always perform a leakage test before each port flow test to establish the amount of leakage that is then subtracted from the total CFM airflow number. This is a step that is often overlooked when doing cylinder head flow testing.

valve lift for both the intake and exhaust.

By solving this simple math problem, you can use this percentage as a quick determiner of exhaust port efficiency, but it should not be accepted as gospel as there appears to be no given E/I number that is ideal for all combinations. If you solve the E/I question for the more popular small-block heads, you will see that the number varies throughout the lift curve as well as varying by cylinder head manufacturer. Residing within the 70 to 80 percentile range is acceptable, so what you're looking for when evaluating an exhaust port is anomalies that fall outside this range. An exhaust port with E/I performance above 90 percent, especially at or near peak valve lifts, does not necessarily indicate a high-flow exhaust port. The first thing to do in this situation is to look more closely at the intake port. Consistently high E/I numbers usually signal a weak intake port rather than an outstanding exhaust port.

For street engines with valve lifts that rarely exceed 0.550 inch, consider that the higher flow potential generated with lower valve lift values will generally create a more efficient evacuation of the exhaust gas. This is a rather simple formula since exhaust gas pressure is highest at the point when the exhaust valve first opens. So it would stand to reason that strong low and mid-lift flow numbers would help to quickly reduce pressure in the cylinder and reduce negative work by not requiring the piston to push oxidized gas out the exhaust port. Again, we get deeper into this subject in Chapter 3.

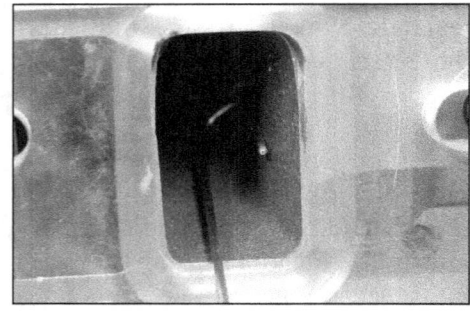

A separate manometer can also be used to map an intake port to establish a velocity profile. The higher the velocity, the higher the reading on the vertical manometer in inches of water. Mapping a port at various locations from the valve will indicate areas of high velocity as well as dead areas where the air is stagnant.

Leakage

Much of what you read in this book originates either from SuperFlow or from many people who have spent years of their lives running a flow bench. Human nature being what it is, shortcuts often occur especially when performing multiple tests very quickly. Often, shops do not perform a leakage test after bolting the heads on the bench. Sometimes the head leaks from between the head and the cylinder adapter but often the leaks can be simple miscues like leaving the spark plug out of the chamber or testing a stock small-block exhaust port that is fitted with an EGR port that is left open.

Even if you discover that the head leaks roughly 3 to 5 cfm for the tests, it is not necessary to eliminate these leaks, as long as that leakage number stays the same for all test pressures. If it does, then the amount, say 3 cfm, can merely be subtracted from the flow total once the test has been performed. If the leakage is not subtracted, this makes the test less accurate than it could be.

Lift-to-Diameter Ratio

An interesting way to compare the efficiencies of different size valves is to employ a technique called the valve lift-to-diameter, or L/D, ratio. This step multiplies the valve diameter by the following ratios: 0.05, 0.10, 0.15, 0.20, 0.25, and 0.30. For example, if we have a 2.02-inch diameter small-block intake valve and we want to compare it to a 2.05-inch diameter valve, doing a straight test will usually reveal the larger valve generating greater flow at the same valve lifts of 0.100, 0.200 inch, and the like.

But by testing these valves using valve lifts that are in direct ratio to their diameters, we can truly evaluate the efficiency of the larger valve. Using this same comparison, the valve lift for a 2.02-inch valve at the 0.30 lift-to-diameter ratio would be 0.606 while the larger 2.05 valve would be 0.615. Clearly, the larger valve also has a larger valve lift test lift, but this way you are evaluating the valves at a common ratio. We've included the following chart to save you doing the math.

L/D	Intake Valve Diameters					Exhaust Valve Diameters		
	1.94	2.02	2.05	2.08	2.10	1.50	1.60	1.625
	Test Valve Lifts							
0.05	0.097	0.101	0.102	0.104	0.105	0.075	0.080	0.081
0.10	0.194	0.202	0.205	0.208	0.210	0.150	0.160	0.162
0.15	0.291	0.303	0.307	0.312	0.315	0.225	0.240	0.244
0.20	0.388	0.404	0.410	0.416	0.420	0.300	0.320	0.325
0.25	0.485	0.505	0.512	0.520	0.525	0.375	0.400	0.406
0.30	0.582	0.606	0.615	0.624	0.630	0.450	0.480	0.487

Most flow numbers listed in this book are tested with an exhaust pipe in place over the exhaust port unless specified in the test. Generally, an exhaust pipe improves flow roughly 5 percent over an exhaust port with no pipe.

Placing a 4-inch cylinder around the combustion chamber on a small-block Chevy head reveals just how tight the area is around the intake valve. This shrouding has a negative impact on flow, which is why a larger cylinder adapter bore will indicate greater flow from the same cylinder head.

Conclusion

This has been a rather quick run through the basic operation of a typical SuperFlow bench. There is probably a Master's thesis equivalent of information if you really want to dive into flow bench operation and the details involved with that, but most enthusiasts are really only interested in what the bench will tell us, rather than exactly how it works. Now that we have a working knowledge of what a good bench delivers, we can take that information, apply it to a cylinder head, and use that data to help determine the best head for your application. The next chapter is where the fun really starts.

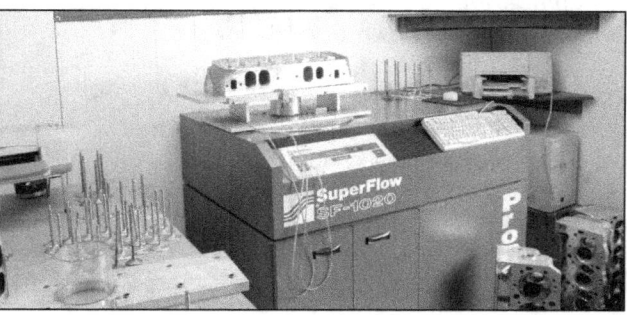

SuperFlow has recently introduced a larger 1020 bench that flows up to 1,000 cfm at 28 inches of test depression. According to the Dart guys, this bench also picks up slight changes in port design that the smaller 600 bench does not.

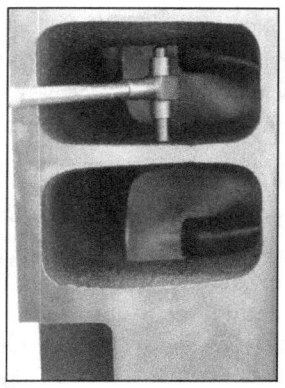

Generally, the greatest potential gains for minor porting efforts are located within 1 inch of the valve seat. The pushrod restriction (being measured here), usually establishes the smallest cross-sectional area of the port.

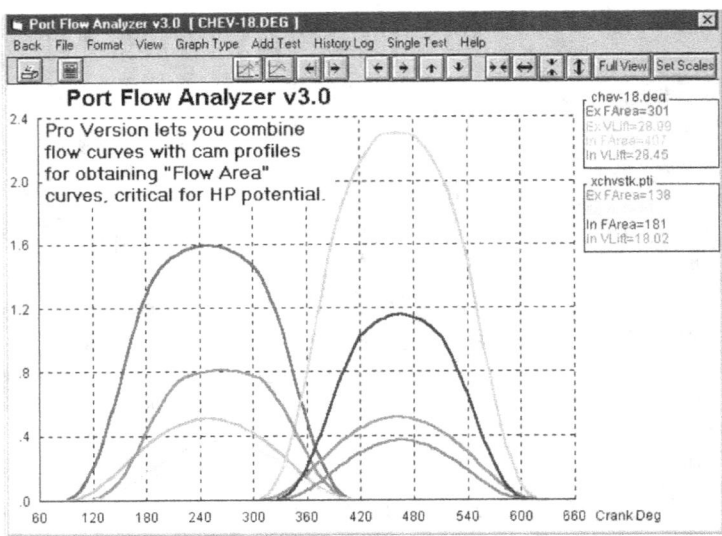

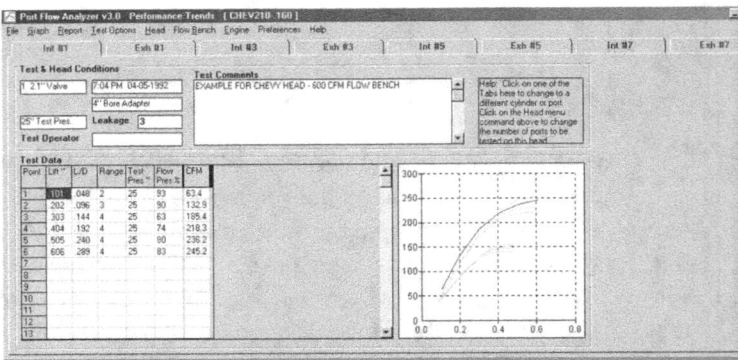

This is the main input screen from the Performance Trends Port Flow Analyzer program that works very well in conjunction with SuperFlow's FlowCom digital output.

SuperFlow has recently added the FlowCom digital update for its SuperFlow 600 bench that automatically establishes the specified test depression and also directly reads out the calculated test CFM. This makes the test procedure a bit less cumbersome, especially when combined with Performance Trends' software where the data is averaged and can be viewed in many user-configured outputs.

Hardly A Bore

Another big variable when performing cylinder head flow bench testing is the diameter of the cylinder bore. One of the limitations of the original small-block Chevy is that the 265-ci Mouse motor utilized relatively small 1.72 and 1.50-inch valves that, for the equally diminutive 3.75-inch bore, was acceptable. Since the bore spacing on a small-block is established at 4.400, the absolutely largest bore available is 4.25, leaving precious little room between cylinders to seal the combustion pressure. More realistically, 4.155 out to 4.200 are practical limits, but even these bore diameters still shroud the valves, which limits flow from even smaller intake valve diameters. Part of the reason for this is the small-block's 23-degree valve angle, as the valve opens, it tends to maintain the position of the valve near the cylinder wall.

All of this is a way of explaining that bore diameter has a direct effect on cylinder head flow potential. This means that as the bore diameter becomes larger, intake (and to a lesser extent, exhaust) flow improves. This is easily seen on a flow bench and is one of the tricks used by some manufacturers to make a cylinder head appear more efficient on a flow bench. For example, almost any performance small-block head will respond with better flow numbers if the bore adapter diameter is increased from 4.00 to 4.250. But if the heads will be used on a 4.030-inch bore 355-ci for example, these are unrealistic numbers. This is also why most all race engines are built with the largest bore, again to improve overall cylinder head flow potential by reducing the shrouding effect of the cylinder wall.

One variable that is often lost when comparing flow numbers on any given cylinder head is the test bore diameter. Larger test bores like this 4.155-inch sleeve allows flow to improve coming out of the intake port. So when comparing flow numbers, strive to use flow numbers using similar sized bore diameters.

Wet Flow

Around the turn of the 21st century, the performance industry earnestly began looking at the effects of intake port wet flow characteristics. The new car companies have spent millions of research dollars in this area, but about the only part of this that has trickled down to the performance industry has to do with swirl and tumble—an area that is still currently debated as to its efficacy in regard to performance engines. More importantly, this has led to more practical study of what happens to the "wet" portion of the air and fuel mixture as it moves its way through the induction system. Carbureted engines turn the entire induction system into a wet flow system since fuel is introduced at the carburetor, as opposed to dry flow EFI systems where fuel is usually injected at the entrance to the intake port.

Until recently, characteristics of wet flow and how the fuel is affected by turns in the intake port and especially what happens to the fuel as it enters the cylinder past the valves has been largely ignored. But several years ago, Joe Mondello began a concentrated effort to construct a realistic wet flow cylinder head test bench that would allow the more dedicated engine builder and cylinder head porter to begin to evaluate wet flow characteristics. Mondello's system is basically an add-on device intended to be used in conjunction with a typical SuperFlow flow bench. The system consists of a reservoir of fluorescent liquid that is introduced into the port and then dispersed past the intake valve inside a clear plexiglass cylinder (simulating the cylinder). After the liquid leaves the cylinder, it is then collected in an adjacent drum to be used again. A non-flammable liquid roughly equivalent to the specific gravity of gasoline is used, and a portable ultraviolet light is used around the plastic cylinder to evaluate how the liquid is dispersed in the cylinder.

We've witnessed a couple of Mondello's systems that had only just recently been installed. Few of the cylinder head people we've spoken to would consider themselves to be really knowledgeable on the subject of wet flow. However, the patterns and characteristics that their early tests have indicated that once changes are made and evaluated, certain parameters are sure to evolve and more experience is gained in this area. One company that has a head start on this program is Dart Machinery. Dick Maskin commissioned Mondello to construct a major wet flow bench in his Detroit area shop, and Dart's Platinum series of street small-block Chevy heads is a direct result of the work that Dart has done with the wet flow bench on these heads. What is bound to

This is Dart's custom-built wet flow bench that can pull an amazing 55 inches of water for a test depression. According to Dart's Tony McAfee, this comes close to the actual depression the engine sees at maximum piston velocity. The bench uses three massive 50-hp electric motors to generate this kind of test pressure. Dart's Platinum line of iron and Pro 1 Platinum aluminum small-block heads were developed on this bench as well as Richard Maskin's current Pro Stock cylinder heads.

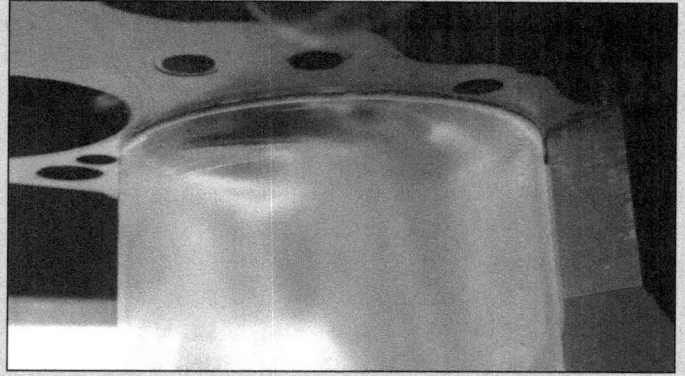

The Mondello wet flow adapter uses a fluorescent liquid that, when exposed to ultraviolet light, reveals the path of the fuel past the intake valve into a clear plastic tube that simulates the cylinder. The liquid is then collected in a downstream drum to be used again.

result from combining wet with dry flow will no doubt redirect certain areas of port flow development that were before this left uncovered.

CHAPTER 3

AIRFLOW BASICS

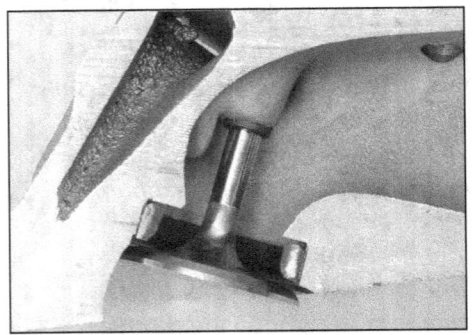

The area defined as from 1 inch below the valve seat to just beyond the valve seat in the chamber is clearly one of the most critical areas that help define flow potential in a small-block Chevy cylinder head.

Stories that deal with airflow always start out with the classic definition that an engine is really just a simple air pump—the air goes in and it comes out. This chapter is no different because that's the most simplistic way to approach an internal combustion engine. In order to do this, we should first know some fundamental facts about the working fluid we will be dealing with.

The atmosphere we breathe and that our performance small-block Chevy inhales is comprised of roughly 21 percent oxygen, 78 percent nitrogen, and one percent miscellaneous components. The part we are most concerned with is the oxygen, since this is the part that actively contributes to combustion. The more air we can stuff into the cylinders and keep there, the more potential power our engine will make. But there's more to this equation than just sheer volume. Atmospheric conditions play a part in this equation as well. The three critical ones are air temperature, air pressure, and the amount of water present in the air. This is generally referred to as humidity, but the engineers like to call it vapor pressure. A discussion of each of these conditions is important since all three play a part in what is generally referred to as air density.

The air that encompasses this planet we live on has both volume and weight. The weight of this air is directly related to where you measure it. For example, if we take one square inch area and measure the pressure at sea level, this column of air will weigh 14.7 pounds per square inch (psi). Up in the mountains, a similar column of air will weigh much less, perhaps only 12.5 psi, because we have shortened the standing height of the air. So the point here is that air pressure changes based on altitude relative to a sea-level standard. With less pressure, there is less atmospheric force pushing the air into our engine. This reduces the amount of air in the cylinders, producing less power. Temperature is an equally important factor in this trilogy. As the temperature of the air increases, the density of oxygen molecules in a cubic foot of air is reduced. This gives us less air to combust the fuel. So it's safe to say that higher inlet air temperatures generally produce less power. The last component is the amount of water vapor present in the air going into the engine. It's no secret that water doesn't burn, so the volume of water present in the air not only displaces a certain amount of air, but also contributes to reducing combustion efficiency, which means less power.

This leads us to a concept called standard temperature and pressure (STP) that is most often used in the performance industry. STP is defined as 60 degrees of dry air (zero vapor pressure) at sea level, or 14.7 psi of air pressure. This combination of atmospheric conditions is used as the atmospheric standard for engine dyno work. No matter what the existing conditions are during a dyno test, the horsepower and torque will be "corrected" to that atmospheric standard. The correction factor is applied to the observed torque and horsepower numbers, which usually means that the corrected numbers are higher than the observed numbers, assuming the existing atmospheric conditions are worse than the STP. This standard used to be the correction factor for original equipment manufacturers (OEM) until the 1970s when more realistic temperature, pressure, and the inclusion of vapor pressure, reduced the corrected power levels slightly. There have been several revisions to this standard, but generally, if you subtract 5 percent from a STP-corrected data, you will be very close to what the OEM's now use as their horsepower correction factor.

Now that we have applied a standard to the air that's moving into the

CFM and Volumetric Efficiency

Air movement through an engine is generally expressed in terms of cubic feet per minute (cfm). This is a term that is tossed about in high-performance circles very freely, but it's important to know exactly what this term means. One cubic foot of air can be represented by an imaginary 1 x 1 x 1-foot box. Inside this imaginary box is a volume of air. This volume can be measured moving into an engine using several devices. On many engine dynos, airflow is measured by something called a laminar flow device that spins a small propeller calibrated to measure airflow based on the speed of the propeller. The faster the propeller spins, the more air enters the engine. This works well as a measurement of the volume of air entering the engine, but it doesn't tell the whole story.

Air also has mass or weight, which is really not taken into consideration when expressed as a volume such as one cubic foot. We know that air has mass because at sea level air pressure equals 14.7 pounds per square inch (psi), or also called one atmosphere. This means that a column of air, one square inch in area that extends from sea level all the way to the edge of our atmosphere, weighs the equivalent of 14.7 pounds. If we drive up into the mountains, to an elevation of 6,000 feet above sea level, a barometer will indicate less air pressure because that column of air is 6,000 feet shorter in height.

So, airflow into an engine can be expressed either in terms of cfm or in mass flow quantities, as in pounds per hour (lbs/hr) or grams per second (g/sec). Most of the supercharger and turbocharger companies express airflow in terms of pounds per hour since this is a more accurate measurement of airflow than cfm because it takes into account the density of the air along with its volume. New car manufacturers use a device to measure mass flow called a Mass Air Flow (MAF) meter. The most common MAF uses a heated wire that extends across the airflow path. A greater mass of air moving across this heated wire tends to cool the wire more than less air. By measuring the amount of current required to maintain the wire's temperature along with the amount of airflow through the MAF, engineers can create a very accurate "map" of airflow density or mass flow in grams per second of air. If we know the density of the air, we can also easily convert that to cfm. For example, you can convert g/sec to cfm with the simple equation:

CFM = g/sec x 1.805
CFM = 400 g/sec x 1.805
CFM = 722

Clearly, increasing airflow through the engine will increase the potential for greater engine performance. One way to rate this efficiency is to compare the amount of air entering the engine with the engine's displacement. This is called volumetric efficiency (VE) and is created by dividing cfm of airflow by the theoretical maximum amount of air the engine could ingest with a given displacement. Let's use a 355-ci small-block Chevy as our example:

(CID / 2) x (RPM / 1,728) = CFM
(355 / 2) x (6,000 / 1,728) = CFM
177.5 x 3.472 = CFM
616.28 = CFM
(1,728 is the number of cubic inches in a cubic foot or, 12 x 12 x 12 = 1,728)

So with this formula, a 355-ci small-block could theoretically move a maximum of 616 cfm at 6,000 rpm. In reality, most naturally aspirated street engines do not achieve 100 percent VE. Let's say that our engine only really moves 500 cfm at 6,000 rpm. Dividing actual cfm by the maximum airflow theoretically possible, we can come up with a VE number.

Actual airflow in cfm / theoretical airflow in cfm = VE
500 cfm / 616 cfm = VE
0.811 = VE or, 81.1 percent VE

Actually, a small-block that can attain between 80 and 90 percent VE is a very efficient street combination. But internal combustion engines do not achieve maximum VE at all engine speeds. In fact, most engines achieve max VE at or near one place—peak torque. Below that speed, there is insufficient air speed to feed the cylinders. At engine speeds above peak torque, there is less time to fill the cylinder, which reduces its efficiency. Some fine-tuned race engines can and do achieve peak VE above peak torque since they are intentionally designed to achieve higher VE numbers.

CHAPTER 3

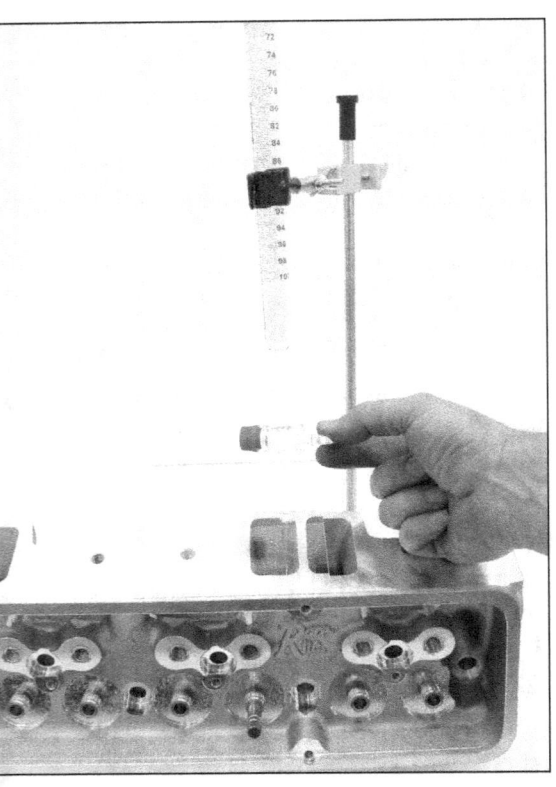

Check port volume by closing the port with a valve and measuring the port using a 100-cc burette. This is a quick and easy way to establish port size for comparison purposes.

engine, we can now begin the investigation of how that air moves through the engine, and, for the subject of this book, through the cylinder heads of a small-block Chevy. In order to quantify size in the cylinder head market, port volume has become the most popular shorthand way to identify port size. While this continues to be the popular shortcut to identify a head, it is not the best. Generally speaking, larger port volumes tend to flow more air and are therefore considered a better application for higher engine speeds and more peak power. In reality, this is a gross overgeneralization and far too simplistic. Frankly, if selecting cylinder heads were that easy, there would be little call for the information in this book!

While port volume does work to categorize heads, and we use that throughout this book, it's merely a signpost to direct the more knowledgeable cylinder head user to more specific data that he can use. We've included a couple of sidebars that deal specifically with intake port cross-sectional area and those two sidebars are among the most important pieces of information in this entire book ("Cross-Sectional Areas" and "Power Secrets"). If you take the time to evaluate any intake port not only by both its cross-sectional area and its port flow, that evaluation technique will always serve to point you in the right direction when it comes time to evaluate and select a cylinder head. Now that we have a basis from which to work, it's time to get down to what really happens in both the intake and exhaust ports.

Intake Flow

This section looks at the basics of airflow in the intake port. The goal here is to explain some basic flow examples, but in no way can this be construed as anything more than a very basic look at airflow. This is a complex and highly specialized area and certainly full of differing theories, many of which are guaranteed to change as we continue to learn more about how an internal combustion engine operates. We can start with the concept that much of the information delivered here has been determined with help from a flow bench, and therein rests the first dilemma. A flow bench, by design, is a steady-state flow measurement tool. In other words, it measures air movement primarily in one direction, either intake or exhaust, and does little to address the intermittent motion and major pressure excursions that are present in a running engine. As a result, many of our theories on airflow, while they may seem to make sense, are in fact flawed. That is what leads us down the path of discovery. This may sound like a giant disclaimer, and that is partially true. The point is that much of what we know is based on assumptions that the future may prove to be not entirely accurate. But it's what is known as contemporary wisdom, and that's the best we can do with what we know.

If we accept that velocity and mass flow are key components in our attempt to shove air and fuel into a cylinder, then it would seem logical to look at what happens to air as it attempts to move from the intake manifold on its way past the intake valve. In the intake port, we have both air and some ratio of fuel mixed with the air. We must also assume that this mixture of air and fuel will behave differently when

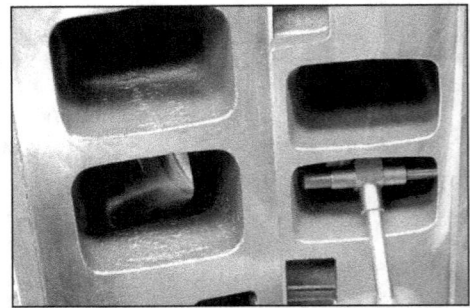

Rectangle-port Rat heads are a classic example of a too-large port. A rectangle port Rat head always outflows a small-block head on the flow bench, but with a monstrous 3.2 square inches of area (or larger), flow velocity is virtually snail-like and volumetric efficiency (VE) suffers. We've seen Rat motors pick up tons of torque and lose minimal peak HP by using smaller, oval port heads (despite their lower flow numbers). That proves the point. Yet somehow, the big-block guys still want those big heads. Go figure....

Port Area Math

While not getting into serious math, there are some simple formulas that allow you to experiment with valve size to approximate port cross-sectional areas. This can be used to help you home in on a recommendation for a street or race cylinder head. Plus, it's fun to see how these simple formulas relate a round valve area to the port's upstream cross-sectional area choke point.

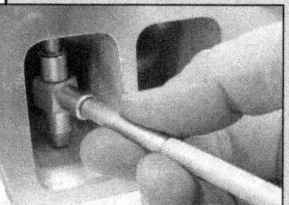

Port cross-sectional area is a term used freely throughout this book. On most small-block Chevy heads, the pushrod wall is generally the area of tightest restriction. To come up with this figure, we merely measure the port height and width at this point to determine cross-sectional area for all the heads in this book.

We're using the same formula, but changing the values slightly to target either a high-output race engine or a somewhat milder street engine. Note that the value used for the race engine assumes a 90 percent area underneath the valve seat while the street engine assumes a more conservative 85 percent. While 5 percent may not sound like much, look what happens to the resultant port cross-sectional area with a "small" 2.02 valve between 85 and 90 percent of valve diameter. By changing this value, the port area changes by 0.28 sq.in., which is a 12 percent increase in port area–a sizable increase. This is why most cylinder head porters suggest the "85 percent" rule for street porting. Others will contend that 90 percent is a more efficient number even for street engines. Where did this number originate? As an example, if you measure a typical 2.02-inch diameter valve for its "flow" diameter at the inside point of the valve seat, you'll discover that it measures around 1.820 inch. This computes out to be almost exactly 90 percent of the valve diameter. The 85 percent idea creates a bit more velocity but does cost some cfm.

Valve Dia. x 0.90 (race) = D
Valve Dia. x 0.85 (street) = D
D squared / 4 x 3.1417 = Port Area

Race Examples:
2.02 x 0.9 = 1.818
Port Area = (1.818 x 1.818) / 4 = 0.8262 x 3.1417 = 2.59
Port Area = 2.59 sq.in.

2.05 x 0.9 = 1.845
Throat Area = (1.845 x 1.845) / 4 = 0.8510 x 3.1417 = 2.67
Throat Area = 2.67 sq.in.

Street Examples:
2.02 x 0.85 = 1.717
Throat Area = (1.717 x 1.717) / 4 = 0.7370 x 3.1417 = 2.31
Throat Area = 2.31 sq.in.

2.05 x 0.85 = 1.74
Throat Area = (1.74 x 1.74) / 4 = 0.7579 x 3.1417 = 2.38
Throat Area = 2.38 sq.in.

By comparing these calculated values to the measured port cross-sectional areas that are elsewhere in this book, you can begin to see how these relationships begin to make sense. There's much more to this concept, but we'll keep this part simple for right now. Elsewhere in this chapter, we'll tie in flow with cross-sectional area and see where that leads us.

---

required to change direction. Physics and common sense tell us that the heavier fuel droplets are less likely to make a change in direction than the lighter air molecules. This means that in order to create a more efficient intake port, we need to ensure that any change in direction includes more of the fuel droplets combined with the air. The more homogenous the mixture, the more efficiently (and quicker!) that mixture will burn in the cylinder.

So how do we accomplish this? Let's start with a poor design and work our way toward a more efficient configuration. Let's start with the current small-block Chevy architecture and what we're forced to work with. These design parameters (some may call them restrictions) include the stock 23-degree valve angle, the intake port angle at the manifold, and limitations on port width because of pushrod placement. These are the realities of the layout of a small-block Chevy. The stock valve angle means that we must force the air and fuel to make a significant change in direction in order to transition past the intake valve. This is measured as the angular valve face relationship to the cylinder. Had the first generation small-block Chevy design engineers realized the value of a less acute angle, we might have been blessed with a taller intake valve angle such as the GEN III small-block, beginning in 1998, came with a more efficient 15-degree valve angle. Of course, airflow was not the only consideration when Chevy designed the small-block. We'll save that discussion for some other time. To show how important this is, in a matter of a scant few years, GM changed the 15-degree valve angle on the LS2 to 12 degrees for the LS7 on its way to an amazing 505 SAE production horsepower.

So given this 23-degree valve angle, one of the first priorities for a port designer is to attempt to "fool" the air into thinking that it has made less of a change from straight ahead flow as possible. Much like auto racing, the wider the radius of the turn, the faster you can negotiate that corner. As we look at older small-block Chevy intake ports, one thing that is quickly identified is that those older ports tend to have very flat floors. This is not a big problem until it comes time for the air to make the change in direction into the bowl just above the valve seat area. Air (and fuel) traveling across this sharp ledge quickly separates, and moves across the valve head toward the roof of the port. Any change in direction of a port will witness this type of movement, but it is especially bad in flat floor ports.

Most port designers and porters refer to the floor of the port where it transitions into the throat area as the short turn radius. At low port velocities, a gentler short side radius helps to maintain contact with the air stream, and this is what often results in improved low and mid-lift flow performance. As velocity and mass flow increases, there comes a point where the air still separates from the short-side radius. The higher the inlet velocity where this separation occurs, the more dead area is created by this separation, which is a major condition in the port's flow curve performance. Of course, increasing the height of the short-side radius also reduces the cross-sectional area of the port, which demands that the top of the port be raised to accommodate the taller short side. The problem here is that the spring seat and valveguide placement limit a taller port roof. This is also determined by the 23-degree valve angle. A 15 or 18-degree valve angle allows more room for this taller roof, which is another reason why a taller valve angle works better for high-RPM engines.

As the air (and fuel) makes the transition into the valve bowl area, almost all intake ports increase the port volume in this area to slow the air to help it turn the corner. Still with sufficient velocity even at partial valve lift, air tends to be pushed toward the high side of the bowl area. This is an inevitable result of increased velocity through the port,

While valve outside diameter (o.d.) is always used for valve sizes, keep in mind that the actual valve seat diameter is smaller, with an actual valve flow diameter of around 1.98 inches on a 2.02-inch valve with a seat placed 0.040 inch inboard of the valve diameter.

which tends to concentrate a majority of the flow around the tall side of the intake valve. If you picture the intake valve at a given lift—say 0.500 inch for example—the circumference of the valve times the lift create a flow window sometimes called a flow curtain area. Adding a larger intake valve increases this flow window by a factor of pi (3.1417), which is one reason why adding a larger valve generally increases flow. In an ideal world, the flow distribution around the intake valve into the cylinder would be symmetrical, meaning flow and a pressure

We couldn't resist picking on the Ford guys. If you need an example of an absolutely low-velocity, sewer-pipe-sized intake port, look no further than the Ford Tunnel Port heads. These are actually small-block heads that were once used on Ford's 302-ci Trans Am effort. Tons of RPM was the only solution to making these heads work.

AIRFLOW BASICS

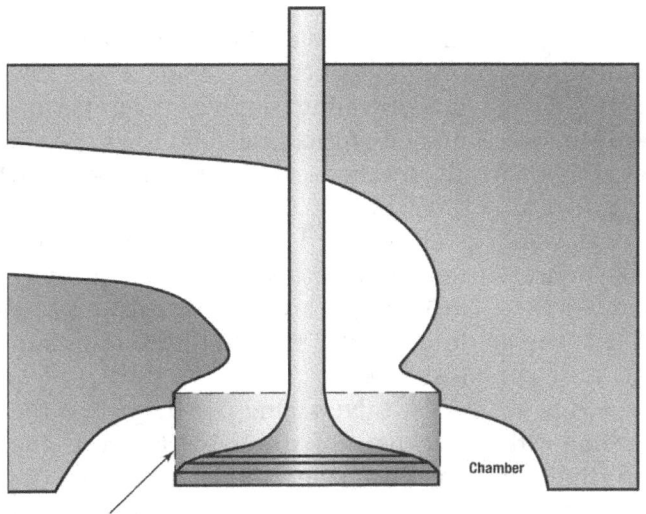

The valve curtain area is defined as the diameter of the valve seat width (not the valve diameter itself) multiplied by valve lift. This curtain area determines flow potential, but does not take into account shrouding by the cylinder wall or the combustion chamber.

distribution around the valve would be the same at every point around the valve. As you can imagine, that rarely happens. One key to a more efficient cylinder head is an intake valve where more of the air and fuel moves past the short-side portion of the valve, and this is what the port designer seeks to achieve.

Tracking the movement of air and fuel in the intake port, we now find the air making that important move past the intake seat, moving between the seat angles and the

Cross-Sectional Area

Intake ports are always a subject of much discussion among engine builders and tuners. The S-A Design book *Desktop Dynos* by Larry Atherton offers a rough rule of thumb for creating an induction system cross-sectional area that may help create balanced intake runner inlet air velocities somewhere on the conservative side of optimal flow potential that does not create a serious restriction. A large intake port that is efficient will always look better on the flow bench because we're measuring mass flow in cfm, but may not do well in an engine because the flow bench does not address port velocity. This simple formula offers an introduction into the cross-sectional area that may help in the search for the best cylinder head. The RPM number represents the peak RPM power point.

The formula looks like this:

Minimum Port Area = (RPM x Stroke x Bore x Bore) / 190,000

We have computed a couple different cubic inch combinations using this formula that may be of some interest. All results are in sq.in. of cross-sectional area.

Engine A	Engine B
355ci	406ci
4.030-inch bore	4.155-inch bore
3.48-inch stroke	3.75-inch stroke
@ 5000 rpm = 1.48	@ 5000 rpm = 1.70
@ 5500 rpm = 1.63	@ 5500 rpm = 1.87
@ 6000 rpm = 1.78	@ 6000 rpm = 2.04
@ 6500 rpm = 1.93	@ 6500 rpm = 2.21

As you can see, if we use the same port cross-section in both of these engines, it forces a higher peak engine speed with the smaller engine or a lower RPM with the larger engine, which is a typical result when using the same heads and/or intake on different displacement engines. This formula is conservative, but clearly illustrates the effect of cross-sectional area on peak horsepower. Compare these figures to the cross-sectional areas of the various cylinder heads in the following chapters and you might have a way to help you choose the right head and intake system for your next engine.

We've included a list of the minimum cross-sectional areas for a few popular small-block cylinder heads for reference. All these heads were measured in the center of the intake port at the pushrod wall restriction. These measurements may vary due to production tolerances and casting variations, but they should give some type of comparison between different heads.

Cylinder Head	Cross-Sectional Area (sq. in.)	Port Volume (cu. cen.)
GM Vortec Iron	1.74	170
Edelbrock Performer RPM	1.81	170
Edelbrock E-Tec 170	1.81	170
TFS 195	1.93	195
AFR 180 (Version 1)	1.93	180
AFR 195 (Version 1)	1.98	195
AFR 210 (Version 1)	2.05	210
Edelbrock Victor Jr.	2.05	215
Dart Pro 1 200	2.06	200
World Sportsman II	2.19	200

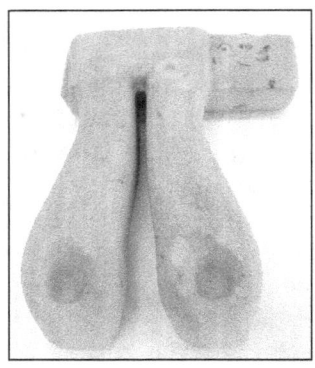

Intake port taper affects intake port velocity. There are plenty of theories about where the "choke point" (or, if you like, the point of highest port velocity) should be in relation to the valve. In the case of the small-block Chevy, this point is at the pushrod restriction as seen here on this intake port sand core. The air then slows down as it approaches the short turn radius where it must make the turn to go past the valve.

angle on the intake valve. While every point in the intake port is important, it's hard to find a single area that is more important than the area surrounding the interface between the valve and the seat. The classic approach is a three-angle seat that begins in the port throat area with a 60-degree angle. The sealing angle that contacts the valve is 45 degrees and then transitions to a top cut (closest to the combustion chamber) of anywhere from 35 to 15 degrees, depending upon the application. While we use three angles as an example, the cylinder head designer is certainly not limited to just three angles. Many performance valve jobs now incorporate up to five angles.

The idea with multiple seat angles is to maximize airflow through the valve curtain area throughout the entire lift curve. This is a critical distinction that deserves discussion because most enthusiasts tend to focus far too much attention on peak valve lift flow numbers, ignoring the low and mid-lift flow numbers. We emphasize this throughout the book, not to bore you but to reinforce just how critical these flow numbers are to overall performance. This is how the three-angle seat evolved. In fact, there is data to support that perhaps a 70 to 75-degree transitional throat cut underneath the 60-degree seat angle is beneficial in certain applications.

Another important point here is the transient nature of all these numbers. Given unlimited time on the flow bench, the goal would be to experiment one degree at a time with each seat angle, along with different valve seat and back-cut angles. For most enthusiasts, this is hardly practical. But we know of many drag racers and cylinder head experts who have performed this exercise. The frustrating part of this process is that as soon as the port is even slightly changed, the very specific valve seat angles do not perform the same way. Often, the difference of 1 degree can be decisive. If you begin to see how complex this whole arrangement is, you are beginning to gain an appreciation for a strong-performing port.

Another important element in all this angle interplay is the position and width of the intake seat on the valve. Positioning the intake seat as far to the outside diameter of the intake valve as possible improves airflow. Most head porters place this seat approximately 0.020 inch inboard of the outside diameter of the valve. To create a durable intake-sealing surface, most performance cylinder head builders specify an intake seat width of between 0.060 and 0.070 inch. A narrower seat width definitely improves airflow, but for a street engine, normal driving quickly pounds this out to a much wider seat that only results in lost flow.

A valve's margin is defined as the thickness of the valve between the chamber side of the valve and the end of the valve sealing face. A margin of at least 0.050 inch is also a good idea and has been used to help create improved flow. Valve manufacturers often specify different margins for their valves since this additional material adds to the overall weight of the valve, and a couple of grams here and there add up pretty quickly. If there is additional flow to be gained, some head builders actually specify a slightly larger valve and then machine the outside diameter down by 0.020 inch or so in order to increase the margin thickness. This additional margin can also then be used to add a 20 to 25-degree top cut in an effort to improve flow. This is a less popular modification for intake valves, and we recommend testing this before blindly adding yet another angle to the flow mix.

The throat diameter can be measured with a simple set of dial calipers. All our research indicates that 90 percent is the limit for throat diameter in relation to the intake valve.

AIRFLOW BASICS

A radius face on the exhaust valve is an easy trick that can often result in flow improvements. Like most other "tricks," this is something that requires testing on your application—we've seen just as many radius efforts that did not improve, or actually hurt, exhaust port flow.

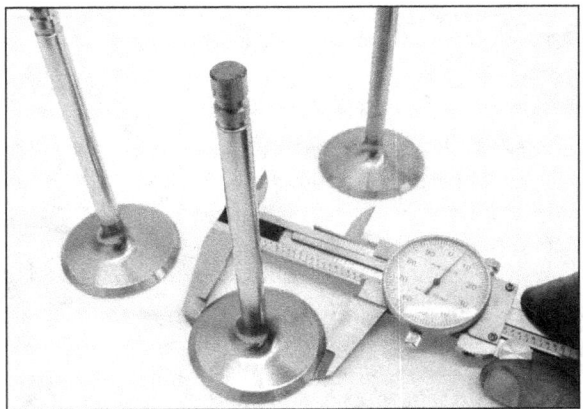

Larger valves almost always improve flow as long as all the other variables remain the same. But as valve diameter increases, this also pushes the valve closer to the cylinder wall.

Earlier in this discussion of intake flow, we mentioned that a majority of the flow exiting the intake port tends to push toward the roof side of the port and valve exit. If you look at the chamber arrangement of a typical 23-degree small-block head mounted on a cylinder block, you'll notice that the flow is predominantly aimed at the combustion chamber wall and then directly into the cylinder wall. This shrouding effect is especially bad on production iron heads with deep chambers. Experiments with top cuts on the combustion chamber can also be worth increased low-lift flow, but again there is less experimentation in this area to support exact details. We leave a more detailed description of chamber configuration to Chapter 11 where we get much deeper into this subject. But suffice it to say that the chamber side of the valve is a big-time player in not only combustion efficiency, but port flow numbers as well.

Exhaust Flow

The exhaust side of the cylinder head always seems to attract less attention than the intake. Perhaps this is because the exhaust side is less "romantic" or maybe it's just because the topic involves lots of hot air, but there's no disputing the fact that, given the air pump analogy, you can't get more good air in if you can't get the bad air out. Dealing with exhaust flow is also substantially different from inlet air because we're dealing with a high-temperature, high-pressure working fluid. Because of this, the exhaust valve can be smaller, roughly 80 percent of the intake valve diameter.

Predicting HP

In using flow bench numbers, SuperFlow offers a simple formula for estimating horsepower based on flow. These are merely simple predictions, but do offer some insight into flow potential and horsepower. For ideal horsepower, the formula looks like this:

HP = 0.257 x (intake cfm @ 28 inches of water) x engine cylinders

This formula assumes that this is flow through the entire intake tract including the intake manifold and carburetor (or throttle body). So if we have an intake system with a flow of 250 cfm at 28 inches of water test depression:

HP = 0.257 x 250 x 8
HP = 64.25 hp/cylinder x 8
HP = 514

This sounds at first to be very optimistic, but keep in mind that a typical induction system will decrease flow through an intake port, which will reduce total flow between 5 and 30 percent. At a 30 percent reduction, this means that the intake port alone would have to flow 325 cfm by itself in order to generate 250 cfm with the induction system in place.

Let's take another example of a small-block head with 250 cfm intake port and a flow loss through the induction system of 20 percent. That makes the overall flow 200 cfm. Plugging that into the formula looks like this:

HP = 0.257 x 200 x 8
HP = 411.2

This is a more realistic (and conservative) HP estimate for a 250-cfm cylinder head.

CHAPTER 3

CFD

The beauty of computers is the ability to do rapid mathematical modeling in a very short period of time. One of the areas that has benefited from this is computer simulation work. While most readers are familiar with the engine simulation programs, several engineering-oriented software firms have developed sophisticated software programs that can simulate movement of air through a passageway like an intake port or intake manifold. These programs are referred to as computation fluid dynamics (CFD) applications and treat air, because it has mass, as a compressible fluid.

These are incredibly powerful and expensive programs that require a tremendous amount of computer power and knowledge to use. First off, solid modeling programs are necessary to create a "mesh" or mathematical model of the inside dimensions of the port. The more accurate this mesh is, the more accurate your evaluation of the results the program will deliver. For the OEM's and some forward-thinking aftermarket companies, this isn't a problem since they are already designing ports and cylinder heads using computer solid modeling programs.

From a layman's standpoint, the CFD modeling results are often displayed like a running video of air movement with hundreds of tiny lines representing airflow movement through an intake port, for example. These lines are different colors depending upon pressure and velocity. Generally, high pressure is indicated in red while low pressures are indicated in blue. Port designers can look at a pressure gradient from high pressure to low pressure in a port and get an idea of not only how the air moves through a port, but also where they can eliminate dead areas in the port or perhaps slow the air down if the velocity appears too great. The idea is to eliminate flow losses and improve overall port flow. Of course, once changes in the port configuration are indicated, the user must then make changes to his mesh model in order to then evaluate those changes and hope that he has made a positive change. This is where the application engineer really earns his pay since he must not only be a competent software user, but also know what kinds of changes to make to improve flow. From what we've seen in our extremely limited access to these programs, this is where the essential work is performed. Tim Collins works for Managed Programs, LLC (a

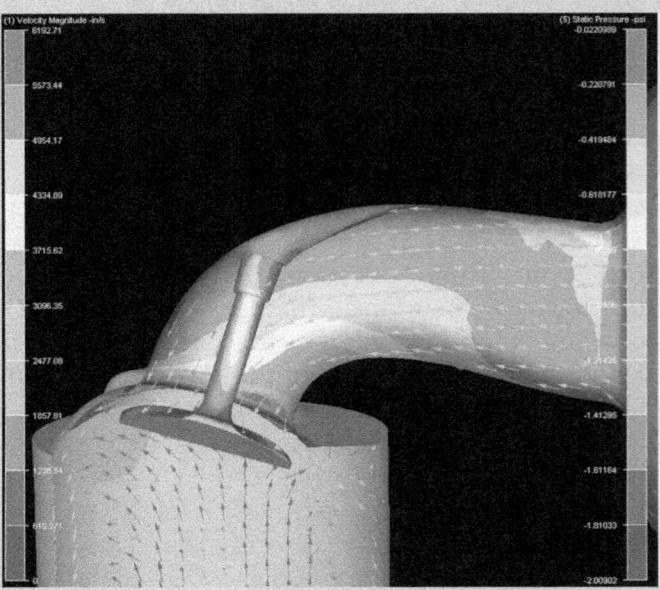

CFD simulations are beyond the realm of most hot rodders, but they do represent the next level of design and testing port configurations. One thing to look for are areas of low velocity where flow can often create eddies or even reverse the flow direction.

CFD company out of the Detroit area). As stated by Tim in a presentation to the Advanced Engine Technology Conference in 2005–"All computer models are wrong. Some are useful." What that means is that simulation programs are merely another useful tool that help a designer "see" what air is doing in a port and how to manipulate it to more efficiently move between the air inlet, into the cylinder, and out.

These programs are currently not intended for use by the average enthusiast mainly because they are both incredibly expensive and even more time consuming to both set up and operate. However, like most other expensive programs, over time these companies will learn how to simplify the programs to the point where it may be possible to one day run a simplistic version of a CFD program on your home computer to help create a more efficient intake port for racers and street enthusiasts.

Ironically, on the flow bench, we flow test the exhaust port much like the intake except in the opposite direction. The temperature and the test pressure are usually the same as the intake. Perhaps because of these differences, the industry has created its own unique way of measuring the efficiency of the exhaust by comparing it to the intake side. This E/I (exhaust-to-intake) index is a percentage created by dividing the exhaust flow by the intake port flow at the same valve lift to come up with one type of rating system for the exhaust port.

One interesting point about this is that the exhaust rarely achieves more than around 80 to 85 percent flow compared to the intake port. Generally, if the exhaust port

AIRFLOW BASICS

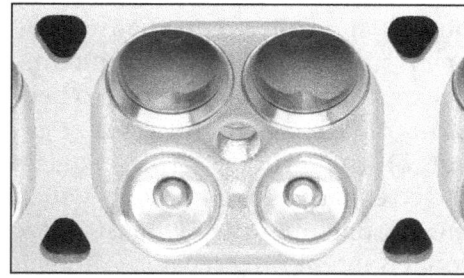

A 4-valve head offers greater flow curtain area since more of the chamber is filled with valves. This increased flow curtain area, combined with smaller intake ports with higher velocity curves, is why 4-valve heads always offer increased power potential. This is a shot of the combustion chamber on a GM 4.6L Northstar 4-valve engine.

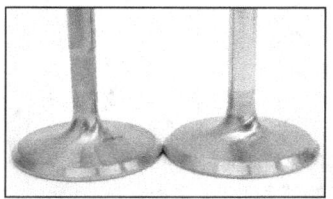

Manley was the first to champion a necked-down valve as the stem approaches the head of the valve. The concept is sound, but we've rarely seen appreciable improvements in flow with a quality head. The gains claimed were originally achieved with an undersized production intake port.

Port-matching the face of the port to the intake manifold is a simple operation, but unless the intake manifold runner is larger than the port opening on the heads, this is a job you can save for when you have nothing else to do. In this photo, the gasket indicates the runner is smaller than the intake port.

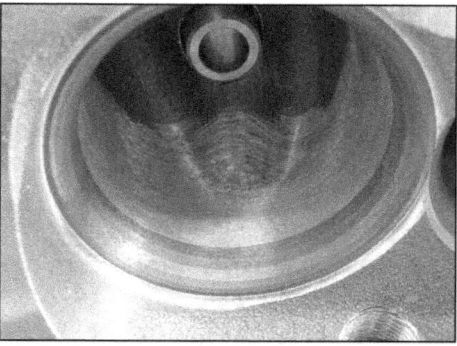

The classic three-angle valve job is not easy to see in this photo, but the idea is to form a gentle radius between the seat and the valve in order to direct air through this area as efficiently as possible.

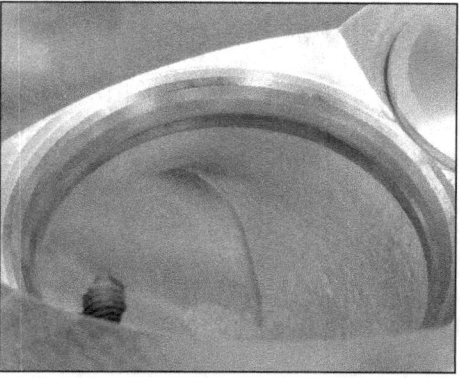

Besides the angles themselves, one key to a good valve job is to ensure a sharp edge delineating each separate angle. These sharp angles pay off in improved airflow, but also enhance wet flow by shearing the wet stream, which helps atomize the fuel as it enters the chamber.

achieves this value, it's not because the exhaust port is that great, but because the intake port flow value used for the comparison at that valve lift is generally weak. There is also much contention and discussion around what the "optimal" E/I value is for a particular cylinder head or engine family. Generally, these numbers revolve around the 75 to 80 percent value, but we don't lay claim to any hard and fast rule. If the exhaust port is too efficient, it tends to over-scavenge the cylinder and pull fresh inlet air right out of the port during overlap. If this occurs, the solution is generally to reduce cam overlap and/or reduce exhaust camshaft duration.

Exhaust port size is also critical to engine performance. Just as velocity is important to the intake side, it is an essential component on the exhaust side as well. Just like all other components for a street head, the port designer is forced to fit his exhaust port exit within a relatively narrow area of real estate in the cylinder head. Port exit location is dictated by the location of the exhaust header flange bolts in order for the headers to fit the chassis. This means the designer cannot arbitrarily raise the exhaust port location to improve exhaust flow such as could be accomplished in a pure race head. The width of the port is also limited because of the location and factory spacing of the exhaust bolts holes. But still, within this area there is much that can be done to improve exhaust flow. This is evident by the wide variety of flow numbers generated by the different cylinder head manufacturers. It appears that some cylinder head companies spend much more time on their exhaust ports than others. This is revealed not necessarily by the E/I number, but by the actual flow numbers themselves. What we are looking for is coefficient of flow numbers that take into account the cross-sectional area and the actual flow numbers.

If the cross-sectional area of the exhaust port is too large, velocity is reduced and it becomes more difficult for the exhaust port to purge all existing combustion residue from the cylinder. If the port cross-sectional area is too small, it's easy to see how the port itself is a restriction, and more exhaust residue will remain in the cylinder. Either way, peak power is limited because at higher engine speeds, there is precious little time for the exhaust port to do its job. Cylinder displacement plays a part in this scenario as well since a larger cylinder with a longer stroke has the potential to ingest more air and fuel, consequently requiring a larger exhaust port to help evacuate the cylinder of this combustion residue.

It's also important to think about the combustion process and what occurs along each step of the four-stroke cycle to truly appreciate the functionality required of each component on the cylinder head. In a performance engine, long before the piston reaches BDC, the exhaust valve opens to begin the exhaust phase. The earlier the exhaust valve opens, the more time it has (in terms of engine degrees of rotation) to help blow or push most of the exhaust gas out of the cylinder. This requires more exhaust lobe timing, which means opening the exhaust valve sooner and closing it later. A longer exhaust duration helps an under-performing exhaust port to improve

Flow Curtain Area vs. Port Cross-Sectional Area

The following chart calculates the flow curtain area by combining valve circumference and valve lift. Big valves garner a lot of attention in the high-performance community, but funny things happen when you calculate the area difference between a 1.94 and 2.10-inches diameter intake valve at 0.600-inches lift. Larger valves create very large flow curtain areas, especially above 0.400-inch of valve lift that far exceed the port's minimal cross-sectional area. The accompanying chart lists the flow window area of each valve at a given valve lift. Use this chart to determine when valve lift exceeds the minimal port cross-sectional area.

Valve Lift	Valve Size				
	1.94	2.02	2.055	2.08	2.10
0.100	0.609	0.634	0.645	0.653	0.660
0.200	1.218	1.269	1.291	1.306	1.319
0.300	1.828	1.904	1.936	1.960	1.979
0.400	2.438	2.538	2.582	2.614	2.639
0.500	3.047	3.173	3.228	3.267	3.299
0.600	3.656	3.808	3.874	3.921	3.958

Valve curtain area in sq.in.

As an example, let's say we have an intake port with a minimum cross sectional area of 2.00 sq.in. at the pushrod restriction, employing a standard 2.02-inch intake valve. Looking at the chart, you can see that somewhere just past 0.300 inch of valve lift, the flow window achieves this 2.00 sq.in. of area. To find out exactly where this occurs, we have to solve a simple proportion problem. Here's where that high school math you thought you'd never use again comes in to help you learn about cylinder head flow.

$$\frac{0.400}{2.538} = \frac{Y}{2.00}$$

This equates to: $(0.400 \times 2) = 2.538 \times Y$
$0.800 = 2.538Y$
$0.800/2.538 = Y$
$0.315 = Y$

So at 0.315 inches of valve lift, our flow window equals the intake port restriction. That's a fairly small window if you think about it. If this same intake port were fitted with a 1.94-inch intake valve, it would require 0.328 inch of valve lift to equal the flow with the port restriction. It follows then that as the intake valve becomes larger, the flow window area increases for the same valve lift. Conversely, as the valve becomes smaller in diameter, it requires more lift to achieve that intake port cross-sectional area with the flow window.

Armed with a basic understanding of valve flow curtain area, we can now get into the relationship between the valve curtain flow area and the minimum port cross-sectional area. The point where flow measured on the flow bench in cfm most often levels off is generally around 0.400-inch valve lift. At this point, the flow curtain area determined by the combination of valve diameter and valve lift usually equals or exceeds the area of the port cross-section. Increasing valve lift from this point can, at best, be expected to increase flow only slightly. It will not increase dramatically because the port has become the restriction. Smaller heads will cross over sooner because of their smaller cross-sectional areas, but between 0.400 and 0.500-inch valve lift is where this most often occurs with 23-degree valve angle heads. Race heads with taller valve angles and larger ports increase this saturation point to higher valve lift numbers. This also requires us to remember that the cylinder wall also affects flow as well.

We've created a graph that illustrates this concept very simply. This graph also appears in the information packet that comes with every SuperFlow bench. What's missing from the SuperFlow material is the explanation to make it more useful. As you can see from the graph, the top-end power, but this sooner-opening exhaust valve point also potentially robs the engine of mid-range power with the exhaust valve opening too soon at lower engine speeds.

Here's where we get to discuss an interesting concept making the rounds in high-output naturally aspirated engine applications that

While few enthusiasts are aware of it, the chamber has a direct affect on intake and exhaust port flow based on the proximity of the chamber wall to the valve as well as the angle of the chamber wall relative to the valve. Steep chamber walls only reduce flow into or out of the chamber.

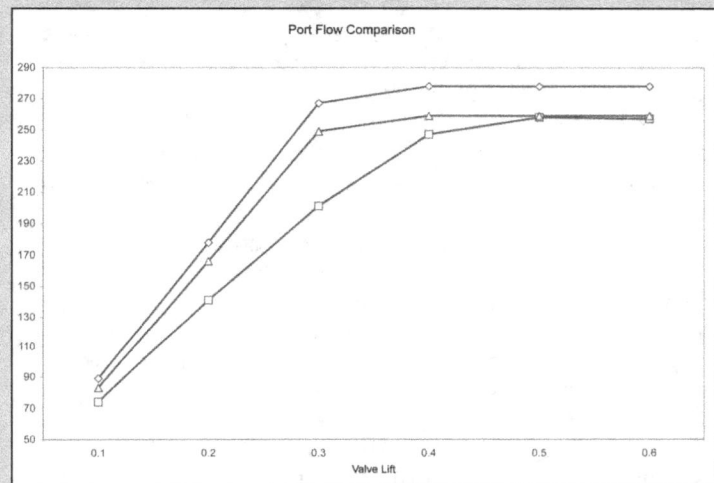

top curve represents optimal flow in cfm for each valve lift. This particular chart uses the flow curtain area for a 2.02-inch valve to calculate optimal flow based on the theoretical maximum flow of 140.5 cfm per square inch. This is a number that is calculated as being optimal flow per square inch and uses some rather intense math based on Bernoulli's equation that we won't get into since this chapter is already too long. We didn't create the formula, but based on calculations created by Edelbrock's Rick Roberts (who has a PhD in this stuff) you'll have to trust that this number is accurate. Each optimal data point is calculated by multiplying the valve curtain area for a given valve diameter times 140.5 cfm/square inch. For this particular chart, we also used a given port minimal cross-sectional area as the tip-over point. In this case, it was 1.98 sq.in., but this will vary with each port's actual cross-section.

The upper curve represents the theoretical optimal flow per square inch, which is difficult (if not impossible) to achieve. Rather than send a bunch of enthusiastic head porters in search of this 140.5 cfm/sq.in. holy grail, we've added a second plot to the graph that uses a much more achievable optimal flow number of 131 cfm/sq.in. According to Patrick Hale, who owns Racing Systems Analysis and the creator of the Quarter, Jr. and Quarter Pro computer drag strip simulation programs, this figure is a cfm/sq.in number that is achievable and can be used to evaluate different heads. Note that our test head (the bottom curve) is significantly below both curves until 0.500-inch valve lift. At 0.500-inches of valve lift, the test head overlaps the 131 cfm per square inch number—represented by the middle curve in the graph.

There are several very key points to this exercise. First, you can divide this chart into two portions. The first area is the point from 0.100-inch valve lift up until the optimal flow curve flattens out—roughly at 0.400 on this particular chart. The "low-lift" portion of the curve is the area dictated by the valve diameter, valve angles, and throat area portion of the intake port. The portion of the curve represented by valve lifts from 0.400 and higher can be used to evaluate the port's minimal cross-sectional area. Using that information as an evaluation tool for the test head, it's clear that any attempt to improve upper valve lift flow potential is going to be tough without increasing the intake port's cross-sectional area. Could the port be improved further? Certainly, but the results may require weeks of development work to achieve minimal improvements because the head has already achieved decent cfm/sq.in. velocity numbers compared to the optimal velocity of 140.5 cfm/sq.in.

However, looking at the area of the test head curve in the valve throat/valve job portion of the curve, we can see there is plenty of room for improvement merely to increase flow up to the 131 cfm/sq.in. curve. Add to this the notion that mid-lift flow combined with excellent flow velocity will drastically improve cylinder filling, which will result in excellent volumetric efficiency numbers. Herein lies what this author believes is the greatest potential for additional power for street engines. We deal with this subject in more detail in the "Power Secrets" sidebar.

Power Secrets

This is a very important point worth emphasizing. Think about airflow in terms of the induction cycle. As the piston reaches BDC on the induction cycle and begins its upward movement, the area in the cylinder becomes increasingly smaller. The intake tract from the bottom of the carburetor (or throttle body) all the way to the intake valve has now had sufficient time to achieve peak intake velocity. Think of this as a train that has now achieved its maximum speed and atmospheric pressure is sending that long chain of air and fuel into the cylinder. On the closing side of the valve lift curve, the piston is rising in the cylinder. Pressure is also increasing due both to cylinder filling and the reduction in cylinder volume. If the intake tract has sufficient velocity, which is the mass component of air and fuel combined with a given velocity, this has energy that can overcome the rising pressure and continue to fill the cylinder. Ultimate cylinder filling is achieved when the intake valve closes just as peak cylinder pressure is achieved. This can and often does result in cylinder filling that exceeds 100 percent volumetric efficiency (VE). This equates to achieving cylinder pressures much like what could be accomplished with a small supercharger.

The trick to attaining a higher level of volumetric efficiency may be found by enhancing flow efficiencies within the mid-lift areas. According to performance author Jim McFarland, his discussions with both Smokey Yunick and GM engineer Zora Arkus-Duntov revealed that both men reinforced the concept of emphasizing intake port flow at 65 to 70 percent of maximum intake valve lift and 80 percent of exhaust peak lift. So, if peak valve lift is 0.550 inch, this means that 0.350 to 0.400 inch of valve lift becomes an area where the port designer should emphasize intake flow efficiency. An ideal port would be one where all the valve lift points have achieved maximum flow, but if you want to find a place to start your improvements, the mid-lift flow area would be the place. This makes sense for several reasons. First, the valve lift curve achieves these values twice within its lift cycle. More importantly, if the intake port offers excellent coefficients of flow in this area, it offers both increased velocity and increased flow to help pack the cylinder with additional air and fuel near the end of the intake cycle as the piston is moving toward TDC. If there is sufficient kinetic port energy, created by the combination of mass flow (cfm) and velocity, then this energy is sufficient to fill the cylinder beyond 100 percent of its capacity. This will improve power throughout the entire RPM curve.

Many enthusiasts make the mistake of concentrating only on the peak flow numbers when evaluating cylinder heads. We hope you would agree that the idea is to enhance the entire flow curve, but if the engine builder is interested in building a very powerful engine combination, then attention to the mid-lift flow numbers becomes critically important.

Let's now take this information and add yet another factor. We've established that large valves radically increase the flow curtain area at higher valve lifts. Large valves drastically increase this flow curtain area. Some contend that this large area creates a flow loss because of the reduced velocity. This also occurs at the turn in the port bowl where the air and fuel must slow down to make the turn and begin to exit past the valve. While the velocity does drop off, Bernoulli's principal also states that as velocity decreases the pressure increases and that pressure and velocity are inversely proportional. This explains how an airplane wing creates lift. A wing is shaped so that the top portion creates a curved, longer path. With enough airspeed, the air traveling over the top of the wing must accelerate, creating high velocity and lower pressure. Because the wing is flat on the bottom, the air has a shorter distance to travel, creating less velocity and therefore more pressure. With a large enough surface area and sufficient speed, the pressure pushing up on the bottom of the wing lifts the aircraft. Early airplanes needed two wings to create sufficient lift at the low speeds generated by heavy, low horsepower engines.

This same pressure versus velocity relationship now comes into play in the flow window area of the intake port. With a large valve and subsequently larger flow curtain area, the inlet velocity slows down. As the speed decreases, the pressure increases in the flow curtain area. This is how an intake port with a smaller port cross-sectional area helps to fill the cylinder. It creates velocity at the intake pushrod restriction. This higher inlet speed then slows as it moves past the valve. This creates pressure. Despite the rising pressure in the cylinder, additional cylinder filling can be achieved because of this greater pressure at the valve. This incoming pressure charge can then push its way into the cylinder even as the pressure in the cylinder is rising on intake valve closing. If you've ever wondered why a cylinder can continue to fill as its pressure is rising in the cylinder, this interesting trick of physics is what makes it possible. This is most prevalent at peak torque where a well-tuned engine can achieve volumetric efficiency numbers above 100 percent.

This is important information since it reinforces the concept of enhancing mid-lift flow on any cylinder head for any engine. Sure, peak valve lift flow is still important, but it's entirely possible that sacrificing peak valve lift flow in favor of increasing mid-lift flow will contribute to an overall power gain. If you begin to see how all this theory weaves itself together toward the common goal of making more power then you have just made a very critical and important step in your understanding of how engines make power. We can't emphasize too strongly how critical this information is to properly evaluating intake port flow potential. Every time we study a new cylinder head, if the intake port offers a strong mid-lift flow curve, it generally becomes a very successful cylinder head. Those heads that offer weak or compromised mid-lift curves tend to be less successful when it comes to making power. There are certainly many other hurdles to value in terms of achieving the greatest reduction of exhaust gas volume in the cylinder. Many drag race cylinder head designers and builders ignore low-lift exhaust flow rates, claiming they are of insignificant value, and perhaps they know something about race engines that we don't. Several cylinder head manufacturers do not even list 0.100-inch valve lift numbers in their catalogs, choosing to start the flow curves at 0.200 inch. However, there are a few respected cylinder head specialists who contend the low-lift exhaust flow numbers are important. In fact, one cylinder head porter we spoke to stated he'd prefer if we didn't discuss this in our book since he was concerned about acknowledging this point to the

Flowing an intake manifold on the head to measure flow reduction is a good way to judge the effectiveness of the intake. A single-plane-style intake will always test better than a dual plane, so the best test is to see which style intake among dual planes or single planes is the best.

Coefficient of Flow

Any work with airflow through an orifice can be evaluated by a process called flow coefficients, which is defined as the relative measurement of a device's ability to flow air against a known standard. As an example, let's say we have a simple hole in a plate. If we push air through the hole at a given pressure, we can apply a mathematical calculation based on flow and the pressure drop across this orifice based on Bernoulli's principals that will establish the maximum theoretical flow potential for that orifice. That maximum is then given a rating of 100 percent. At standard temperature and pressure (60 degrees of dry air and 29.92 inches of Mercury with no humidity), we'll save you the headache of the math and tell you that the number is 140.5 cfm per square inch. The one assumption we must make when using this number is actually a big one. This assumes the incompressibility of the working fluid—air. Since we all know that air is certainly compressible, there is an error that creeps into these calculations, but in order to take that into account, the math gets really messy. So for the sake of our sanity and the very slight error that it creates, we'll use the concept that we're dealing with an incompressible working fluid.

Keep in mind that this 140.5 cfm/sq.in. standard is for flow through a simple orifice or a pipe. It's unlikely that any complex small-block intake or exhaust port that's forced to move around pushrods and incorporate valve seats and other restrictions would attain this theoretical maximum. So given that, all flow coefficients are rated as a percentage of this maximum of 140.5 cfm/sq.in. So, we could flow an intake port for example at 0.500 inch of valve lift and generate a cfm. Next, we divide the flow by the port's minimum cross-sectional area and then use this cfm per square inch (cfm/sq.in.) component to evaluate it compared to the maximum flow coefficient standard.

As an example, let's say we have a head that flows 260 cfm at 0.500-inch lift with a port cross-sectional area of 2.00 sq.in. This creates a 130 cfm/sq.in. flow versus the theoretical 140.5. Dividing 130 by 140.5, we come up with a flow coefficient of 0.925, which is outstanding. This means that the port flows 92.5 percent of what an ideal port of that size could flow. When using the minimum port cross-section area for calculation, be sure that the flow window area exceeds the minimum port cross-sectional area. This means that the sq.in. of flow window created by the combination of the valve diameter and valve lift is larger than the minimum port area so that you are actually evaluating the port and not the valve job. For all of our calculated flow velocity numbers you will see in this book, the velocities are calculated in exactly this fashion where the flow curtain area is used until the valve lift equals the area of the port cross-section and then the port's area is used from then on.

Attempts to enhance or improve swirl or tumble out of the intake port does little to affect power. In fact, this Dart wet flow bench photo illustrates that minimal swirl occurs and that tumble may not exist at all. Of course, this is also based on static piston position testing.

Increasing the height of the exhaust port is perhaps the single best way to bump up exhaust port flow. Of course, a radically raised exhaust port also requires custom headers, but if you're looking for an excellent exhaust port for a supercharged or nitroused engine, this may be worth the effort.

benefit of other cylinder head companies! So perhaps there is something to this concept.

As far as street cylinder heads are concerned, even 0.100 inch of valve lift becomes critical if you consider that peak valve lift often occurs at 0.450 to 0.500 inch, making even 0.100 inch represent 20 percent or more of the total valve lift figure. Port work is often a game of compromises. It's rare to find a change that is worth improved flow throughout the entire valve lift curve. More often it's a case where a slight change in the seat angles or throat approach angle improve the flow at low lift while hurting high-lift flow. The opposite can also be true. Taking this low-lift flow concept one step further, it's possible that sacrificing peak valve lift flow to enhance flow at 0.050 or 0.100 inch of valve lift might just be beneficial.

Further evidence supporting this low-lift flow theory states that in-cylinder pressure analysis of a race engine indicates that the majority of exhaust port flow occurs before the exhaust valve reaches peak valve lift. This also indicates that only a minor amount of flow occurs on the closing side of the exhaust valve curve. While this is only one test on one engine, it does indicate that this is a fairly typical situation that is probably duplicated in most every street engine.

One detracting component of improving low-lift exhaust flow is that most camshafts tend to accelerate the valve through 0.100 inch rather quickly, which is why certainly 0.200 inch valve lift is also an important exhaust flow number as well. Flat tappet cams are not limited in acceleration, so they pump the lifter through the 0.100-inch valve lift point rather quickly compared to roller cam followers that are a bit more lazy off the base circle. This would then mean that, in theory, good low-lift flow numbers would be of more positive consequence for roller cam motors than flat tappet cammed engines.

Another point worth considering is valve overlap, where both the intake and exhaust valves are open at the same time. This occurs as the exhaust valve is closing and the intake valve is just opening. It's possible that exhaust gas exiting the cylinder past the exhaust valve tends to enhance intake low-lift flow. The negative side of this is that a strong low-lift flowing exhaust valve might also pull a portion of the inlet charge directly from the intake right out the exhaust. This probably does occur, but could be minimized by reducing the amount of valve overlap that is designed into the camshaft. As you can see, this is very much an open-ended discussion with proponents and detractors on both sides.

We only know what works for us on many different naturally aspirated small-block Chevys. While we have never actually tested the concept of improved low-lift exhaust port flow, we do know that every cylinder head that offers an excellent performing exhaust port in the low lift region tends to perform very well and usually requires less cam duration on the exhaust side than heads that do not offer good low-lift exhaust port flow numbers. To support this statement, we canvassed every single head in our flow inventory and came up with a list of five heads that offered no less than 67 exhaust cfm at 0.100-inch valve lift. A couple of heads, like the AFR 210 and the TFS 195 head, tested at 70-plus cfm at this same valve lift. All of these heads also perform in the top 10 percent of all the castings that we've tested. This example encompasses much more than just low-lift exhaust flow, but certainly this component must be a contributing factor.

Getting back to more specific app-lication recommendations, exhaust ports with a taller exit exhibit far superior flow characteristics than ports forced to pinch off the exit line for the exhaust gas. Some cylinder head manufacturers even raise the ports to the extent that headers no longer fit the chassis they were designed for. Another trick employed by the cylinder head porter to increase flow is to widen the exhaust port floor to even out the pressure distribution from the port into the header.

AIRFLOW BASICS

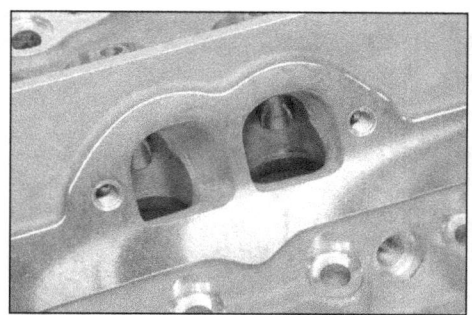

A flat-floor or D-port style exhaust port is also a good exercise in improving exhaust port flow. Not all exhaust ports respond to this change, so tread carefully here before you hog the exhaust ports without testing.

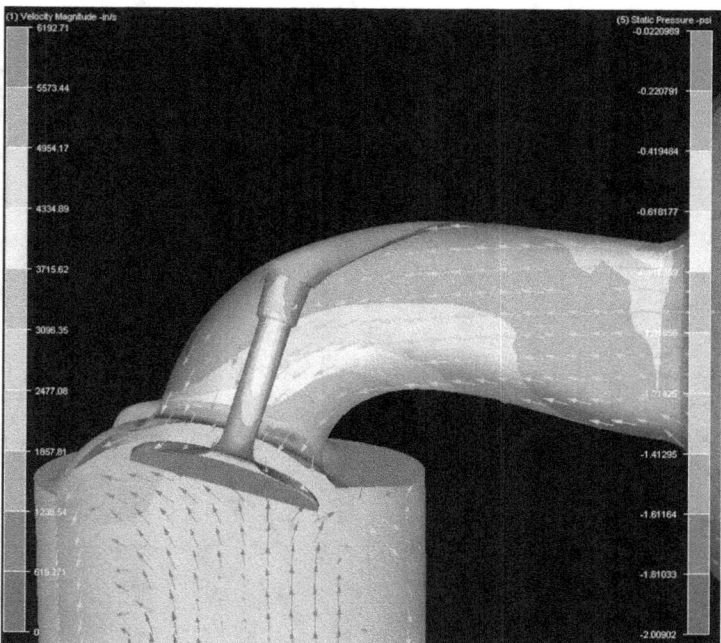

CFD simulations are beyond the realm of most hot rodders, but they do represent the next level of design and testing port configurations. One thing to look for are areas of low velocity where flow can often create eddies or even reverse the flow direction.

Because the exhaust port does not have to be concerned with wet flow characteristics, a full radius valve job can often be employed on the exhaust side with favorable results. These valve jobs enhance low and mid-lift flow by using smooth transitions between the valve angles. While this works on the exhaust side, don't try this on the intake—the results will not be favorable. A wider margin on the exhaust valve is always preferable not just for the additional material as a heat sink, but also to enhance flow around the valve. Some head specialists prefer to fully radius the chamber side of the exhaust valve, while other ports respond negatively to this technique. A wider seat of around 0.100 inch is a good idea, especially because the valve seat along with the valvestem are the two primary heat transfer areas that pull heat out of the exhaust valve.

We discuss back cutting the valve in more detail in Chapter 10, but this is a quick way to enhance exhaust port flow. A 30-degree back-cut placed inboard of the 45-degree seat on the valve tends to especially enhance low-lift flow, and often it can be beneficial throughout the entire lift curve. If you have the time and resources to test, it may also be of value to try other back-cut angles besides 30 degrees. The guys at Lingenfelter Performance Engineering have found that even one-degree changes can be beneficial, but this requires precise and repeatable testing techniques to verify. But that's how the fast guys become fast.

Conclusion

As we began this chapter, it became apparent that there was no way to adequately cover this subject in the amount of room we originally budgeted. In fact, this chapter is much larger than intended because we kept coming across more information that we couldn't resist including. Our goal was to hit the major points of cylinder head airflow characteristics, but it is impossible to cover everything. There is clearly enough material for a complete book just on the physics and theory of airflow in an internal combustion engine. It was our intent to introduce you to this subject and perhaps open enough doors to intrigue you to continue your personal search for increased knowledge on the subject. If so, then this chapter has been successful. It was definitely fun to write.

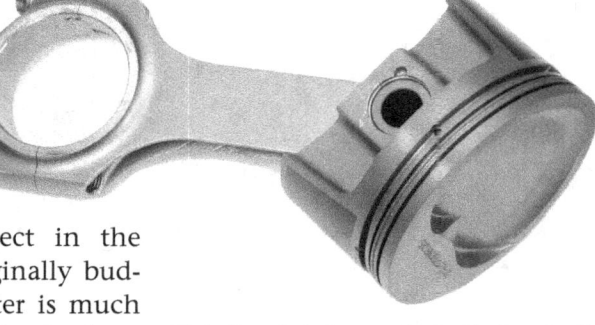

Relating intake ports to the rest of the engine combination, large intake port combinations tend to work best with large displacements, supercharged, or nitroused combinations. Large ports also respond better to short connecting rods. Higher-velocity ports tend to work well with longer connecting rods and slightly longer intake manifold runner lengths, such as those found in dual-plane intakes.

The Velocity Factor

Now that we have an idea of the relationship of valve size, flow curtain areas, and port cross-sectional area, let's add flow in cubic feet per minute (cfm) into the recipe and see what settles out. If we take the cfm flow of a given intake port at a valve lift of 0.500 inch or above and divide it by the port's minimum cross-sectional area—or choke point—we should come up with a velocity value that we can use to compare different cylinder heads. Basically, if we have two cylinder heads under consideration, it's not just simply the head with the most flow that wins. The selection process must acknowledge inlet velocity. If we measure both heads on a flow bench at the same test depression (28 inches of water), then we can combine this volumetric data with the port's cross-sectional area to compute a velocity. Let's see how this works.

To start, let's take two cylinder heads. Head A has an intake flow of 225 cfm at 0.500-inch valve lift with a cross-sectional area of 2.35 sq.in. as measured at the pushrod restriction in the port, just downstream of the port opening in the head. Head B offers 215 cfm at the same valve lift using a smaller cross-sectional area of 2.15 sq.in. also measured at the pushrod restriction. Let's do the math:

Head A:
225 / 2.35 = 95.74 cfm per square inch (cfm/sq.in.)

Head B:
215 / 2.15 = 100 cfm/sq.in.

The results from this simple evaluation indicate that even though Head B flows less volume of air at the same test depression and valve lift compared to Head A, it offers a higher cfm of airflow per square inch. These numbers also reinforce the concept that the head with the smaller cross-sectional area will deliver higher inlet velocity numbers, which tends to increase overall power and especially torque—which is a good thing for a street engine. Of course, this also means the smaller port may not be the best choice for peak RPM horsepower. That's where the larger head will shine. But in terms of a street engine where the goal is great overall power with an emphasis on mid-range torque and good acceleration—the smaller head should be given serious consideration.

If you have read the sidebar on Flow Curtain Area versus Port Cross-Sectional Area, then you already know that below roughly 0.500-inch valve lift that the valve curtain area is smaller than the port cross-sectional area. This means that at these lower lift numbers, the valve curtain is the restriction to port flow. But once valve lift achieves roughly 0.500 inch of lift, the port becomes the restriction. Valve diameter plays a big part in this equation as well. Smaller valves require more lift to achieve what we will call the merge point, the specific valve lift at which the port cross-section and the valve curtain area are the same. Larger valves will achieve the merge point at lower valve lift while smaller valves will merge at higher valve lifts.

As an example, let's take a look at a pair of cylinder heads and their velocity numbers.

Vortec Iron
Port Area = 1.74 sq.in.
Port Flow @ 0.500-inches lift = 239 cfm
239 cfm / 1.74 = 137 cfm/sq.in.

Sportsman II
Port Area = 2.19 sq.in.
Port Flow @ 0.500-inches lift = 240 cfm
240 cfm / 2.19 = 109 cfm/sq.in.

By themselves, these velocity numbers are only valuable when compared to the 140.5 cfm/sq.in. standard. But when we use them to compare velocity values at the same valve lift, they become more relevant. For example, examining the cfm flow of both these heads at 0.500 inch of valve lift, there is only one cfm difference between them. But the difference in velocity is enormous with a full 25 percent increase (137 vs. 109). This reveals in sharp detail the difference in cross-sectional area. The heads flow the same, but the Sportsman II is much larger in cross-sectional area. The Vortec port area is roughly 20 percent smaller in cross-sectional area than the Sportsman II yet flows virtually the same at 0.500-inch lift. This means the Vortec offers much higher velocity with the same or better airflow, which is a great situation for any street engine. We chose this pairing for its obvious disparity, but you can use this same velocity comparison technique anytime there is a question of which cylinder head to choose. Clearly, the higher the velocity, the more efficiently the intake port will fill the cylinder, improving the engine's volumetric efficiency (VE). You can also see now how following the simplistic approach of looking only at peak valve lift flow numbers, the Sportsman II head would appear to be the better of the two heads.

It's also worth noting a couple of simple parameters that will help you choose between cylinder heads even when you do not know a given intake port's cross-sectional area. Basically, you can use intake port volume for any 23-degree small-block Chevy head as a rough comparator of port cross-sectional area. Larger-volume heads generally employ a larger cross-sectional port area. Given this, if you have two heads with similar flow numbers but one port has a larger volume, you can assume that the smaller of the two heads will most likely offer a higher velocity number. There are probably exceptions to this rule of thumb, but in the majority of cases, it will work to your advantage.

CHAPTER 4

PRODUCTION HEADS

This is the classic small-block production iron head from the mid 1970s. Back in its day, it was a decent cylinder head, but with today's wide spectrum of heads to choose from, there are far better heads out there at a decent price that put these original iron castings at the bottom of the choice list.

Every step of the small-block Chevy's performance history has originated out of production parts. High-performance efforts have always begun by improving upon what the factory built, and the small-block Chevy is the poster child for that effort. This is a quick walk through the history and evolution of some of the better production heads, but the reality is that there are very few that are of any note. In fact, there's really only one production head (and iron at that) that is really worthy of consideration for a 21st century performance small-block Chevy. But in deference to the millions of castings that have made their way down the assembly line, we take a look at the few that are worthy of mention.

Head History

The selection list is basically rather thin for today's performance engines. The earliest 265 and 283 small-blocks relied on an iron Power Pack head that featured 58-cc chambers and tiny 1.72/1.50-inch valves. The bigger heads to follow were the "double-hump" heads championed by the mid-'60s 327 engines. The easiest way to reference any production head is with the last three digits of its casting number. The most famous heads are the 461 and 462 heads that offer 160-cc intake ports, 64-cc chambers, and 2.02/1.60-inch valve sizes. For years, these were coveted castings in the performance community that were not superseded until the advent of the Chevy over-the-counter Turbo and Bow Tie iron pieces. Even for many years after their introduction, the Bow Tie was considered exotic fare for street engines.

Around the mid 1980s, several companies including Brownfield (which was eventually purchased by AirFlow Research), World Products, Brodix, Dart, and others began producing aftermarket iron and aluminum cylinder heads that were substantially better than the original small-block Chevy castings. For a while the Bow Tie head held its own, and there was even furtive interest in the '88 and later aluminum Corvette heads. The Corvette heads turned out to be marginal, and by this time production heads were

Even older is the troglodyte-like 64-cc chamber heads, often referred to as "double hump" or "camel hump" heads because of their distinctive casting marks on the ends of the heads. These smaller chamber heads had better flowing ports than the later 441 or 882 castings.

HIGH-PERFORMANCE CHEVY SMALL-BLOCK CYLINDER HEADS

only considered for low-budget street engines. Even the older performance "double hump" heads are now considered passé. Then, in 1996, GM came up with the L31 Vortec engine package for light-duty trucks, using a new production cylinder head that quickly gained favor first among the roundy-pounders and then on the street.

To look at the Vortec head, it appears to be just another iron production head. Its cosmetic changes include using centerbolt valve covers and a strange sawtooth i.d. pattern on the front of the head. It also uses the later-model 8-bolt intake manifold pattern that is different from the small-block's traditional 12-bolt pattern. Otherwise, its 170-cc intake port volume, 64-cc chamber, and 1.94/1.50-inch valve sizes offer little clue as to its performance potential. But the chamber shape is much improved and the ports were born of performance heritage. Without a doubt, it is the best iron GEN I small-block production cylinder head Chevrolet has ever produced. Topping that, the word soon spread that you could purchase these heads, complete for around $500 per pair, straight from Chevrolet. Virtually overnight, a new subculture of budget small-block Chevy engines was created.

Since then, the price from GM has risen steadily, but as this book is written, the heads are still available from several sources and can still be purchased in stock condition for between $600 and $650, which is still an excellent deal for the performance they produce. We look at a few iron and aluminum production predecessors in more detail, but the majority of this chapter is devoted to the Vortec for obvious reasons. Let's just say it now so there's no confusion—the Vortec head is the only real mild production head to use if you're on a budget and your power goals are 400 hp or less with a 355-ci small-block.

Iron Maidens

We can classify iron production heads with several different categories, but the simplest is by combustion chamber volume. The early (before 1970) factory iron performance heads

The older iron 76-cc chambers suffered not only from increased volume, but the steep chamber walls also restricted flow from the intake and out the exhaust.

Beginning in 1969, Chevy added accessory holes to the front of all its cylinder heads to facilitate mounting alternator and air conditioning brackets to the front of the engine. Older heads like the 461 and 462 heads do not have these bolt holes, requiring the use of a short water pump and different brackets.

Factory Production Heads

The following list is a quick reference guide to some of the more popular iron and aluminum factory heads. Only production heads are listed here. Aftermarket heads are listed in Chapter 5. We have not listed the cross-sectional area of these heads, since most are rather small. With the exception of the Vortec iron heads, these production heads are around 1.80 sq.in., which is slightly larger than the Vortec head that specs out at 1.74 sq.in.

Casting Number	Material	Port Vol.	Valve Size (Intake) (inches)	Chamber Vol. (cc)
441	Iron	160	1.94/1.50	76
461/462	Iron	160	2.02/1.60	64
492	Iron	161	1.94/1.50	64
882	Iron	160	1.94/1.50	76
624	Iron	161	2.02/1.60	76
993	Iron	159	1.94/1.50	76
113	Alum.	163	1.94/1.50	58

PRODUCTION HEADS

Exhaust to Intake

If you want an object lesson in why the Vortec head works so well, don't just look at the excellent intake flow numbers. Comparing the exhaust flow numbers of the Vortec to the older 462 iron head for example, the percentage increase is significant. At 0.400-inch valve lift, the Vortec flowed 22 cfm more than the iron 462 head (147 cfm vs. 125) using the same size valve. That's an improvement of 17 percent! The worst differential between the two heads was at 0.100-inch lift–the Vortec was not as good by 4 cfm. The average improvement across the entire valve lift range was around 9 percent.

These improved exhaust flow numbers are one reason why the Vortec head makes more power. The improved intake flow certainly helps, but the exhaust is better. Of course, it could be even better. We've spoken to a couple of head porters who believe there is another 25 to 30 hp more in modifying the exhaust port, and perhaps even more. If you think about what has to happen at higher engine speeds, you must have an efficient exhaust port to blow the spent exhaust gas out quickly because there is precious little time to perform this task efficiently.

---

such as the 461, 462, and 291 heads were all 64-cc chamber heads because they were used mainly on the earlier small displacement 327 and 302-ci engines. As displacement grew and smog laws took precedence over performance, combustion chambers expanded to 76-cc. They constitute the later-model iron heads such as the 882, 441, and other casting number heads. These large chamber heads shrouded the valves even more than the older 64-cc chambers and did nothing to improve airflow. Not so ironically, the Vortec returned to a 64-cc chamber mainly because the current trend for all engines is with smaller, tighter chambers to improve both flow and chamber activity. This has to do with reducing the surface area to volume relationship that helps keep heat in the chamber rather than allowing it to escape into the cooling system.

Another major difference between the older 64-cc heads and the later 76-cc heads are the accessory drive holes located in the front of each pair of heads. With the '69 model year, Chevy went to a long water pump design that placed the accessory drive units more inboard and mounted them on the front of the cylinder head using the accessory drive holes. Early 64-cc chamber heads do not use these mounting points and it's a bit of a challenge to drill holes in the earlier heads for fear of hitting water. Without the accessory bolt holes, it's not possible to use the alternator, power steering, and A/C mounts with the long water pump.

We minimize production iron heads, but with a little bit of work they can be made to perform admirably. A classic example is the GM Performance Parts 492 (casting number) stock replacement head for the early 64-cc iron heads. We included this head in our test data, and it flowed well. Out of the box, GM must have realized how bad the stock exhaust port was and added a 1.60-inch exhaust valve to help the exhaust flow. The stock valve size for this head is the 1.94-inch diameter. The test data included in our flow info is a little different in that this head was fitted with a 2.02-inch valve. The catalog states that the larger valve can be added with a new valve job, which is what happened on this head. The combination of the larger intake valve and a good three-angle aftermarket valve job produced some decent flow numbers. These improved flow numbers also produced some interesting and mildly impressive velocity numbers. We didn't have time to do the work, but it appears that it would be a great candidate for a mild pocket porting effort, which would, based on our experience, improve the flow slightly over the current numbers, but only another 5 to perhaps 10 cfm in the mid-lift numbers. In addition, this

If you are looking for a replacement set of stock heads, try to avoid the later-model iron non-Vortec heads that are lighter castings and prone to cracking. The scallops around the lower row of head bolt-holes can quickly identify these heads. Earlier and more durable heads did not have these scallops.

work would actually help the exhaust side far more along with a 30-degree back cut on both the intake and exhaust. Again, the big gains would be on the exhaust side. We've seen improvements in low-lift flow as much as 10 to 15 cfm on the hot side of the head with the back cut trick and that's worth about 10 to 15 percent! That's a great return on a minimal investment.

There are several weak points with the older iron heads, not the least of which is that after 30 years or so of service, there is a distinct possibility that they are cracked (or soon will). We discuss the late '60s and mid '70s style heads like the 441 and 882 castings because they offer decent performance and were produced with sufficient iron. In later years, the factory began lightening these heads to reduce weight, and these heads are the ones that suffer from cracking. If you are considering rebuilding a set of production iron heads, the first step is to have the heads Magnafluxed to ensure there are no fissures. Places to look for cracks include the combustion chamber area between the valves and also in the top part of the head around the spring pockets.

The big cork for better horsepower is really on the exhaust side of all production small-block Chevy heads. Chapter 10 gets into the details on how to pocket port a set of iron small-block castings, but we can give you a sneak preview with the tip that almost all the horsepower rewards are gained on the exhaust side rather than the intake like many enthusiasts think.

If you are really on a budget and can't afford anything more than a stock rebuild on a set of heads, then the best approach is to at the very least invest in new guides and not scrimp by trying to get by with used valves. Valves can be re-used if the stems are not worn. The problem with used valves is that if the stems are worn, even new guides will not last long with tapered valvestem wear. The key here is that proper valveguide clearance means the valves won't dance around and beat up a good valve job. This should point out that investing in a performance 3-angle valve job is wasted if the guide clearance is not idealized to keep the valve centered on the seat.

Aluminum Upgrade

In 1986, Chevy debuted the L-98 Corvette engine with aluminum heads. At first these seemed to be an excellent way to upgrade a small-block with factory aluminum castings. The heads are a 40-lb weight

In 1986 Chevy introduced the first production aluminum small-block head on the Corvette, but it has turned out to be mediocre at best. These heads were used only on Corvette TPI engines used between 1986 and when the LT1 engine debuted in 1992.

Perhaps the biggest difference with the Vortec head is that it requires a specific 4-bolt intake manifold bolt pattern that is quite different from the standard 6-bolt small-block intake manifold pattern. This GM Fast Burn head offers both intake patterns on the same head, which makes intake selection easier with this head.

saver, but these heads are completely underwhelming as a street performance candidate. While significantly lighter by 20 pounds per casting than its iron cousins, the intake ports feature marginal improvements on the exhaust side. In addition, the chamber size comes in around 58-cc, which means a flat top 355 small-block with a near-zero deck and a 0.040-inch thick gasket will spike the static compression ratio to 10.9:1, which is too high for a mild street engine.

These aluminum castings can be mildly ported to improve flow, but because of Chevy's thin-wall casting techniques, it's difficult to increase port cross-section sufficiently without making the heads inherently weak and prone to cracking. Plus, unless you are capable of doing the porting work yourself, the cost involved in improving these heads could easily be invested in an aftermarket set of aluminum heads that will easily outperform even a ported L-98 style casting.

Price vs. Performance

Many enthusiasts believe that they're money ahead to rebuild an older set of heads rather than buy a brand new set of aftermarket heads. This is worth investigating because while that may have been true 30 years ago, the same cannot be said today. If you ever studied economics, there is a situation known as economy of scale. What this means is that major manufacturers like GM, World Products, or Dart have such a large production capacity that they can actually build a set of iron replacement cylinder heads much cheaper than you can have your set of heads rebuilt. Let's run through a typical rebuild on a set of iron small-block heads and then compare that to the price of a brand new set of Dart 180-cc iron heads. The prices we are using here are from a local machine shop. You might be able to find prices at your local machine shop that are less expensive depending upon your geographic location. Prices for parts were pulled from Summit Racing for budget-based valves, springs, retainers, keepers, and screw-in studs.

Production Head Procedure	Price
Hot tank and Magnaflux	$90
New guides installed (includes guides)	144
Machine guides for PC style seals	50
Valve job and assembly	275
Surface heads	50
Machine for screw-in studs	175

Component	Price
Valves, 2.02-inch intake	$64
Valves, 1.60-inch exhaust	64
Springs, single 1.250-inch	60
Retainers	55
Locks	7
Screw-in studs	32
Guideplates	13
Total	$1,079
Dart 180-cc Iron Eagle head from Scoggin-Dickey Parts Center	$953.98

The iron Vortec head is an incredibly durable and strong flowing head for a production casting. All Vortec heads have taller intake ports that make using a standard small-block intake difficult.

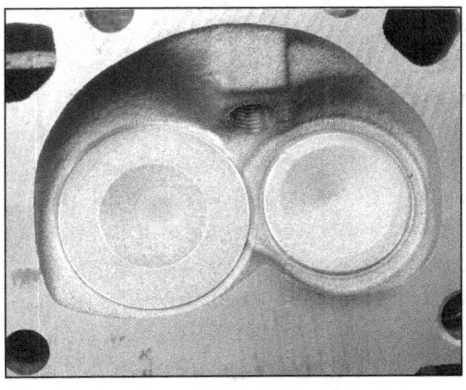

The Vortec head illustrates what Chevy engineers learned about constructing a more efficient chamber where the walls are not as steep, and the heart shape pushes the combustion activity toward the exhaust side of the chamber.

If you are just looking for a set of inexpensive aluminum heads to use on a street cruiser, the L-98 Corvette heads perform decently. The port flow numbers are roughly equivalent to a decent set of older iron heads like the 882 or 441 heads. On the plus side, the aluminum Corvette head offers a slightly better exhaust port than the older iron heads which helps produce slightly better peak horsepower numbers compared to iron production heads. These heads feature the older-style intake bolt pattern so they will accept the standard small-block Chevy intake manifold bolt pattern. These heads do require a centerbolt-style valve cover and look especially good fitted with a set of the magnesium Corvette-style valve covers. If you're on a budget, the stock tin production centerbolt valve covers will also bolt right on.

Another interesting point worth mentioning is that all these aluminum heads came with what appear to be factory guideplates. But if you look carefully, these heads also used guided rocker arms that use guides on either side of the rocker arm tip to center the rocker arm over the valve. Because the aluminum heads were not cast with guide holes in the heads, GM needed a way to retain the pushrods before the rockers were installed, so these "guideplates" are only used to position the pushrods on the assembly line. These plates are not hardened, which means if you use hardened pushrods, the guides will quickly wear. This means you must use guided rocker arms with these heads. It's worth noting that you should never combine guided rocker arms with guideplates since this may put most if not all the pushrods into a bind condition that quickly contributes to broken parts. Of course, these aluminum L-98 heads can also be converted over to aftermarket-hardened guideplates and hardened pushrods, which do not require the use of guided rockers.

Vortec Heads

The Vortec head was first produced for light-duty trucks in 1996, and at first no one really gave these new castings much more than a cursory look. But the word soon spread by way of the performance magazines, especially with one story that pitted the venerated Bow Tie performance head against the Vortec with the Vortec coming out on top. Considering that the Vortec came with conservative 1.94/1.50-inch valves and a mere 170-cc intake port, there were many who were skeptical. After all, the Bow Tie sported a bigger intake port with larger 2.02/1.60-inch valves. So how could this puny production head be better than the Bow Tie? The answer lies hidden in the confines of the port design and with the GM engineers who paid attention to a couple of keys, not the least of which was that intake velocity is a key player in the

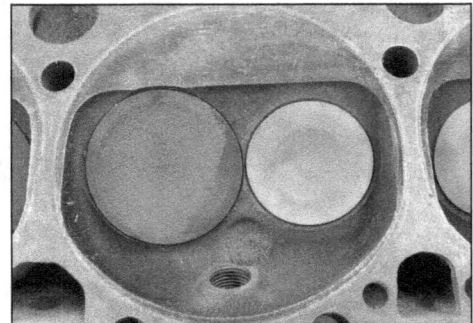
The older 76-cc chambers, such as this 882 head chamber, feature deep chamber walls that shroud both intake and exhaust flow. Plus this bathtub shape does little to enhance combustion efficiency.

torque game. And after all, this was supposed to be a truck head, so mid-lift flow and high velocities were key. Along the way, it didn't take long for performance enthusiasts to learn that the head was a perfect replacement for those older iron castings.

There turns out to be several changes to this head that deserve investigation before blindly diving into the small-block Vortec head game. There are actually two different casting numbers for the Vortec head, the 10239906 and the 1255062. We'll start with the basics around the 64-cc chamber design. For a 350-ci small-block, this smaller chamber automatically pushes the compression envelope, considering that with a flat-top piston with a 0.020-inch deck height, and a 0.040-inch thick gasket, this creates a 9.7:1 compression ratio, which is right on the edge. Certainly with a small cam, this would contribute to detonation problems even with 93-octane fuel, especially on hot days.

The smaller chamber is matched with rather conservative valve sizes of 1.94 and 1.50-inch diameters for the intake and exhaust. While these might seem small, the valve sizes are

The newer Vortec heads also come stock with excellent positive-style Viton rubber seals on both the intake and exhaust guides. Also note that different seals are used on the intake and exhaust.

The stock Vortec combination of a tall valveguide and a deep retainer make retainer-to-seal clearance marginal. GM claims you can run a 0.475-inch lift cam, but that's with virtually zero clearance between the seal and the retainer. This photo shows measuring this clearance on a different head, but the procedure is the same.

GM also learned one way to enhance the Vortec's mid-lift flow is with a 30-degree back cut on both the intake and exhaust valves.

PRODUCTION HEADS

Vortec Head Parts List

The following GM Performance Parts and GM Service Parts numbers relate directly to the iron Vortec head that can be useful if you are considering using a set of Vortec heads.

Part numbers that include (SDPC) are parts available only from Scoggin-Dickey Performance Center, a major GM Performance Parts dealer in Texas. This organization is also a great resource if you have questions on any GM Performance Parts.

Component	Part Number
Vortec head assembly	12558060
Vortec head assembly, SDPC-modified	SD8060AGP2 (SDPC)
Valve, intake, 1.94-inches	1 0241743
Valve, exhaust, 1.50-inches	12550909
Intake seal	10212810
Exhaust seal	12564852
Valvestem seal kit	12511890
Intake gasket, both Vortec and std. bolt pattern	12497760
Intake gasket, Vortec only (w/ pins)	12529094
GM intake bolts	12550027
Head gasket, 0.028-inches thick (400 engines)	12363763
Head gasket, 0.028-inches thick	14096405
GM roller rockers, 1.6, LT1 style, guided	12370839
GM roller rockers, 1.5, LT1 style, guided	12370838
GM stamped 1.5 rockers, guided	12495490
Valvespring kit, LT4, 1.32-inches dia.	12495494
Retainer kit for LT4 springs	12495492
Locks for LT4 retainers	12495503
Valve cover, chrome, bow tie, centerbolt	12355350
Valve cover, polished aluminum, centerbolt	12497978
Valve cover gasket	10046089
Bolt and seal kit	12497980
Vortec intake, dual plane, GMPP	12366573
Vortec intake, single plane, GMPP	12496822
COMP Cams spring seat cutter	4718
COMP Cams valveguide cutter	4726
COMP Cams arbor for 11/32-inches stem dia.	4732

If you choose to add a larger diameter, more aggressive valvespring to the Vortec head, you must enlarge the spring seat in the head and reduce the outside diameter of the valveguide to create sufficient inside diameter clearance for the larger spring.

The more elegant solution to adding a stiffer spring to the Vortec head is a set of COMP Cams' conical or beehive springs like this 26915 spring, which fits into the stock spring pocket and does not require a narrowed guide. These are excellent springs that literally bolt on.

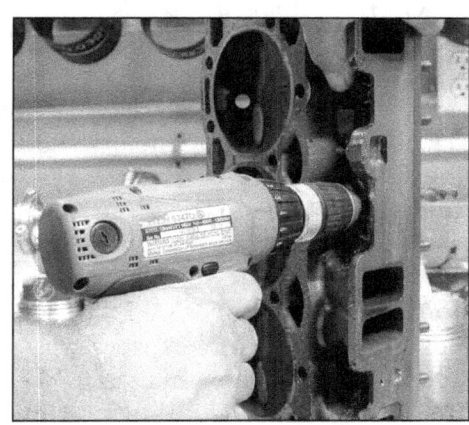

If a 1.6:1 roller rocker arm is in your Vortec future, remember to drill out the pushrod holes to a larger 3/8-inch diameter to ensure that the pushrods don't rub on the cylinder head.

actually well matched to the high velocity intake port. As we saw in Chapter 3 in respect to flow basics, velocity is an important key to cylinder filling, especially when the intake port is properly matched to the intake valve diameter and throat area. To this end, despite its diminutive port dimensions, the Vortec creates outstanding velocity (as measured in CFM flow per square inch of port area) especially in the 0.300 and 0.400 inch of valve lift areas. Just the flow numbers by themselves are good, but when you include the velocity numbers, its true potential begins to take shape. Frankly, there are few heads in this book that can top its intake velocity numbers, and it is the intake speed ratings that are this head's strength.

Vortec Springs

The stock springs used on a Vortec head offer minimal performance potential. The stock spring rate is weak and offers limited lift potential. GM Performance Parts has several alternate performance springs, and aftermarket cam companies like COMP and Crane have literally dozens of choices. We've listed a few here that we know work well. Some springs require machining springs seats and guides in order to fit.

Description	Outside Dia. (inches)	Load at Installed Ht. (lbs @ inches) Lift	Load @ .500 (in.)	Coil Bind	Valve Lift* (lbs/inch)	Spring Rate (lbs)
GMPP 3927142	1.273	110 @ 1.700	289	1.16	0.490	358
GMPP 10206040	1.300	85 @ 1.78	271	1.26	0.470	373
GMPP 12551483	1.320	101 @ 1.78	267	1.22	0.510	332
COMP 26915 conical	1.290 (base)	105 @ 1.800	261	1.085	0.665	313
COMP 26918 conical	1.290	130 @ 1.800	286	1.085	0.665	313
COMP 983 ovate	1.440	105 @ 1.700	310	1.150	0.500	410
COMP 981	1.254	105 @ 1.700	316	1.150	0.500	423

*Valve lift is listed here for reference only to coil bind, not to retainer-to-seal clearance, which could be less than the potential lift indicated. This valve lift capacity figure includes 0.050 inch of coil bind clearance. The safe valve lift figure is calculated by subtracting the coil bind height from the installed height, minus 0.050 inch for coil bind clearance.

On the exhaust side, this head is much more typical of a production small-block head. The original small-block Chevy has always been plagued with weak exhaust port flow, and the Vortec is no different. Its best exhaust-to-intake (E/I) flow relationship numbers are at the lowest flow points and get decidedly worse as valve lift opens up to 0.500 inch of lift. The entire exhaust cross-section is just too small for the intake port. For a truck application where torque is everything, this is acceptable. But to pull out a decent horsepower number from these heads, your attention for modifications should be directed almost exclusively toward the exhaust side of this head. To help peak flow while still maintaining low-lift flow velocity is key to improving these heads. We know cylinder head porters who claim they can pull another 35 to 40 hp out of a stock iron Vortec head with work only on the exhaust side.

At this point, you may have more invested in a set of production iron heads than it would cost to buy a good set of Edelbrock or even TFS aluminum heads, so the goal should be carefully evaluated. But it can be done.

If serious performance is your aim with these heads, there are other situations that must be addressed as well before you bolt these heads on an engine. Because this head was originally designed as a production piece, the stock Vortec's max valve lift potential is definitely limited. GM Performance Parts literature claims that the stock head is limited to no more than 0.475 inch of valve lift, but this is a very tight number. The standard clearance spec for seal-to-retainer clearance is 0.050 inch, but in a head that we measured, we barely had 0.460 inch total from the retainer to the seal. At a true 0.475 inch of valve lift, this results in a crushed valvestem seal. To retain a true 0.050 inch of retainer-to-seal clearance, this leaves roughly 0.410 inch of allowable lift, with perhaps 0.420 to 0.430 inch if you feel lucky. Some of the newer Vortec heads may offer additional clearance to allow that 0.475-inch lift figure, but you must measure your heads to ensure there is sufficient valve lift clearance.

There are several solutions to this problem depending upon how much money you want to spend. The easiest solution is to purchase a set of modified Vortec heads from companies like Scoggin-Dickey Performance Center or Jim Pace Chevrolet. Both of these reputable GM Performance Parts dealerships offer professionally modified heads that have had the valveguides machined to increase the clearance to allow you to run up to 0.550 inch valve lifts. Of course, if you already have a set of stock Vortec heads, you can also have your local machine shop do the machine work. Further, if you have

PRODUCTION HEADS

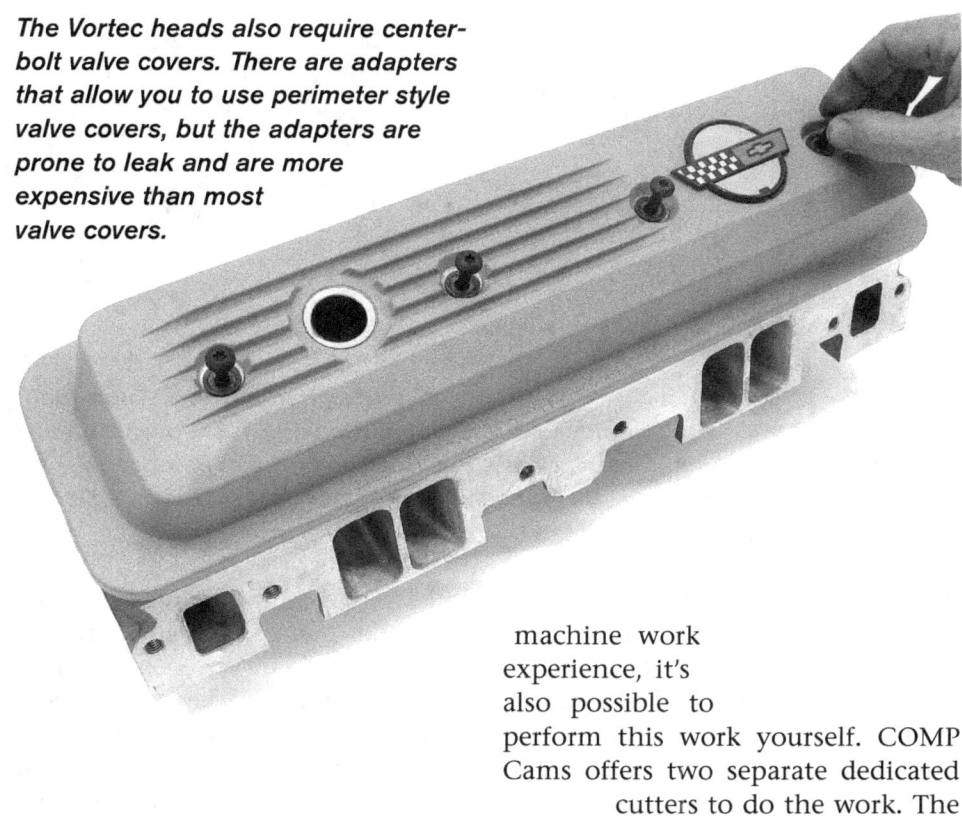

The Vortec heads also require center-bolt valve covers. There are adapters that allow you to use perimeter style valve covers, but the adapters are prone to leak and are more expensive than most valve covers.

The centerbolt-style covers also demand narrow body rocker arms to offer sufficient clearance to prevent rubbing on the valve cover. Some stock covers like the original equipment manufacturer (OEM) TPI magnesium covers require minor surgery to clear even the narrow body Crane rockers.

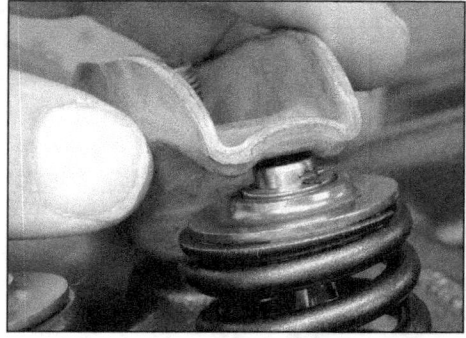

Vortec heads also use guided rocker arms. Stamped rockers use these mild guides while the Crane Gold Race rockers use stamped steel guides. These guides do require a valve tip that protrudes above the retainer more so than other valvestems.

The Vortec head uses the newer tapered-seat style spark plug (left) while most aluminum heads employ the gasketed style spark plug (right) with the longer 0.750-inch thread length.

machine work experience, it's also possible to perform this work yourself. COMP Cams offers two separate dedicated cutters to do the work. The first opens up the stock spring pad diameter from 1.300 inch to while also cutting the guide outside diameter from 0.850 inch to a smaller 0.630 inch at the bottom. The second tool lowers the height of the guide while also reducing the top of the guide dia-meter from 0.560 to 0.530. By lowering the guide height, this increases the retainer-to-seal clearance, allowing more valve lift.

Increasing the spring seat diameter creates room for a larger diameter spring, which can accommodate more valve lift. The stock springs are somewhat weak and with the retainer-to-seal limitation, any more cam than 0.450-inch lift is treading on dangerous ground, especially if you were to over-rev the engine and put the engine into valve float. The simplest trick to upgrading the Vortec head to a better performance valvespring is to use one of the new-generation conical or beehive valvesprings from COMP Cams. The 26915 or 26918 springs offer several bolt-in advantages over standard spring designs.

The conical shape of the spring by design reduces the mass (weight) of the spring at its uppermost por-

HIGH-PERFORMANCE CHEVY SMALL-BLOCK CYLINDER HEADS

CHAPTER 4

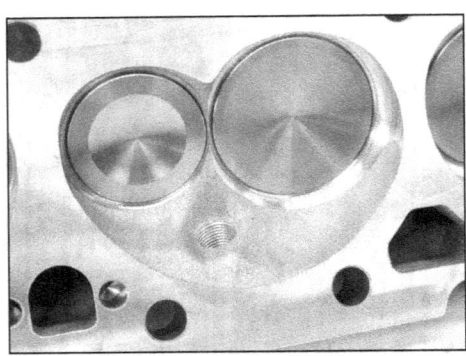

The LT1/LT4 engines, while similar, do not use the same cylinder heads as a typical GEN I small-block. The water jacket deployment within the cylinder heads is significantly different and GEN II heads are not interchangeable with GEN I engines.

When GM redesigned the small-block and introduced it in the 1997 Corvette, it set a whole new standard for the small-block Chevy, especially in terms of production head cylinder head flow and combustion chamber design. This is a Dart version of the LS1 head.

tion. Reducing the mass of the spring as well as drastically reducing the mass of the retainer allows more spring rate to be used to control the valve at higher engine speeds as opposed to using a significant amount of the spring load to control the spring itself. Consider that the top portion of the spring travels the most distance during valve lift. So if we reduce this mass, we can use more of the spring's load to control the rest of the valvetrain. Also, by design, the conical spring offers a variable spring rate, which means it is far less susceptible to harmonics and therefore does not need a damper to help control spring surge. If you are interested in learning more about valvesprings and their effect on valvetrain dynamics, this is covered in my book, *High-Performance Small-Block Cams & Valvetrains*, also available through S-A Design and CarTech.

The only drawback to using conical valvesprings is that they are roughly twice as expensive as typical single-wound valvesprings. But the advantage of these springs is that they drop right into place on a stock Vortec head, fitting tightly into the stock valvespring seat diameter, and they also clear the large Vortec valveguide diameter at the base. This positively locates the spring, which helps in a dynamic situation, and along with the smaller-diameter retainer, it is also shorter, which allows much more valve lift room. If your engine is already equipped with a set of Vortec heads, these springs make the swap simple since all you have to do is pump each cylinder full of compressed air with both valves closed, remove the original units, and install the conical springs. This eliminates the hassle of machining the heads for the larger-diameter springs, which also requires purchasing new valveguide seals as well. That's not necessarily bad, but it seems a waste when the factory seals are particularly good and worth keeping, which is again a plus when using the conical springs. Overall, the conical springs end up being only slightly more expensive than removing the heads, having a machine shop modify them for bigger springs, and also installing new seals.

The Vortec heads also do not use a guideplate to position the stamped rockers over the valve as is done in traditional small-block heads. Instead, the factory went to what is called a guided rocker arm. These rockers use two small bumps or guides that straddle the valve tip to properly position the rocker over the valve. Both COMP Cams and Crane offer guided roller rockers as performance upgrades for these heads, or you can modify the heads for screw-in studs and guideplates that allow you to run non-guided rockers on these heads.

Keep in mind that in addition to all the other non-traditional aspects of the Vortec head, this head also uses a centerbolt valve cover design. This means the bolts run down through the center of the valve cover. This makes the real estate in between the rocker arms somewhat restricted, which means that typical budget aluminum roller rockers generally will not clear a Vortec head valve cover. The top-of-the-line Crane roller Gold Race series narrow body rockers not only fit in between the center bolts, but are also guided rockers that do not require guideplates. One addition to these heads that would be a good idea if you plan to run stiffer valvesprings is to machine

PRODUCTION HEADS

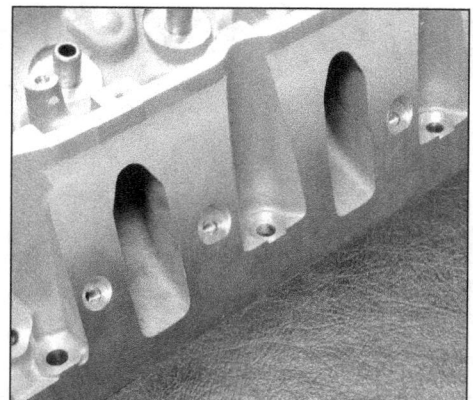

There's been much discussion about the cathedral port design on the GEN III engines. While there may be some minor flow advantage, Ron Sperry and his team of GM engineers designed the port to be narrow to allow more vertical pushrod clearance. The rounded top of the port allows the fuel injector to be aimed directly at the backside of the intake valve that sits at a 15-degree angle versus the original small-block 23-degree valve angle.

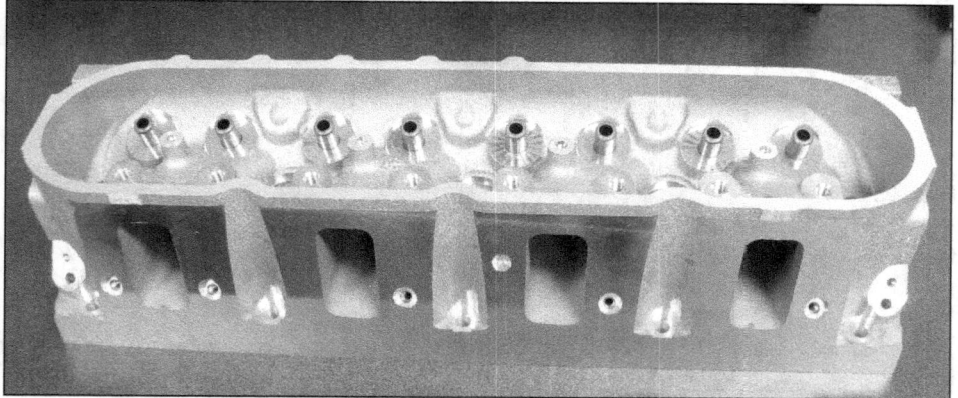

In terms of "production" heads, the most affordable with the highest flow is the GEN IV L-92 aluminum head that offers a 3.160-inch intake valve and 320 cfm right out of the box. The reason for the huge flow numbers is partly due to the large cross-sectional area of the rectangle port intake. These heads are extremely affordable for the flow they offer.

the heads for high-quality screw-in studs such as those from ARP. This is essential because otherwise the stock pressed-in studs will eventually pull out. It's only a matter of time.

Generally, if a set of roller rockers is in the plan, this also means the rockers will probably be a 1.6:1 ratio to take advantage of the greater valve lift. Again, the Vortec heads do require slight modifications should you choose to run a set of 1.6:1 rockers. Increasing the rocker ratio is achieved by moving the pushrod cup closer to the trunion (or pivot) of the rocker arm. This also moves the pushrod more toward the center of the head. The older small-block heads can accommodate this slight change, but the Vortec pushrod holes are much more accurate, and several pushrods generally rub against the head in this area. While elongating the pushrod holes is the solution, this requires specialty machining. A simpler solution is to merely drill out the pushrod holes with a 3/8-inch drill bit. This opens the pushrod hole in the restricted area and prevents damage to the pushrods.

These heads also require a specific centerbolt-style valve cover. If you are on a budget, the boneyards are full of centerbolt-stamped steel valve covers that fill the bill, but if you are looking for something a little nicer, the aftermarket is full of choices. GM Performance Parts offers several covers from chromed stamped steel to polished aluminum covers. Moroso, TD Performance, and many others also offer a multitude of handsome covers that can add a little flair to your engine compartment without spending a ton of cash.

Conclusion

There really is not much of a performance choice when it comes to production cylinder heads for the small-block. If daily driver power is all you need, then any of the older 76-cc heads will do the job, but if you're looking for the best power for the least investment, the Vortec iron is the only real choice.

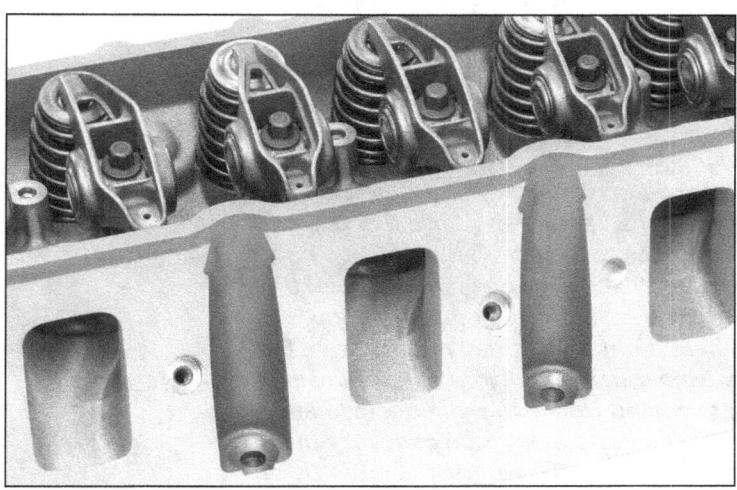

The latest version of the small-block, the GEN IV, is more of a minor evolutionary change rather than yet another clean-sheet redesign. This is the fully CNC machined head for the 427-ci ZO6 engine that makes 505 hp in full production trim.

HIGH-PERFORMANCE CHEVY SMALL-BLOCK CYLINDER HEADS

Heads in Review

Description	Intake Port Volume (cc)	Valve Sizes (Int./Exh.)	Intake Cross Section (sq.in.)	Part Number
Iron 441	157cc	1.94/1.50	1.81	N/A
Iron 462	157cc	1.94/1.50	1.85	N/A
Iron 492	158cc	2.02/1.50*	1.76	12480092
L-98 Aluminum	163cc	1.94/1.50	1.90	12556463
GM Vortec	170cc	1.94/1.50	1.74	12558060
Bow Tie Iron	184cc	2.02/1.60	2.27	12480034

*This particular 492 head is equipped with larger 2.02-inch intake valves versus the standard 1.94-inch valves.

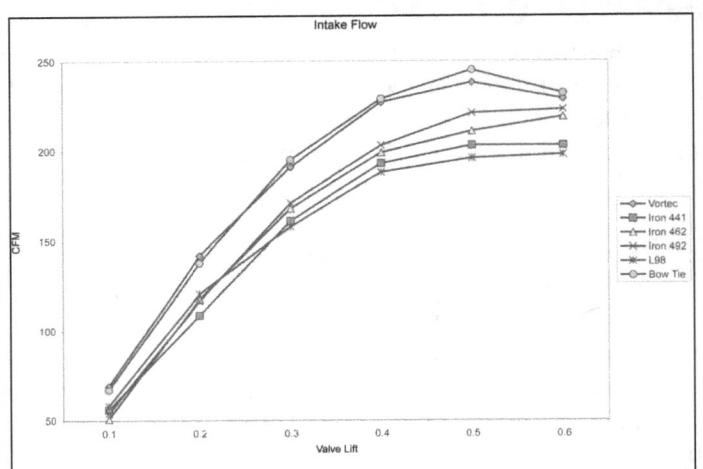

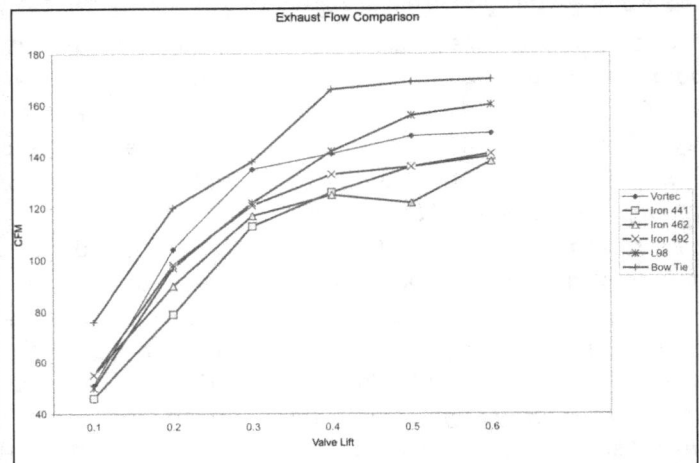

We included the Bow Tie 180 in with the rest of the production heads, which makes the rest of these OEM heads look soft. The reality is, the Bow Tie 180 was only offered as an over-the-counter race head. In this graph, it appears to put the rest of the heads to shame in terms of flow. But this is why you want to look at the velocity chart and the Bow Tie's rather large 2.27 square inch cross-sectional area and what that combination does to the velocity curve. It's also important to look at how well the Vortec flows in the 0.300 to 0.400 inch valve lift area compared to the Bow Tie. We can also realistically ignore the information above 0.500 inch of valve lift since few engine builders would spec a 0.600-inch lift cam with these tiny production heads.

Here the clear winner is the Vortec head in comparison to all the other production heads as well as the Bow Tie. Note how the Bow Tie just lays down above 0.300 inch of valve lift due to its large cross-sectional area. Also note how well that ancient 492 casting does. A few tweaks to the low-lift curve with a solid performance valve job would bring this head right up into the Vortec arena. But the clear velocity winner here is the iron Vortec, which is the main reason this head works so well on a mild street engine. This curve presents a solid case as to why this head works so well—it's all in the velocity.

Again, the Bow Tie head is the clear winner in the exhaust flow department, but then it is also sized much larger than all the other heads in this category. Among the production heads, you can see that the Vortec doesn't really shine here. The word among cylinder head porters reinforces this. But what this also means is that you can pick up 20 hp or more just with some flow improvements to the exhaust side of the Vortec head.

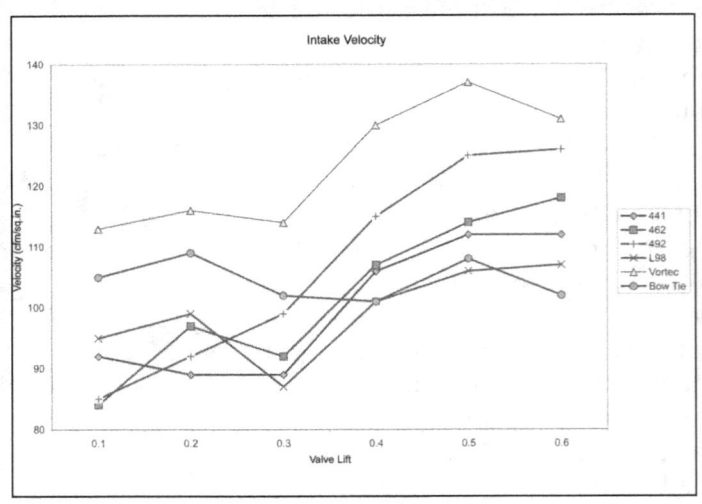

PRODUCTION HEADS

Iron 441 Head

Valve Lift (inches)	Intake	Exhaust	E/I (%)	Intake Port Velocity (cfm/sq.in.)
0.100	56	46	82%	92
0.200	109	79	72%	89
0.300	161	113	70%	89
0.400	193	126	65%	106
0.500	203	136	67%	112
0.600	203	140	69%	112

76-cc Chamber
1.94/1.50-inches valves
1.81 sq.in. intake port cross-section
157-cc intake port volume
Tested on a 4.00-inch bore fixture

Iron 492 Head

Valve Lift (inches)	Intake	Exhaust	E/I (%)	Intake Port Velocity (cfm/sq.in.)
0.100	54	55	102%	85
0.200	117	98	84%	92
0.300	171	121	71%	99
0.400	203	133	65%	115
0.500	221	136	61%	125
0.600	223	141	63%	126

64-cc Chamber
2.02/1.60-inches valves*
1.76 sq.in. intake port cross-section
158-cc intake port
Tested on a 4.06-inch bore fixture
*Note this head was tested with larger 2.02-inch intake valves. Standard valve sizes are 1.94/1.60 inches.

Iron 462 Head

Valve Lift (inches)	Intake	Exhaust	E/I (%)	Intake Port Velocity (cfm/sq.in.)
0.100	51	55	107%	84
0.200	118	90	76%	97
0.300	168	117	70%	92
0.400	199	125	63%	107
0.500	211	133	63%	114
0.600	219	138	63%	118

64-cc Chamber
1.94/1.50-inches valves
1.85 sq.in. intake port cross-section
158-cc intake port
Tested on a 4.00-inch bore fixture

Iron Vortec Head

Valve Lift (inches)	Intake (no pipe)	Exhaust	E/I (%)	Intake Port Velocity (cfm/sq.in.)
0.100	69	51	74%	113
0.200	142	104	73%	116
0.300	191	135	70%	114
0.400	227	141	62%	130
0.500	238	148	62%	137
0.600	229	149	65%	131

58-cc Chamber
1.94/1.50-inches valves
1.74 sq.in. intake port cross-section
170-cc intake port
Tested on a 4.030-inch bore fixture

Aluminum L-98 TPI Head

Valve Lift (inches)	Intake	Exhaust	E/I (%)	Intake Port Velocity (cfm/sq.in.)
0.100	58	50	86%	95
0.200	121	97	80%	99
0.300	158	122	77%	87
0.400	188	142	75%	101
0.500	196	156	79%	106
0.600	198	160	81%	107

58-cc Chamber
1.94/1.50-inches valves
1.85 sq.in. intake port cross-section
164-cc intake port
Tested on a 4.00-inch bore fixture

Bow Tie Iron Head

Valve Lift (inches)	Intake (no pipe)	Exhaust	E/I (%)	Intake Port Velocity (cfm/sq.in.)
0.100	67	76	113%	105
0.200	138	120	87%	109
0.300	195	138	71%	102
0.400	229	166	72%	101
0.500	245	169	69%	108
0.600	232	170	73%	102

64-cc Chamber
2.02/1.60-inches valves
2.27 sq.in. intake port cross-section
184-cc intake port
Tested on a 4.03-inch bore fixture

CHAPTER 5

SMALL AFTERMARKET HEADS

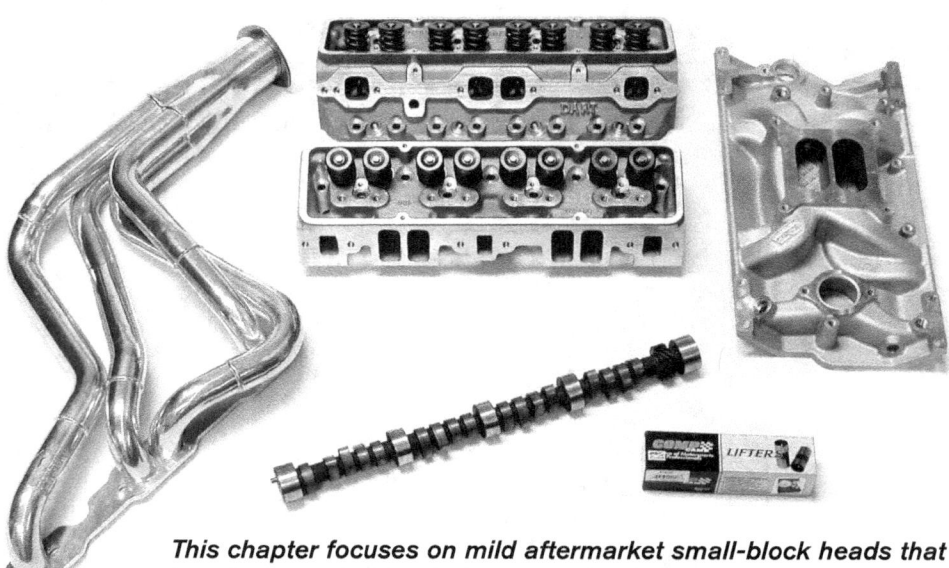

This chapter focuses on mild aftermarket small-block heads that work well when combined with a performance dual-plane intake manifold, a smaller primary header pipe diameter, and a mild flat tappet hydraulic camshaft. These engines may not be number one on the horsepower hit parade, but they are the most popular street engines on the planet.

This may seem like a chapter worth skipping over on the way to the more exotic heads, but if anything stuck with you from Chapter 3, then you know that flow velocity is pre-determined by port cross-sectional area, lift, and valve size. Given that, a small cross-sectional area intake port head with good intake and exhaust flow is an excellent choice for a mild street engine that is intended for miles of trouble-free performance. The heads detailed in this chapter fall in the under-180-cc intake port volume range, and are especially good for 350-ci engines as well as smaller-displacement motors such as 327 and even 302-ci small-blocks that are not intended for high RPM horsepower.

S/R Torquer

In what seems almost like a time forgotten, there was a period in which, besides the iron Chevy Bow Tie, there was little to choose from for a mild small-block other than stock heads. Chevy began building lightweight castings that seemed to crack the moment you unbolted them from an engine and the core market looked in danger of drying up. This was when World Products began casting iron stock replacement (S/R) cylinder heads for both the 305 and 350-ci small-block. The initial run of small-valve S/R heads was so successful that World introduced the S/R Torquer, which was the larger 2.02/1.60-inch valve version of the S/R. As you can see from the flow charts, compared to the Vortec production head, the S/R is down 12 to 20 cfm on the intake side across the board, so performance would be down slightly in comparison.

It's a similar story on the exhaust side, and this head would certainly benefit from simple modifications to the pocket area, especially on the exhaust side. We get into more details in the porting chapter, but typically these heads are cast and machined using high-volume production techniques, which leave a restricted throat area that can use some tweaking. Merely increasing the throat diameter on the exhaust and doing nothing else significantly improves horsepower above 4,000

SMALL AFTERMARKET HEADS

The World Products Torquer S/R is an affordable, iron stock replacement head offering a choice of 1.94/1.50 or 2.02/1.50-inch valves with either 67 or 76-cc combustion chambers. The heads make reasonable power as stock replacement heads, but there are certainly better heads available for a little more money.

rpm while costing no power loss anywhere else. Production and the S/R heads generally have a weak exhaust port as evidenced by the drop in the exhaust-to-intake percentage from 82 to barely 60 percent at 0.600-inch lift. By opening the throat area, this percentage improves significantly.

As an example, we've included a second flow sheet on a mildly ported version of the S/R. Granted, this head received more than mere bowl work, but it also shows the gain from a head that is generally considered a mere stock replacement piece. The intake improvements are minimal since most of the work is concentrated on the exhaust side. Note at 0.300-inch lift, the port flow improves by an amazing 40 cfm, which computes out to a 30 percent gain in exhaust flow at that one data point alone. The average E/I improves to just over 70 percent, which means less camshaft exhaust duration is necessary to make power. If we compare the ported version to a stock Vortec, the intake is still down slightly, while the S/R employs a larger intake valve. However, on the exhaust side it's a completely different story. The ported S/R rocks the Vortec (which admittedly is exhaust limited), revealing a significant potential power gain. The ported S/R is up 30-plus cfm over the stock Vortec, which means that you might be able to get away with a mild dual pattern or even a single pattern cam with exhaust flow numbers of this kind.

While not as good as the Vortec in stock trim, there are times when it's not financially feasible to use the Vortec, which opens the door for the S/R. It's also worth noting that the S/R retains its stock bathtub-shaped combustion chamber which is also a bit lazy when it comes to combustion efficiency. This was done, again, as part of the head's "stock replacement" origins. This head has been around now for two decades and still serves a useful position as an inexpensive improvement over a used production head. The porting information is intended to show that even a relatively obscure, stock replacement head can show promise for a mild street engine if the engine builder is willing to invest a little effort into improving flow. We must also use this occasion to voice the obvious warnings that you cannot just go in and start hogging out exhaust ports in hopes of improving flow. There are important procedures that must be followed if improved flow is to be obtained. But the potential is certainly there if you do a good job of home porting. We go over all that in Chapter 10.

Dart Iron Eagle SS

Dart has long been considered a racing or ultra-high-performance cylinder head company, especially given owner Dick Maskin's extensive experience in drag racing, especially in NHRA Pro Stock. But what many enthusiasts don't know is that the company has also been not-so-quietly building a reputation as a full-line cylinder head company when it comes to the ubiquitous small-block Chevy. Case in point is the 165-cc Iron Eagle SS head, which is Dart's entry-level cylinder head running 1.94/1.50-inch valves and a 72-cc combustion chamber. Right off the mark, Dart's technology advantage is immediately revealed by the combustion chamber. Most of the heads in this category are somewhat dated and rely on the older bathtub-shaped chamber designs of the 1970s. Dart's Eagle SS head steps up with a much more refined heart-shaped chamber that is not only compact with a restrained surface-to-volume relationship for its 72-cc volume, but also utilizes this shape to help push the combustion process over toward the exhaust valve. This is also a straight plug head and is available from Dart either bare or complete with valves and standard production diameter 1.250-inch valvesprings.

The 165-cc intake port is the smallest of this category of heads and therefore enjoys a decent velocity rating compared to the other heads in this category. If you look at the intake and exhaust flow numbers, the head is on a par with a production head. This may not seem like much of an improvement over the older iron heads like a 441 or 882

World Products S/R Torquer

Valve Lift (inches)	Intake	Exhaust (flow pipe)	E/I (%)	Intake Port Velocity (cfm/sq.in.)
0.100	62	53	85%	98
0.200	127	104	82%	100
0.300	178	125	70%	93
0.400	208	131	63%	115
0.500	219	132	60%	121
0.600	215	128	59%	119

72-cc Chamber
2.02/1.60-inches valves
1.81 sq.in. intake port cross-section
170-cc intake port
Tested on a 4.00-inch bore fixture

Ported Version of the S/R Torquer
Majority of work performed on the exhaust side
Valve sizes remained at 2.02/1.60-inches

Valve Lift (inches)	Intake	Exhaust (flow pipe)	E/I (%)	Intake Port Velocity (cfm/sq.in.)
0.100	60	56	93%	94
0.200	130	118	91%	102
0.300	187	165	88%	98
0.400	222	172	77%	122
0.500	227	178	78%	125

Dart Iron Eagle SS

Valve Lift (inches)	Intake	Exhaust (flow pipe)	E/I (%)	Intake Port Velocity (cfm/sq.in.)
0.100	61	47	77%	100
0.200	116	96	83%	95
0.300	162	127	78%	88
0.400	196	135	69%	112
0.500	210	139	66%	120
0.600	209	139	66%	119

72-cc Chamber
1.94/1.50-inch valves
1.75 sq.in. intake port cross-section
165-cc intake port
Tested on a 4.03-inch bore fixture at 28 inches

Edelbrock Performer

Valve Lift (inches)	Intake	Exhaust (flow pipe)	E/I (%)	Intake Port Velocity (cfm/sq.in.)
0.100	65	45	69%	102
0.200	122	97	79%	96
0.300	174	135	77%	97
0.400	216	160	74%	120
0.500	236	177	75%	131
0.600	236	188	79%	131

70-cc Chamber
2.02/1.60-inch valves
1.80 sq.in. intake port cross-section
170-cc intake port
Tested on a 4.03-inch bore fixture

The entry-level head from Dart is the 165-cc Iron Eagle available only with a 72-cc chamber and 1.94/1.50-inch valves. Much like the S/R Torquer, this works as a stock replacement head, but the slightly larger Iron Eagle 180 is a better choice for most mild performance applications.

head, but the chamber offers potential that can only be measured on the engine rather than on a flow bench. Clearly, this head would also respond similarly to the World Products S/R head if lightly ported, especially on the exhaust side. The complete head also comes with guideplates, screw-in studs, and quality valveguide seals. It uses a tapered seat, 5/8-inch hex, and peanut-style spark plug.

Edelbrock Performer

This is the first aluminum head in this small-port aftermarket category. Edelbrock's intake-port philosophy emphasizes port velocity for its mild street heads, and the Performer is the entry-level head in this category with a 170-cc intake port with a rather small 1.80-sq.in. minimum port cross-section. This limits the head's max valve lift flow capacity, but does enhance velocity. The Performer's 0.100 through 0.400-inch lift flow numbers are decent although not as strong as the GM iron Vortec head, which has a similar port volume with a slightly smaller cross-section.

One of the strengths of the Performer is the sheer number of variants that Edelbrock offers. In addition to the Performer, there's also the 50-state legal centerbolt head, which offers EGR passages to make these heads emissions compatible. The heads come with 2.02/1.60-inch valves with a tight chamber design, straight (non-angled) spark plugs, and 3/8-inch screw-in rocker studs along with guideplates that require hardened pushrods. Edelbrock sells the Performer either bare or complete with springs, retainers, and keepers. One point worth noting is that if stock-stamped steel rockers will be used with the Performer or Performer RPM heads, 0.100-inch longer pushrods are required in order to generate the proper rocker geometry. Edelbrock also recommends limiting valve lift to under 0.450 inch when using these heads on engines with smaller bores than 4.00 inches. This includes 283, 305, and 307-ci engines.

The Performer is ideal for the mild street engine applications where the engine builder wants to step up to a set of aluminum heads over the stock iron castings. These heads can be ported while the exhaust-to-intake relationship (E/I) is decent with averages throughout the lift curve around the mid-70 percentages. Part of the reason for the exhaust performance is that the intake port is somewhat limited. This is one case where the head might actually respond to increasing the cross-sectional area slightly to improve upper valve lift flow since the head crosses over in terms of port restriction at just under 0.300-inch valve lift.

If the Performer has a weak spot, it would have to be the combustion chamber. It belies its age since it came about before the new age of heart-shaped chambers that push the combustion process toward the exhaust port. The Performer RPM chamber resembles the production bathtub-shaped chamber.

Perhaps the sleeper head in this category is the Edelbrock Performer with its smallish 170-cc intake port volume. But add in velocity and good flow for such a small cross-sectional area and this head has great potential for torque and decent HP in a mild street small-block.

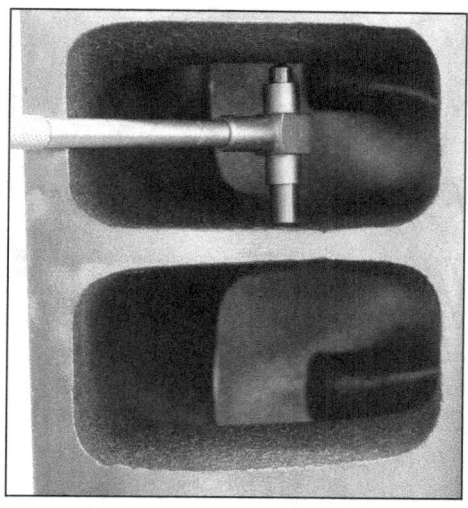

In Chapter 3, we spent a significant period of time discussing flow velocity based on the cylinder head's smallest port cross-sectional area. With most 23-degree small-block heads, the pushrod wall intrusion into the port just downstream from the port entry ends up being the smallest cross-sectional area of the port. This position makes it easy to measure with a set of snap gauges and calipers.

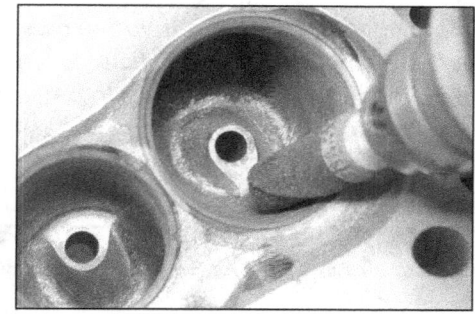

Most of the conservative cylinder heads can really benefit from slight port work within the port throat area, just underneath the valve job. Always go easy here and concentrate your attention on the exhaust side of the head.

Edelbrock E-Tec 170

Edelbrock capitalized on the Vortec iron head phenomenon by introducing an aluminum version of

CHAPTER 5

Virtually every aluminum small-block head that we've ever seen uses a long (0.750-inch) thread reach spark plug (similar to older big-block Chevy heads) with a gasket for sealing. If you use anti-seize on the threads, use it sparingly. If it gets on the insulator, it will kill the plug because anti-seize is a conductor.

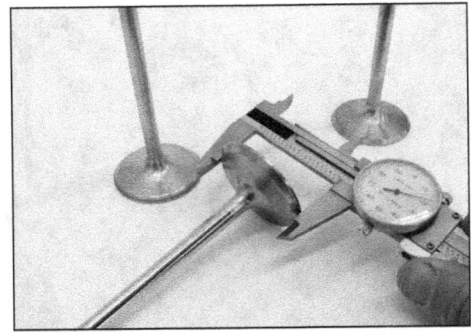

Most small-port heads use a 1.94/1.50-inch valve package in an attempt to keep the price down. The biggest percentage of gain in performance can often be gained by increasing the exhaust valve diameter rather than the intake.

the GM head. This resulted in two different intake port heads, the E-Tec 170 and its larger E-Tec 200-cc cousin. We deal with the smaller of the two heads in this chapter. The 170-cc E-Tec features the same port configuration, 4-bolt Vortec intake flange, and 64-cc chamber volume so that the heads are easily interchanged. The valve sizes vary slightly, with the intake the same as the GM iron at 1.94 inches, but Edelbrock snuck in a slightly larger 1.55-inch exhaust valve.

By comparing flow figures, you can see that the E-Tec intake port is actually not quite as good as its GM iron progenitor. Perhaps we expect too much from Edelbrock, but if the company is going to come out with an aluminum version, we expected it to be far

Edelbrock's E-Tec line of aluminum heads strives to improve upon the GM iron Vortec head. The exhaust port is improved with more flow, which means it may make better power with a single-pattern camshaft as opposed to the dual-pattern cam demanded by the original iron Vortec.

The Edelbrock Performer RPM head may look very similar to the Performer, but it offers a slightly larger port cross-section and concurrently more flow, especially in the mid-lift areas.

Edelbrock E-Tec 170

Valve Lift (inches)	Intake	Exhaust (flow pipe)	E/I (%)	Intake Port Velocity (cfm/sq.in.)
0.100	64	49	76%	105
0.200	127	105	82%	105
0.300	179	139	77%	99
0.400	216	170	79%	119
0.500	240	180	75%	132
0.600	241	191	79%	133

64-cc Chamber
1.94/1.55-inch valves
1.81 sq.in. intake port cross-section
170-cc port
Tested on a 4.030-inch bore fixture at 28 inches

Edelbrock Performer RPM

Valve Lift (inches)	Intake	Exhaust (flow pipe)	E/I (%)	Intake Port Velocity (cfm/sq.in.)
0.100	66	52	79%	104
0.200	129	105	81%	101
0.300	182	133	73%	95
0.400	220	159	72%	113
0.500	239	174	73%	122
0.600	225	182	81%	115

72-cc Chamber
2.02/1.60-inch valves
1.95 sq.in. intake port cross-section
170-cc intake port
Tested on a 4.030-inch bore fixture

SMALL AFTERMARKET HEADS

better than the stock iron version. Edelbrock claims that its engineering effort was placed on the exhaust side, which makes sense since the stock Vortec is clearly exhaust limited. But you must look closely to see the flow improvements on the exhaust side. First, Edelbrock raised the exhaust port exit by 0.200 inch to help the port flow and create a more generous short-side radius. Our flow numbers indicate that at 0.400 inch of valve lift and above, the E-Tec is significantly better than the Vortec. For example, at 0.600 inch, the E-Tec is almost 30 cfm up over the stock iron Vortec, which is a 17 percent flow improvement. But this begs the question of how often are you going to run a 0.600-inch lift cam with a relatively small 170-cc intake port head? At the lower exhaust valve lifts, the E-Tec is virtually even with the Vortec, so it offers little improvement.

On the intake side, it doesn't take long to realize that the E-Tec does not perform as well as the stock iron Vortec, especially in the mid-lift flow range. At the critical 0.400 inch of valve lift on the intake side, the E-Tec actually flows roughly 10 cfm less than the Vortec. This lack of performance on the intake side, combined with an exhaust port that only flows better at valve lifts that will rarely be attained, underscores why in a dyno test comparison with a relatively mild camshaft there is little E-Tec power improvement (with the 170-cc head) over the stock iron Vortec. Here's a case where your money might be better spent elsewhere unless having an aluminum head is worth the price of admission. We deal with the larger 200-cc E-Tec head in a subsequent chapter.

Edelbrock Performer RPM

If Edelbrock whiffed on the E-Tec, its earlier entry with a conservative port size, high-velocity, aluminum street head it certainly smacked a solid hit with the Performer RPM head. One reason for splitting up the heads in this book by chapters as well as port area (and volume) is because it's important to emphasize that heads of like cross-sectional area should be compared on this level playing field, not against much larger heads that can easily out-flow the smaller castings.

Edelbrock chose to build a decent, standard small-block intake bolt pattern head that emphasizes flow velocity for street-driven engines that could benefit from significant torque gains. Again, it is this velocity that creates

A good cam can only deliver maximum power when combined with a solid, reliable valvetrain. That means accurately matching the pushrods, springs, and rocker arms to ensure that the valve is doing exactly what the cam tells it to do.

Most cylinder head companies such as Edelbrock, Dart, World, and others offer bare heads at a reduced cost that allow you to outfit the heads with your own personal valves, springs, and the rest of the attendant valvetrain. This may end up costing more money, but it gives you control over all the components in the valvetrain.

RHS Vortec				
Valve Lift (inches)	Intake	Exhaust	E/I (%)	Intake Port Velocity (cfm/sq.in.)
0.100	75	67	89%	118
0.200	132	122	92%	104
0.300	186	145	78%	98
0.400	225	164	73%	119
0.500	258	165	64%	136
0.600	230	165	72%	122

64-cc Chamber
2.02/1.60-inch valves
1.89 sq.in. intake port cross-section
170-cc port
Tested on a 4.030-inch bore fixture

CHAPTER 5

Both the Performer and the Performer RPM are aimed at conservative street engines that are looking to make torque by creating strong velocity curves in the middle of the engine's torque curve. A 383 with a set of Performer RPM heads, an Edelbrock Performer RPM intake, and a 230/236-degree cam with 0.500-inch valve lift would make excellent torque of around 430 ft-lbs and around 390 hp at a relatively conservative 5,500 rpm.

Most of the heads in this category primarily use 1.250-inch standard diameter valvesprings. There are dozens of similar-diameter springs that do not require spring seat machining and offer improved performance. Among the best of these new springs is the conical or beehive COMP spring such as the part number 26918 that uses a smaller, lighter retainer that reduces total spring/retainer mass that the spring must also control.

the mid-range torque, especially in relatively small-displacement engines like a 327 or a 350-ci small-block. The comparison against the Vortec street standard works well in this case since it can outflow that production head at the higher valve lifts mainly based on a slightly larger cross-sectional area. This is despite the fact that the Performer is an older design that predates the Vortec. This makes the RPM more appealing to an engine builder looking for a bit more horsepower from an affordable aftermarket aluminum head. In Chapter 13 we detail a 355-ci small-block combination that includes these cylinder heads that made a solid 438 ft-lbs of torque at 4,000 rpm while making 424 hp at 6,000 rpm. With a power band between peak torque and peak horsepower of an impressive 2,000 rpm, this is a great engine for use in an automatic where the engine speed drops more between gears, demanding a wider power band. The Performer RPM heads are a bit of an underdog in the current world of high-flow heads, but it should not be overlooked when it comes to price versus performance. This head outperforms most of the heads in this chapter and yet still qualifies as easily affordable.

Racing Head Service Vortec Iron

The most recent player in the replacement Vortec head genre comes from the revitalized Racing Head Service (RHS)—now the brand name for what once was the Pro Action cylinder head company out of New Zealand. The owners of the COMP Cams family of companies recently purchased the offshore cylinder head concern, and the Vortec replacement head is the first of a new line of cylinder heads from the reorganized business.

The original Vortec set the bar rather high for mild street cylinder heads, and by looking at both the intake and exhaust numbers, the new RHS head achieves an interesting level that might make it a player in the mild street head category. The RHS head manages to achieve

All intake port flow numbers used in this book also use a radius flow adapter on the intake port that both improves the flow and also serves as a standard for all intake ports.

SMALL AFTERMARKET HEADS

The focus of this chapter has been on mild street engines that see plenty of street miles with some type of mild hydraulic flat-tappet camshaft and a dual-plane intake manifold.

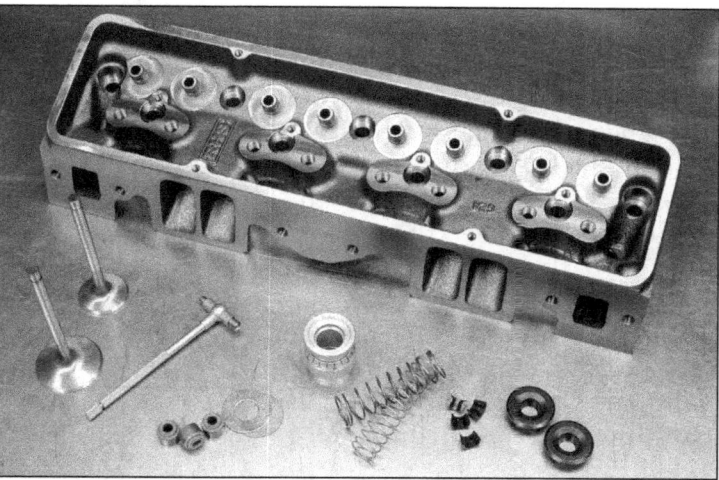

Racing Head Service (RHS) was a performance name back in the 1980s and COMP has recently revived the brand to reintroduce the Pro Topline iron and aluminum cylinder head lineup. Literally as this book was written, RHS released its own upgraded version of the GM Vortec head, but we have not dyno tested this head to see how well it lives up to its claims.

Simulated Power

We have had very good success in using the ProRacing Sim DeskTop Dyno engine simulation program to simulate small-block Chevy naturally aspirated engine packages. So just for fun, we decided to digitally assemble a streetable small-block 350-ci engine with a 9.0:1 compression ratio, a COMP Cams Xtreme Energy camshaft, a dual-plane intake manifold like a Performer RPM, a 750-cfm carburetor, and a mild set of 1-5/8-inch diameter headers along with a set of street-type mufflers. Using this package, we decided to run all the cylinder heads in this chapter and a couple of heads from Chapter 4 across this simulation to see which one would give us a decent power reading. Keep in mind that this is a simulation; we did not actually perform these tests. However, the results mirror what we've seen in actual dyno tests on many of these heads, and these results also fall in line with what the flow bench tests indicate. While peak horsepower is always where everyone looks first, also note the torque levels of even the stock heads. This is where even a set of stock heads will deliver fun power and only fall down because the exhaust ports are so inefficient at higher engine speeds. If you look at these power numbers and the RPM at which they occur, then really study the flow bench curves for each head, you begin to see how the relationship of the exhaust to the intake affects horsepower. Also note how much torque the stock iron heads make with their tiny intake ports and at a relatively low RPM.

We should point out that the World Products S/R Torquer results are a bit of a surprise in terms of simulated horsepower. That peak number might be optimistic by about 10 hp. But as a budget iron small-block head, the World S/R Torquer has shown that it can make good power. The choice between the top three or four heads might come down to price since the difference in horsepower between the top two is only 8 points, and the RHS Vortec appears to make more torque. Then you have the question of iron versus aluminum. It's not easy, is it?

Cylinder Head	Peak HP	Peak Torque (ft-lb)
Dart SS Iron	326 @ 5,000	402 @ 3,500
Iron 441 GM	334 @ 5,000	404 @ 3,500
Edelbrock Performer	349 @ 5,000	409 @ 3,500
World S/R Torquer	360 @ 5,000	413 @ 3,500
Edelbrock E-Tec 170	366 @ 5,500	415 @ 4,000
GM Vortec Iron	367 @ 5,500	412 @ 4,000
RHS Vortec Iron	382 @ 5,500	416 @ 4,000
Edelbrock RPM	390 @ 5,500	409 @ 4,000

HIGH-PERFORMANCE CHEVY SMALL-BLOCK CYLINDER HEADS

equality with the original Vortec on the intake from the low lift through the mid-lift numbers up to 0.400 inch. Then at the half-inch valve lift position, the RHS Vortec jumps up to 258 cfm, a solid 20 cfm better than the stock Vortec. Then the RHS head drops off back to stock Vortec numbers at 0.600 inch of valve lift.

The RHS head uses a larger 2.02 inches of valve size to achieve these numbers, which instantly means that with equal flow numbers in the mid-lift areas that its velocity past the valve will be slower (but the pressure will be higher) compared to the stock 1.94-inch Vortec head. Plus, the RHS Vortec offers a significantly larger 1.89 sq.in. of cross-sectional area compared to the GM Vortec with its smaller 1.74 sq.in. This bump in area along with the larger intake valve is the main reason for the increase in the high-lift flow.

On the exhaust side of things, the RHS head offers dramatically better numbers that promise to make this head worth some power. The stock GM Vortec is most definitely exhaust port limited, and it appears this is where RHS spent its development time. Again, it all starts with not only a larger exhaust valve at 1.60 inches, but also a slightly larger exhaust port cross-sectional area matched with a slightly taller exhaust port exit height compared to the stock Vortec. While this points to improvements in flow at higher lift, the RHS head offers a dramatic increase in low-lift flow right off the mark at 0.100-inch valve lift. Compared to the GM Vortec, the RHS head pumps the flow up with a solid 67 cfm compared to the GM head's 51 cfm. That alone is a 16-cfm improvement, which represents a hefty 31-percent increase.

We simulated these two heads against each other on the ProRacing Sim DeskTop Dyno program, and with a mild 268H COMP Cams flat tappet hydraulic cam, the stock Vortec heads came up with 367 hp at 5,500 rpm with a peak torque of 412 ft-lbs at 4,000. By simply replacing the GM Vortec with the RHS version, the simulation reported an increase to 382 hp at the same peak RPM along with 416 ft-lbs of torque. That's 16 more hp and 5 ft-lbs of increased torque based on the improved airflow. Averages were less dramatic, with horsepower gaining roughly 3.5 and torque 3 ft-lbs. This reinforces the concept that these new RHS heads are worth a slight power increase. Granted, this is a simulation, but we've had amazing success with this simple computer program in predicting naturally aspirated small-block engine packages.

Heads in Review

Description	Intake Port Volume (cc)	Valve Sizes (Int./Exh.)	Intake Cross Section (sq.in.)	Part Number
Dart Iron Eagle SS	165	1.94/1.50	1.75	10021171
Performer	170	2.02/1.60	1.80	60759
Performer RPM	170	2.02/1.60	1.95	60719
E-Tec 170	170	1.94/1.55	1.81	60979
World S/R Torquer	170	2.02/1.60	1.81	042660-1
RHS Vortec Iron	170	2.02/1.60	1.89	12410

Conclusion

The heads discussed in this chapter may seem tame, but they represent some of the most popular in terms of units sold within the small-block market. This is because they are intended to fit the area between daily driver and mid-point performance applications that are used far more than the popular press likes to admit. In the performance magazines, it's all about the horsepower race, so it's rare to read about mild performance heads because most of the editors gravitate toward the castings that can generate big flow and equally big horsepower numbers. While those are enticing and attract readers, the truth is that most of those readers are more interested in a set of heads that they can both afford and match to the rest of the engine combination they currently point in the direction of the local cruise spot on Saturday night. The beauty of the small-block Chevy is that there are so many potential buyers that the market can afford the broad selection offering that no other engine can attain.

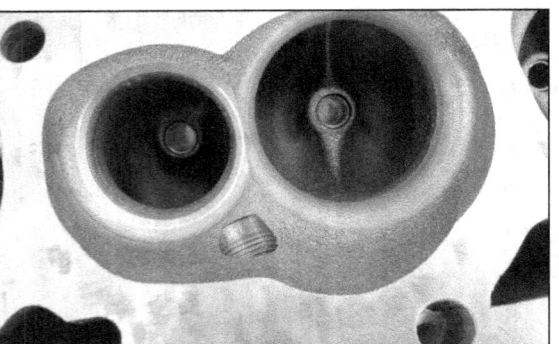

One area not to be overlooked is combustion chamber design. An excellent head is one that offers solid flow, high velocity, and a high-tech-shaped combustion chamber.

Flow Graphs

The two graphs included here plot the intake and exhaust flow numbers that may help you coordinate this mass of information into a somewhat more useable form. On the intake side, the heads tend to overlap in the low and mid-lift areas, and the only real jump in flow is the RHS head at 0.500-inch lift. Keep in mind that the cam profile only sees this peak flow point once in the flow curve, and even then only for a short period of time. But in our "Simulated Power" sidebar, this is worth some peak horsepower, although average power for the RHS Vortec head is only marginally better than the production Vortec.

On the exhaust side of the heads, the RHS exhaust port tends to lay down at higher lifts while the E-Tec 170 seems to take off at around 0.350 inch of valve lift to achieve the big peak flow numbers. But again, these numbers can be deceiving. A closer look at the low- to mid-lift flow numbers reveals that all the heads are clustered together with the exception of the RHS Vortec head, which shows a decided flow advantage in this area. Apparently, RHS concentrated its efforts on the low and mid-lift flow numbers to complement the head's conservative intake in order to enhance mid-range power. This may account for its better performance in the engine simulation estimates.

The top four heads in the exhaust flow category virtually overlap through 0.500 inch of valve lift. The RHS Vortec and the Edelbrock E-Tec appear to be the strong performers in this exhaust flow category.

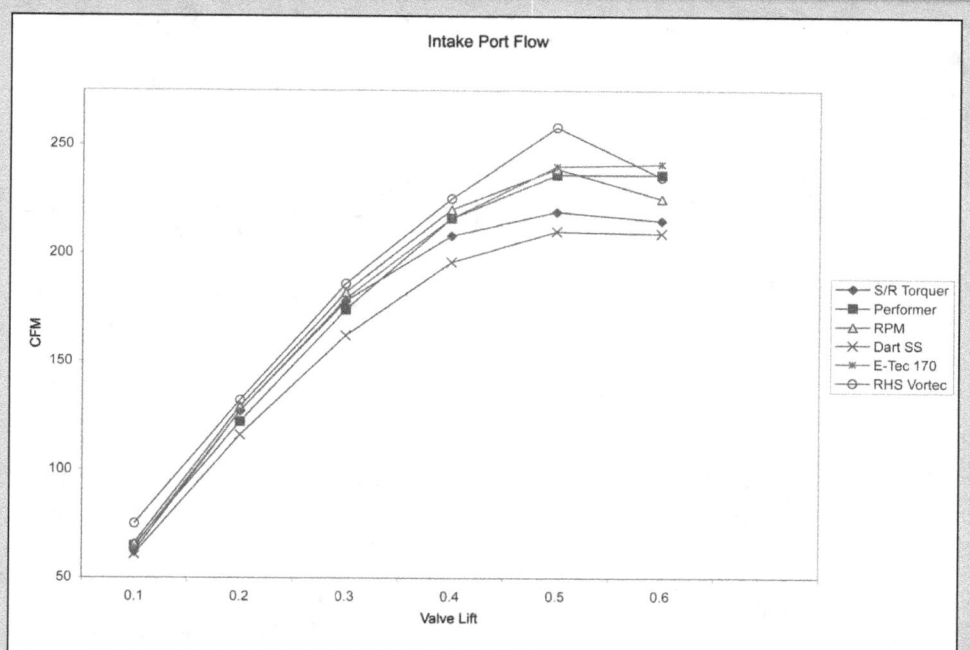

All intake ports flow comparably through 0.300 inch of valve lift. The RHS Vortec, Edelbrock E-Tec, and Edelbrock Performer RPM heads all do well up through 0.500 inch of valve lift. The 0.600-inch lift flow numbers are not all that useful because few engine builders would spec a 0.600-inch lift cam with any of these small intake port heads.

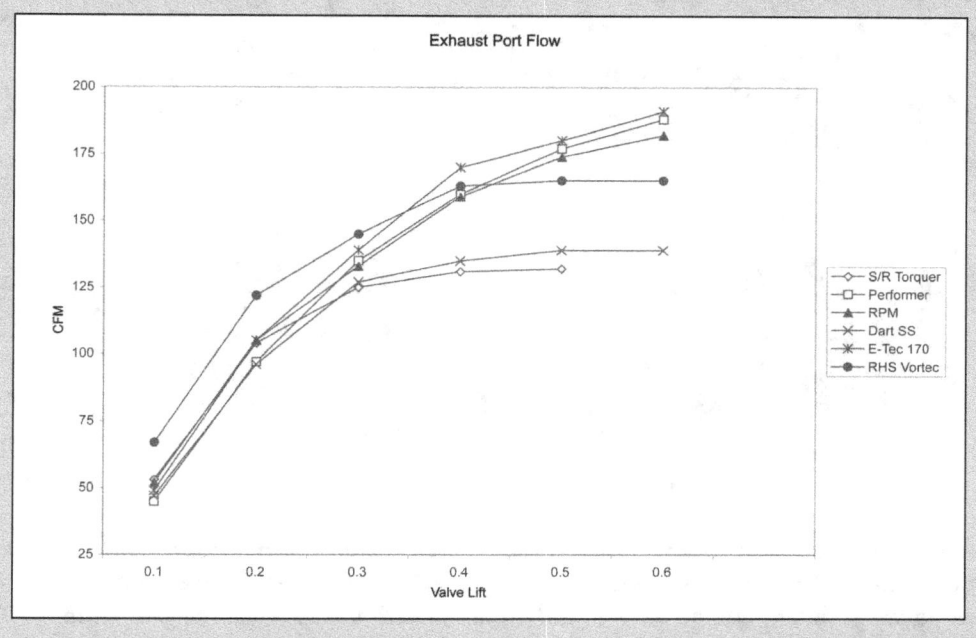

CHAPTER 6

MEDIUM AFTERMARKET HEADS 180 TO 199-CC PORT VOLUME

If there is one category of small-block heads that is best suited to performance street small-block Chevy engines, it is the heads in the 180 to 199-cc intake port volume zip code. Sized to nestle into the 350 to 383 to 406-ci small-block displacement range, these heads are intended to produce a street-friendly broad RPM power band. This range of intake port volume also represents an excellent choice for that dual-purpose small-block that spends most of its time on the boulevard sprinkled with a few forays a year to the drag strip.

Since we're diving right into this category, it would be a good idea to begin the discussion with a word on torque. If we combine the idea of a conservative port cross-section with a larger-displacement engine like a 400-ci small-block, it's possible to

Most of the aftermarket heads in this category such as the AFR, Brodix, and Dart heads all offer the option of straight versus angled spark plugs. There is a minimal power difference between the two choices. A good reason for choosing one over the other is header clearance for the spark plug wires. Most headers are now designed for angled spark plugs.

Keep in mind that the intake manifold also plays a big part in creating the torque curve. A good dual-plane intake like the Edelbrock Performer RPM Air Gap is an excellent choice for a street engine, while the Victor Jr. single plane tends to sacrifice torque to maximize peak horsepower. For a primarily street-driven engine, a good dual plane is most often a better choice.

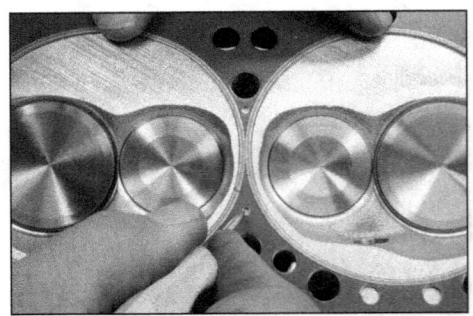

If you plan to run a set of heads on a production 400-ci small-block, make sure to properly drill the steam holes that match the holes in the block. These holes are important for street engines in order to vent steam pockets that tend to form in the block.

MEDIUM AFTERMARKET HEADS

Bare Naked Performance

While most enthusiasts purchase cylinder heads completely assembled so that they merely pop the heads out of the box and bolt them on, most cylinder head companies also offer their heads as bare castings that have their seats installed complete with a finished valve job, but come without valves, springs, retainers, keepers, or seals. Most heads also are sent with screw-in studs and guideplates, but you should check with the manufacturer.

This obviously requires you to purchase your valves and other components separately, but if you have a valve preference for example, it's possible to improve port flow on both the intake and exhaust side by adding better valves. Because of cost considerations, many cylinder head companies look for the least expensive valves that will do the job. This does not make these components a bad choice, just perhaps not the best choice if you're looking for ultimate flow. For example, by making slight changes to the radius on the exhaust valve between the stem and the valve head, it's possible to gain flow with just this change.

Another important point is that you can specify a back cut angle with your new valves and perhaps also choose a slightly wider margin that can also be of benefit. We'll go into more detail on these ideas in Chapter 10 or basic porting techniques, but you might consider the idea of purchasing a set of heads bare for your next hot street engine. It just might be worth some horsepower.

create an incredibly torquey small-block that can grunt out of any situation. This deserves more than just a passing consideration because the rest of the world seems bent on horsepower numbers, but the reality for virtually all street-driven cars is that torque is what moves or accelerates the car, while horsepower pushes it past the finish line at a decent MPH trap speed. We're not trying to sell you on the idea that torque is the only answer—it's not. But in this category, where many of these heads can offer substantial torque gains, it's especially important not to miss those opportunities. The reality is that a careful blend of torque and horsepower is the key to a successful street engine.

As an example, we can categorize most street cars as relatively heavy cruisers moving the scale between 3,600 and 4,000 pounds, fully loaded with driver and full of fuel. Add a tall rear gear and a tight converter and you have a vehicle that demands a torquey small-block just to help it get moving. This is where a combination of a high velocity, good-flowing cylinder head along with the properly matched camshaft can make all the difference in the world in terms of throttle response and acceleration from a dead stop. If making lots of torque from a small-block has some appeal, consider a 406-ci small-block with a 180-cc set of heads with a tall dual-plane intake like an Edelbrock Performer RPM Air Gap and watch the torque soar. It's not unusual to see a motor like this make 480 ft-lbs of grunt at around 4,000 rpm. Generally, this combo won't make a ton of horsepower, but it would feel just like a mild big-block without all the extra weight. We save the discussion of matching camshafts to cylinder heads for Chapter 12, but this is where it all comes together to make outstanding power without sacrificing anything except for a few dollars out of your wallet.

In this chapter, we go through each of the most important and powerful cylinder heads in this mid-size category. Unfortunately, as soon as this book is printed several new heads will no doubt hit the marketplace. But even with this constant influx of new products, there only seems to be a handful of heads that really perform. That's a big part of why we wrote this book, to give you the tools to evaluate these heads on their own merits as opposed to just believing all the advertising hype.

AFR 180 Version 1

While this head is among the smallest intake ports in this category, don't discount it. As this book was being written, AirFlow Research was just releasing its latest versions of the 180, 195, and 210-cc intake port heads called the Eliminator series. But the

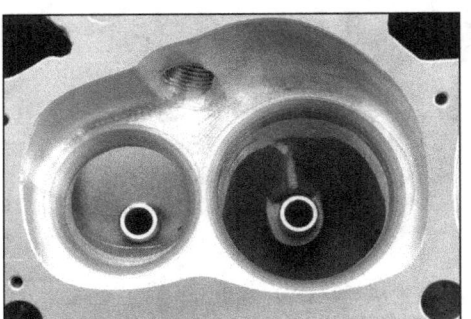

The main difference between the Motown Lite aluminum head over the iron casting is its CNC-machined chamber. Beyond looking cool, the machined chamber is worth a small amount of power over a production cast chamber.

head that the company introduced only a few years before this was the smallest of its small-block Chevy castings. With its recent pedigree, this head benefited from all the flow tuning the company had learned up to that point. There are even several of the more dated 200-cc intake port volume heads that cannot compete with this little 180. This is significant since the small port cross-section generates high inlet port velocities, which in turn generates torque. As good as this head was, the next generation head improved upon that level of performance.

On the exhaust side of the head, the exhaust port maintains an 83 percent average in terms of the exhaust-to-intake (E/I) flow relationship. This is an excellent number that rewards the more astute engine builders who decide to choose a single-pattern camshaft as a complement. While there is no end to the discussion and debate around what, if any, E/I percentage represents the "ideal," the point is that most small-block Chevy heads are exhaust limited. This tends to reinforce the concept that all small-blocks should run a dual-pattern cam with more duration and lift on the exhaust side. This is not really true with this AFR 180 head. We've run a small-block with the 180 heads and a dual pattern camshaft (roughly a 268/276 style grind) that didn't perform nearly as well as it should have. By selecting a single pattern cam (a 268/268 for example), peak power improved, as did the mid-range torque. This occurs because the AFR 180's efficient exhaust port, allows the cam to delay the onset of exhaust valve opening, taking additional advantage of the heat generated in the cylinder. Plus, because of the more efficient exhaust port there is less residual exhaust gas in the chamber when the intake valve opens, which is like built-in EGR—and that's not the best path to horsepower. A more efficient exhaust port also reduces pumping losses where the engine must exert power to pump the exhaust gas out. The concept of matching the camshaft to the cylinder head flow characteristics is detailed in Chapter 12.

While average CFM over the entire flow curve is not nearly as useful as the specific flow numbers, it does serve to indicate this head is no slouch. The AFR is the smallest of the 10 different heads listed in this category, yet its average flow is better than almost half the field. It actually compares favorably to heads with much larger port cross-sectional areas. In Chapter 3 we talked about how important mid-lift flow is to engine performance. If we use 0.400 inch as our mid-lift point, there are only three other heads that fare better than the AFR 180, and two of those heads are the old and new versions of the AFR 195 head. The only other head that beats the 180 at this lift point is the Canfield 195 head.

Given this information, the AFR 180 would be a great addition to smaller-displacement Mouse motors in the 327 to 331 to 355-ci range, and perhaps even a mildly cammed 383. The combination promises to make excellent torque and over 400 hp even from a 355-ci motor, as long as it uses decent headers, exhaust, and a tall dual-plane intake like the Edelbrock Performer RPM Air Gap matched with a 750-cfm carburetor.

AFR 180 Eliminator

As good as the original AFR 180 was and is, the new Eliminator is just that much better. We tested a brand new production Eliminator head with the full Competition CNC porting

AFR 180 (Version 1)

Valve Lift (inches)	Intake	Exhaust (flow pipe)	E/I (%)	Intake Port Velocity (cfm/sq.in.)
0.100	67	56	83%	105
0.200	138	114	82%	109
0.300	192	165	86%	101
0.400	231	192	83%	109
0.500	252	209	83%	119
0.600	256	215	84%	121

68-cc Chamber
2.02/1.60-inches valves
1.97 sq.in. intake port cross-section
180-cc intake port
Tested on a 4.03-inch bore fixture

AFR Eliminator 180

Valve Lift (inches)	Intake	Exhaust	E/I (%)	Intake Port Velocity (cfm/sq.in.)
0.100	65	55	84%	102
	135	107	79%	106
0.300	192	157	82%	101
0.400	241	185	77%	125
0.500	264	197	75%	137
0.600	258	202	78%	134

74-cc Chamber
2.02/1.60-inches valves
1.92 sq.in. port cross-section
180-cc intake port
Tested on a 4.030-inch bore fixture

MEDIUM AFTERMARKET HEADS

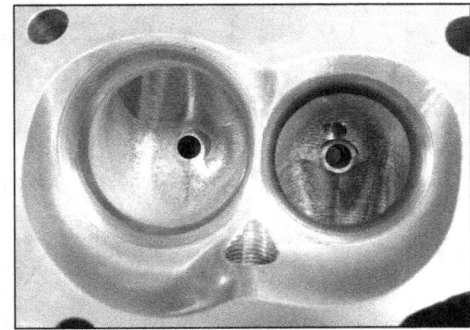

Matching the excellent quality of the AFR 180 port work is the fully CNC-ported combustion chamber. A compact chamber with the spark plug aimed toward the exhaust side means this head requires less ignition timing to make peak power.

Most manufacturers use CNC machines, like the AFR machine seen here, to do the majority of their machine work on heads. This makes the placement of all the drilled and tapped holes very precise, not to mention repeatable from one head to the next.

effort. Our flow numbers are often not quite as good as AFR's published levels, which are typically based on their prototype intake port. We know this because the new AFR catalog came out before the new line of Eliminator heads went into production. Nonetheless, this head is a strong effort. At lower intake valve lifts, this head is equal to the older version, but then at 0.400 inches lift, it stacks another 10 cfm over the first version and adds another 12 cfm at 0.500 inches of lift. Of course, this jacks the velocity curve up at the higher valve lifts, bumping the velocity per square inch number up to 137 cfm/sq.in., which is damn near as good as you can get. Obviously, for a smaller-displacement small-block like a 355 or even a 383, these numbers are roughly equal to what we got out of the larger first-version AFR 195 heads. Add the drastic increase of velocity and it's hard not to recommend these heads for any 355 to 383-ci street engine looking for a combination of awesome torque and excellent horsepower.

Our test revealed exhaust numbers not quite as good as the older AFR 180, but still good enough to outflow all the other heads in its category. We did not get a chance to measure the port volume, so it might be smaller in anticipation of its use on smaller-displacement engines to maintain velocity. This head might actually work well with a single-pattern cam, based on what we've seen with the original 180 AFR head on a 355 small-block Chevy.

Anytime you can decrease port cross-sectional area and still increase flow, that's a home run of major proportions for a street cylinder head, and this appears to be what AFR has accomplished. The flow numbers for an as-cast head will be lower by roughly 10 cfm or so in the lower valve lift flow numbers. It will also have less of a discrepancy at higher flow numbers, so this might be a great way to get into these heads without the additional expense of the full CNC porting. The best way would be to

This is the new AFR 180 Eliminator head with the full Competition CNC porting. With the one-two punch of an excellent intake flow and small cross-sectional area velocity curves, this is a strong head for medium displacement street engines.

Brodix recently introduced the Race-Rite series with RR180 and RR200 cubic centimeter intake ports. The RR180 offers decent flow numbers and could be considered a mid-pack performer. With a 2.00-inch cross-sectional area, its velocity numbers are down since its flow numbers are not as strong.

HIGH-PERFORMANCE CHEVY SMALL-BLOCK CYLINDER HEADS

Brodix Race-Rite 180

Valve Lift (inches)	Intake	Exhaust	E/I (%)	Intake Port Velocity (cfm/sq.in.)
0.100	63	48	76%	99
0.200	118	78	66%	93
0.300	159	114	72%	83
0.400	206	155	75%	103
0.500	248	171	69%	124
0.600	239	184	77%	119

67-cc Chamber
2.02/1.60-inches valves
2.00 sq.in. intake port cross-section
180-cc intake port
Tested on a 4.030-inch bore fixture

Brodix –8 Pro (185cc)

Valve Lift (inches)	Intake	Exhaust	E/I (%)	Intake Port Velocity (cfm/sq.in.)
0.100	64	53	83%	101
0.200	126	95	75%	99
0.300	179	124	69%	94
0.400	221	145	65%	105
0.500	255	166	65%	121
0.600	228	171	75%	108

64-cc Chamber
2.02/1.60-inches valves
2.10 sq.in. intake port cross-section
185-cc intake port
Tested on a 4.030-inch bore fixture

simulate both flow numbers on an engine simulation and then look at the cost difference between the two different heads. Either way, you can't lose, especially when it comes time to take the car out on the streets!

Other features worth noting on the AFR 180 Eliminator are the use of GEN III technology with smaller 8-mm valvestems and lighter valvetrain components. AFR claims these drop the valvetrain weight by an impressive 50 grams. This means you can spin the engine a little higher without losing control of the valvetrain. All the Eliminator heads are drilled for both types of valve covers—either perimeter or center-bolt.

Brodix Race-Rite 180

The Race-Rite is one of two new heads from Brodix intended to supplement its already monstrous selection of iron and aluminum heads for the small-block Chevy. We once tried to count up all the different applications they have for the small-block, but gave up because the list was so long. The Race-Rite (RR) 180 is the smaller cousin to the RR 200 head, with 2.02/1.60-inches valves and a relatively tight 67-cc chamber that promises decent velocity from its 2.00-inch cross-sectional area intake port.

The 180 head can be ordered with either a straight or angled spark plug location, and uses all standard 23-degree small-block valvetrain components. Looking at the flow bench results, the Race-Rite didn't fare as well as its competitors. And oddly, it did not flow as well on the intake side as its older, similar-sized cousin the –8 Pro Brodix. The exhaust side is not much better, with an average flow that is the lowest among the heads that we tested. This is not to say it is a poor head, just that there are other castings, some with smaller intake cross-sections that can generate better flow numbers. But if you run across a set of these heads for a good price, they would make a good investment.

Brodix –8 Pro

This head is another selection from the Mena, Arkansas, manufacturer that has actually been around for many years. Like it does for all its cylinder heads, Brodix offers the –8 in several versions. The head we tested was the –8 Pro fitted with the smallest of the intake valve packages with a 2.02/1.60-inch valve combination. Brodix also offers this head in 2.05 and 2.08-inch intake valve sizes, as well with the exhaust valve sizes remaining at 1.600. While the –8 Pro's

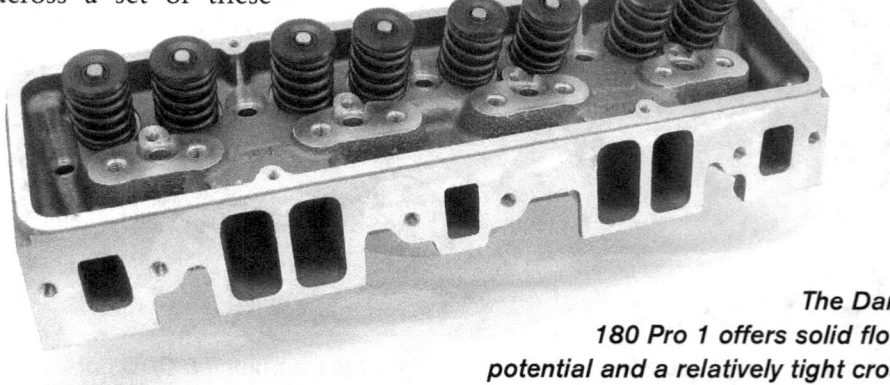

The Dart 180 Pro 1 offers solid flow potential and a relatively tight cross-sectional area that lends well to a mild small-block with displacements between 350 and 383 inches.

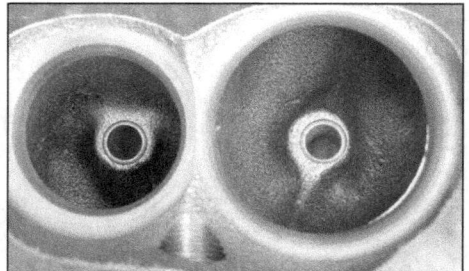

Dart's Platinum series iron heads offer increased power potential because of development time spent on the intake ports using Dart's new wet flow bench. The most obvious clue on a Dart wet-flow technology head is the flow director vane in the intake port. Other heads use these vanes, but only the wet-flow heads angle the inlet charge into the chamber.

If you can handle the price, the CNC Competition ported option for the AFR 195 heads make these heads tough to beat in either airflow or power. Both the intake and exhaust ports pull down outstanding numbers, especially in the lower valve lift areas where they contribute to excellent overall power.

mid-lift flow numbers on the intake side are lower than some of the other heads in this arena, it did pull out a solid 255 cfm at 0.500-inches of lift; however, given a choice, we'd rather see more flow in the mid-lift area and be willing to give up that peak flow to get there.

Unfortunately, the exhaust side is weak in comparison to the other heads in this category. Average flow ends up toward the bottom of the scale, with the mid-lift numbers only creating a 65 percent E/I, which isn't encouraging since the intake numbers are not all that strong to begin with. Again, this head can make respectable power in a mild small-block, but the –8 Pro is showing its age compared to the newest generation of small-block heads.

Dart 180 Pro 1

The testing on these heads is based on the older Pro 1 version of the Dart 180, but by the time you read this Dart will have released the wet-flow Platinum version of the head, which initial reports indicate are better than their iron casting counterparts.

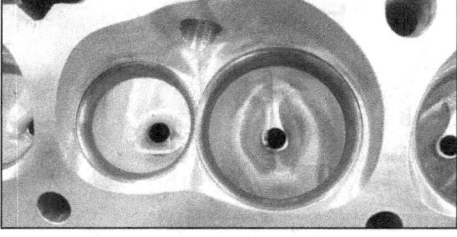

This is a CNC'd combustion chamber for the version 1 AFR 195 head that offers an interesting mix of parameters. Our experience is that the chambers require a couple more degrees of timing than similar-sized chambers, yet are not detonation sensitive. A poorly designed chamber generally requires more timing and is prone to detonation as a result.

Dart 180 Pro 1 Aluminum				
Valve Lift (inches)	Intake	Exhaust	E/I (%)	Intake Port Velocity (cfm/sq.in.)
0.100	63	58	92%	99
0.200	133	102	77%	105
0.300	178	131	73%	93
0.400	216	162	75%	109
0.500	236	181	77%	120
0.600	243	193	79%	123

67-cc Chamber
2.02/1.60-inches valves
1.97 sq.in. intake port cross-section
180-cc intake port
Tested on a 4.060-inch bore fixture

AFR 195 (Version 1)				
Valve Lift (inches)	Intake	Exhaust	E/I (%)	Intake Port Velocity (cfm/sq.in.)
0.100	72	68	94%	113
0.200	145	122	84%	114
0.300	209	159	76%	110
0.400	246	187	76%	111
0.500	263	204	77%	119
0.600	260	211	81%	117

74-cc Chamber
2.02/1.60-inches valves
2.21 sq.in. intake port cross-section
195-cc intake port
Tested on a 4.030-inch bore fixture

This is where dry flow numbers tend to not tell the whole story since the wet-flowed Flow Technology heads show up better on the engine dyno than on a dry flow bench. This is not to make excuses for the Dart Pro 1 heads. Our testing for the older version of the Dart Pro 1 revealed that it lacks a little on the intake flow side in comparison to like-sized heads such as the AFR 180 and both of the Brodix heads. Since this is a somewhat older design, by the time the new version Dart 180 is released, the numbers will be better.

AFR 195 Version 1

Now we get to one of the best small-block heads on the market today. This head has just been updated (we evaluate the new Eliminator head separately in this chapter) because the port design is now well over a decade old and the competition has finally closed the performance gap. In fact, within the category of 180 to 199-cc heads, the first version of this head is only exceeded in the overall intake flow curve average by the AFR Eliminator head with its outstanding mid-lift flow numbers. We believe this is why the head runs so strong even on engines with a modest duration camshaft. We discussed why the mid-lift curves are so important in Chapter 3, and if you skipped the chapter on airflow basics, it would be highly beneficial for you to spend time with this information before going further. Otherwise, much of the data presented in these subsequent chapters will not be as meaningful.

Taking a look at the 0.300 and 0.400 inch of valve lift numbers, the AFR 195 version 1 head certainly holds its own. Taken together, this first version is outstanding. Of all the small-block heads that we've ever tested both on the flow bench and on the engine dyno, the connection between a strong mid-lift flow curve and excellent overall power is indisputable. This is the reason we continue to emphasize this area of the flow curve, and it is obvious that AFR has spent a tremendous amount of time doing exactly this with even this first-generation casting. If it sounds like we are fans of the AFR 195 head for any street-driven small-block, you are correct. While it is one of the most expensive small-block aluminum heads on the market, it is also an example of power-per-dollar where the additional few hundred dollars spent for this head is money well spent in terms of quality and performance. This is also a good place to mention that AFR used to offer a 190-cc intake port head as well. The only difference between the 190 and 195 heads is that the smaller version offered a reduced intake port opening to accommodate more conservative intake manifolds. AFR dropped that practice, eventually selling only the 195-cc intake port version. If you run across a set of used AFR 190s for sale for a good price, consider picking them up since they can be quickly increased to the standard 1.280-wide by 2.090-tall opening that matches a typical Fel-Pro 1205 or 1206 intake gasket. This head has now been discontinued, but AFR did offer two versions, a standard 195 and a competition fully CNC-ported package. The flow numbers we list in this book are for the fully CNC-ported competition heads. Flow numbers for the standard package will be slightly lower on both the intake and exhaust side.

We should also address the exhaust side, which is another AFR strong suit. Right alongside the intake is exhaust port flow efficiency with E/I numbers that average over 81 percent. In the 0.100-inch exhaust lift category, the AFR 195 is only exceeded by

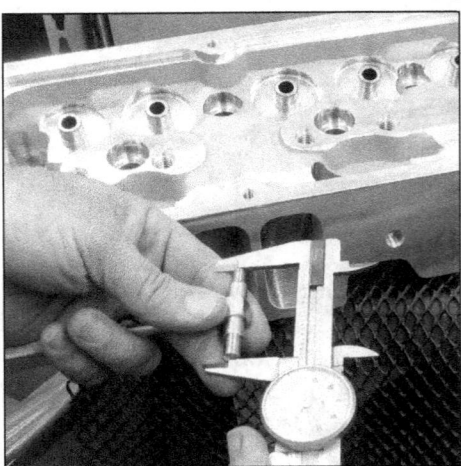

The latest version of the AFR 195 called the Eliminator not only exceeds the excellent flow numbers of its predecessor, but also does so with a smaller cross-sectional area at the pushrod restriction. This promises to be one killer cylinder head.

the TFS head. With an average 89 percent E/I between 0.100 and 0.200-inch valve lift, if you subscribe to the notion that a very efficient exhaust port at low lift is important, then it's hard to argue with these numbers. Not only that, but the AFR also pulls off superior exhaust flow numbers throughout the entire exhaust flow curve. This head is another example of a head that would perform exceptionally well with a single-pattern camshaft as opposed to additional exhaust event duration and lift. It's probably not needed.

By the time this book goes to print, the version 1 head will no longer be in production. But AFR has sold thousands of these castings that will no doubt end up on eBay at some point. For the right price, these heads will be players for years to come.

AFR 195 Eliminator

When we first heard about AFR's revision of the classic 195 head, our first thought was: "Wow, it's the best

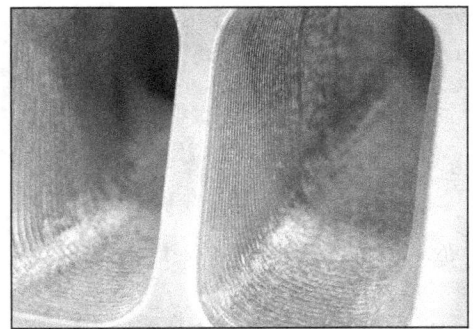

The top-of-the-line AFR heads are fully CNC machined to optimize port flow, while the standard heads are machined only an inch or so into the port entry. You can identify CNC machining by the close parallel lines that extend down the port. Full-port CNC machining is expensive since this requires very precise machine tolerances.

now, what can they do to make it better?" The numbers tell the story. The AFR's prototype numbers for the full CNC version of this head hit 300 cfm at the peak valve lift. AFR's port designer Tony Mamo had an interesting marketing dilemma because the intake port volume tested at barely 190-odd cubic centimeters. The company was concerned that many enthusiasts would feel the head was inferior only because it was smaller. Nothing could be farther from the truth.

With the new Eliminator's smaller intake port cross-sectional, the velocity has increased simultaneously along with the intake flow volume. By now, hopefully your airflow education tells you that this means very positive things for this head. As an example, how about a 383-ci small-block that made over 520 hp with a set of these AFR 195 Eliminators, 10:1 compression, and a 240 at 0.050 duration camshaft. Because of the long duration camshaft, the peak horsepower was around 6,300 rpm. That isn't excessive for a street engine, but with a milder street mechanical roller with 230 or 236 degrees of duration and perhaps a 1.6:1 rocker ratio, you could still benefit from the high-lift flow numbers and not have to buzz the engine. This would also increase the mid-range torque, perfect for a street engine.

The flow numbers tell the story. On the intake side with the full CNC competition package, the intake cranks out an amazing 285 at 0.600-inch lift, which is at the ragged edge of maximum lift that most engine builders would put into this head. At 0.500-inch valve lift this head is pulling almost 280 cfm which clearly bests all the other heads in this cate-

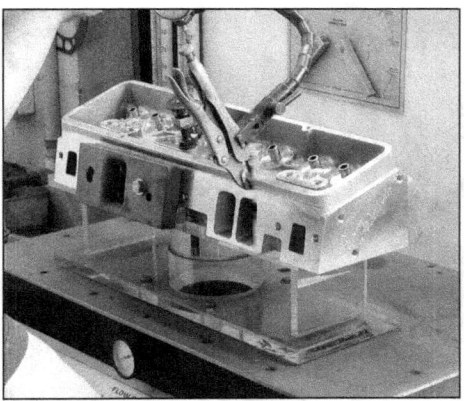

Perhaps one of the best buys in 23-degree aluminum small-block Chevy cylinder heads is the Ken Duttweiler signature TFS piece. This 195-cc intake port head offers excellent intake and exhaust port flow for the price. TFS is owned by Summit, so this is the only place you can buy these heads, but they offer excellent performance potential for the price.

gory and at 0.600-inch lift, we're still looking at a clear CFM flow advantage of roughly 30 cfm—that's impressive. The mid-lift numbers do not enjoy this same level of dominance, but with higher velocity numbers with a small cross-sectional area, the combination still bodes well for this casting.

On the exhaust side, the Eliminator commands the entire flow chart

AFR 195 Eliminator

Valve Lift (inches)	Intake	Exhaust	E/I (%)	Intake Port Velocity (cfm/sq.in.)
0.100	--	--	--	--
0.200	140	115	82%	110
0.300	201	165	82%	106
0.400	247	197	80%	113
0.500	278	218	78%	127
0.600	285	220	77%	130

68-cc Chamber
2.02/1.60-inches valves
2.18 sq.in. port cross-section
195-cc intake port
Tested on a 4.060-inch bore fixture

TFS 195cc

Valve Lift (inches)	Intake	Exhaust	E/I (%)	Intake Port Velocity (cfm/sq.in.)
0.100	66	71	107%	104
0.200	135	103	76%	106
0.300	190	142	75%	100
0.400	226	165	73%	115
0.500	251	183	73%	127
0.600	250	182	73%	127

65-cc Chamber
2.02/1.60-inches valves
1.97 sq.in. intake port cross-section
195-cc intake port
Tested on a 4.030-inch bore fixture

CHAPTER 6

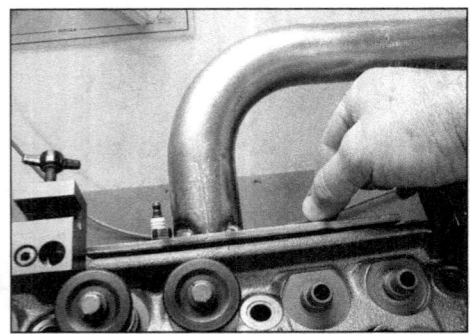

Unless otherwise specified, all exhaust port flow numbers in this book are with a flow pipe attached to the exhaust port. Generally, the exhaust pipe adds around 5 percent flow, and the percentages are slightly higher at higher valve lift numbers.

with the exception of 0.200-inch lift. Looking at the overall flow graph, the peak exhaust flow numbers are impressive, but so are the mid-lift numbers which again help produce impressive horsepower when this head exhibits over 80 percent average E/I. Again, those are solid numbers that predict an engine that can make big torque and horsepower.

TFS 195

A couple of other heads within this port volume category gave the first version AFR 195 strong competition, and one of those heads is the Trick Flow Specialties (TFS) 195 head. Recently, Ken Duttweiler has offered TFS some input into the design of this head and in return, TFS has put Duttweiler's endorsement on the casting. The numbers tell the story. With an almost identical cross-sectional area as the first version AFR 195, the TFS head comes up a little shy in the mid-lift intake flow numbers compared to the first version AFR, but on the exhaust side, the head we tested came up with an amazing 107 percent E/I number with a 71-cfm flow at 0.100-inch valve lift using just a 1.60-inch exhaust valve. The TFS 0.200-inch exhaust flow number is not nearly as efficient, but combined with its other attributes, this makes for a solid performing cylinder head.

One other major contributing factor to this head's success has to do with price. TFS is owned by Summit Racing, which means Summit is the only place you can purchase this head. But that's an advantage since Summit also prices this head very competitively. Generally, this head can be purchased for several hundred dollars less than many of its competitors, including both versions of the AFR 195. For enthusiasts on a budget where $200 to $400 is a deal breaker, the TFS 195 is an outstanding choice that makes the dollar-per-horsepower deal that much sweeter.

Canfield 195

The Canfield cylinder head company is probably one of the best-kept secrets in the street performance industry. John Fenton has been quietly casting aluminum ports with excellent flow numbers for several years, but the heads have yet to really

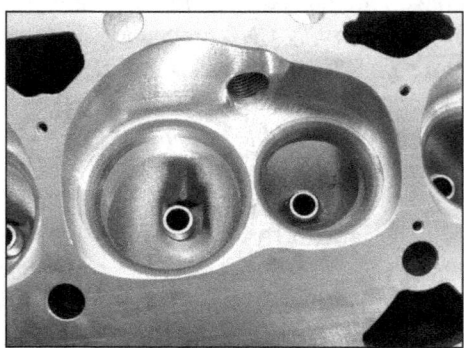

Most good aftermarket aluminum cylinder heads come with either CNC machine or handwork performed in the area directly underneath the valve seat insert. Once the seat is installed, there is a sharp edge or lip created in the transition from the port to the seat insert. A smooth transition in this area is essential to good port flow numbers.

The Canfield 195 is perhaps the least known of the small-block Chevy cylinder heads, but don't let its lack of notoriety dissuade you from giving it due consideration. This is an excellent cylinder head for a small-block.

Canfield 195cc				
Valve Lift (inches)	Intake	Exhaust	E/I (%)	Intake Port Velocity (cfm/sq.in.)
0.100	75	65	87%	118
0.200	142	106	74%	119
0.300	203	144	71%	106
0.400	249	175	70%	117
0.500	258	191	74%	122
0.600	256	200	78%	120

64-cc Chamber
2.02/1.60-inches valves
2.12 sq.in. intake port cross-section
195-cc intake port
Tested on a 4.030-inch bore fixture

68 HIGH-PERFORMANCE CHEVY SMALL-BLOCK CYLINDER HEADS

take off in terms of big sales. This is partly due to the fact that Canfield as a company does very little marketing, and the days of the "if you build it, they will come" marketing approach with performance products is long gone. The company is located in Canfield, Ohio, and apparently the owner likes to maintain its rather low-key image and production size in order to produce a quality product.

Canfield's conservative volume has nothing in common with its port performance since the 195-cc version is a worthy competitor for the first generation AFR 195. On the intake side, the Canfield is a virtual match for the early AFR 195 head. The Canfield is not quite as strong on the exhaust side, especially at 0.200-inch, but still offers front-half of the field performance across both sides of the head.

Conclusion

Intake velocity is a key component to building a streetable small-block for no other reason than it helps the torque curve in the mid-range, which makes the car much more fun to drive on the street. It's akin to having a mini-big-block under the hood. In fact, go back in time to the magazines from 20 years ago, and the power numbers that we take for granted on mid-sized 383 and 406-ci small-blocks used to be impressive big-block 454 power numbers. In fact, we know some hydraulic roller-cammed 454 big-blocks that can't pull down the kind of power that a well-designed 406-ci small-block can create. One key is the wide variety of mid-sized intake port cylinder heads that combine excellent flow numbers with higher inlet velocities. Heads like the AFR, Canfield, and TFS 195 heads help make that happen.

Heads in Review

Description	Intake Port Volume (cc)	Valve Sizes (Int./Exh.)	Intake Cross Section (sq.in.)	Part Number
AFR 180 (Ver. 1)	180	2.02/1.60	2.11	899
AFR 180 Eliminator	180	2.02/1.60	1.92	0985
Dart Pro 1 180	180	2.02/1.60	1.97	11121111
Brodix RR180	180	2.02/1.60	2.00	1011000A
Brodix -8	180	2.02/1.60	2.10	1080001
AFR 195 (Ver. 1)	195	2.02/1.60	2.21	1091
AFR 195 Eliminator	195	2.02/1.60	2.18	7016
TFS 195	195	2.02/1.60	1.97	30400001
Canfield 195	195	2.02/1.60	2.12	See Canfield

All intake ports were tested on a 4.030-inch bore adapter unless noted.
All exhaust ports were tested with a flow pipe unless noted.

Bottom left: The two AFR 180 heads are the obvious front-runners in this graph that details the intake flow for all the 180-cc heads. Through 0.300 inch you can see they are all fairly close, while the AFR heads tend to pull away above 0.400 inch of lift. Also note how the Brodix head is certainly a player.

Bottom right: You can see how strong the new AFR 195 Eliminator head is especially at 0.600-inch valve lift. Of course, this is only useful if you are using a cam that can generate over 0.600 inch of lift. Otherwise, the early version AFR is very strong, as is the Canfield head.

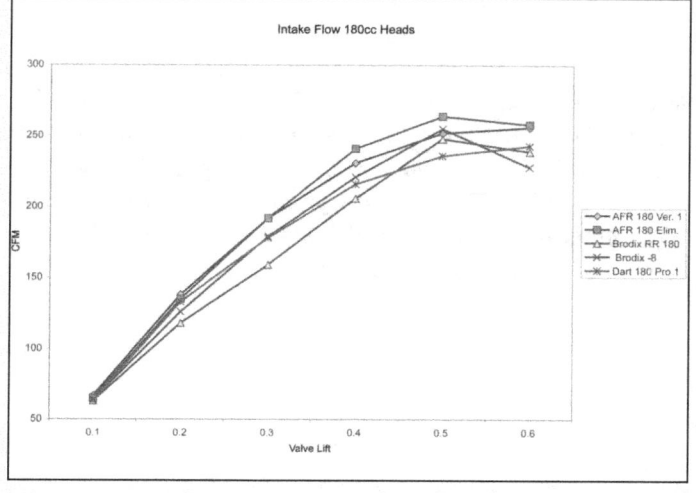

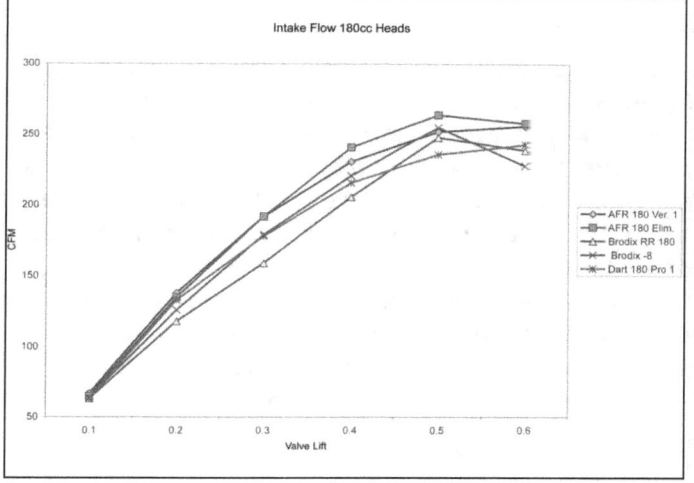

Heads in Review continued

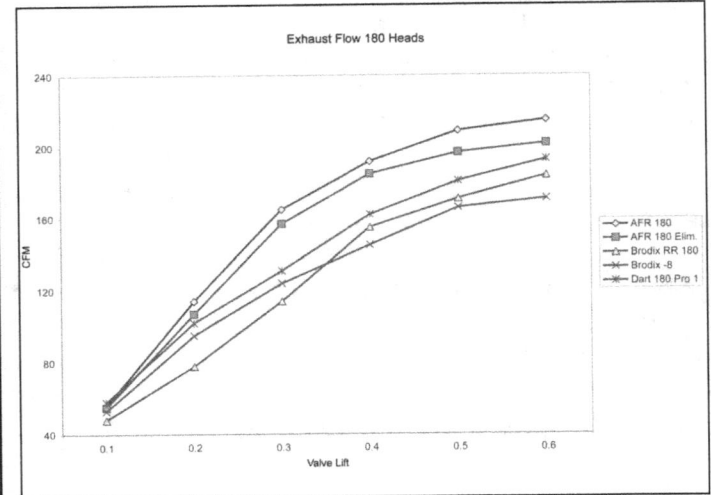

On the exhaust side of the 180-cc heads, it appears the older AFR 180 head is a little stronger on the exhaust side than the new version. The Dart 180 head also appears to have a strong exhaust flow curve.

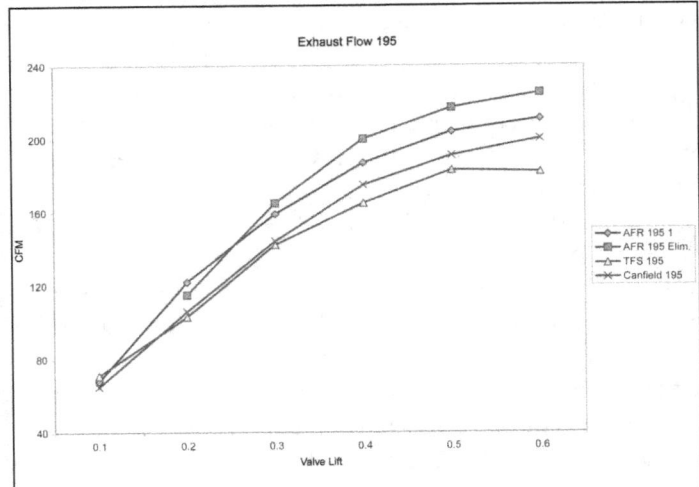

For the 195-cc heads, the AFR Eliminator is the clear exhaust flow front-runner closely followed by the first version AFR exhaust port. The Canfield also does well in comparison.

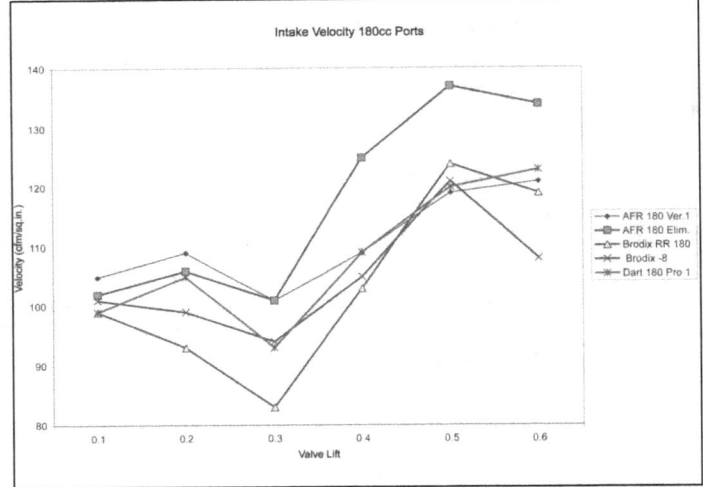

In terms of intake port velocity, the AFR 180 Eliminator starts slowly, but then commands the upper portion of the curve. It's worth noting that every velocity graph this author has created all produce this basic shape with a distinctive dip around 0.300 inch of valve lift. In the case of the Brodix Race-Rite 180, it would be especially beneficial to work on improving intake flow at both 0.200 and 0.300 inch of valve lift since this head clearly suffers from weak velocity at this valve lift. Increasing flow at this valve lift will also increase the velocity.

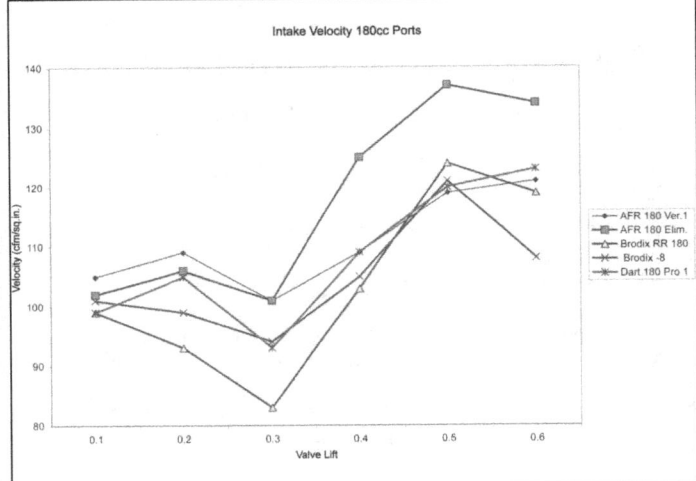

Note how the AFR Eliminator 195 does not take command of this velocity curve graph until the peak valve lift area. The Canfield head starts out strong at the lower lift portion of the curve then lays down while the AFR 195 Eliminator could be considered having the strongest overall velocity curve.

CHAPTER 7

LARGE-PORT HEADS
200-CC AND LARGER PORT VOLUME

Increasingly, the term "small-block Chevy" is becoming almost a contradiction of terms since the aftermarket is bent on building increasingly larger versions of the Mouse. You can now build or buy a standard deck height "small"-block that displaces 454 cubic inches. It wasn't all that long ago that a 454 was a big displacement Rat that everyone lusted after. Today, that's an exotic small-block while the slightly smaller 434, 420, and other displacement variations have become almost plentiful. All this added displacement has an effect on cylinder heads since a 454-ci small-block is almost 30 percent larger than its 350-ci ancestor. This added cylinder volume puts a premium

This category of heads is intended for small-blocks larger than 400-ci or engines that are designed to run at engine speeds up to or more than 7,000 rpm. Larger intake ports need either a larger engine or more RPM to create the velocity necessary to make power.

Longer Valves

With larger intake port cylinder heads, it's common for the ports to intrude into the spring pocket area of the standard 23-degree valve angle small-block head. The easiest way to remedy this real estate rivalry is to raise the spring pocket in the casting. This creates more intake port area to transition into the valve pocket area, which also allows the short side radius to become taller without restricting the port. All of these are positive steps that improve flow. This also requires a longer intake valve because now the spring seat must be raised up. Most larger intake port heads increase the valve length by 0.100 inch, which requires the exhaust valve to be longer so that all the valves are the same length. While all this work is handled by the cylinder head designer, it's important to note this fact because the taller valve lengths generally demand a longer pushrod in order to maintain proper valvetrain geometry.

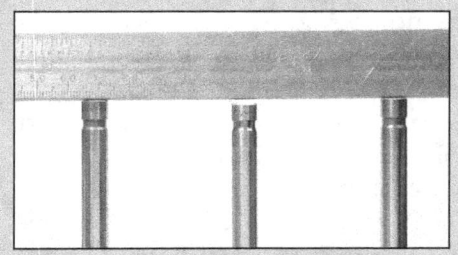

Oversize intake ports also mean longer intake and exhaust valves. These pieces increase the overall cost of building a head, but also require specific valvetrain parts to make them work. Generally, longer intake valves also demand longer pushrods to create proper valvetrain geometry.

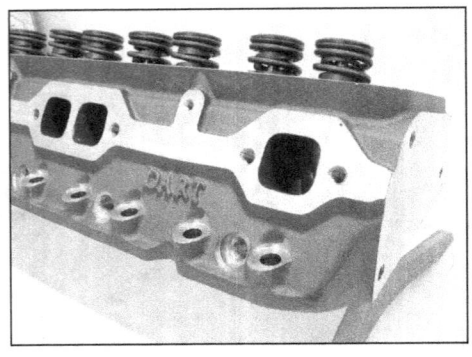

Especially with the larger intake port heads, some manufacturers raise the exhaust port in search of more exhaust flow to match the larger intakes. Be aware of this because a taller exhaust port creates header-to-chassis fitment problems.

on port flow, and the easiest way to accomplish extra flow is with a larger port.

The largest growing portion of the small-block Chevy head market has to be the 200-cc and larger intake port volume segment. These heads are not only great for larger displacement engines, but also for smaller engines looking to make power at higher engine speeds. With a rather small area to work with on a small-block, port volumes for standard 23-degree heads range all the way up to 230-cc.

Of course, intake port volume is just a convenient starting point from which to categorize these heads. What we really want to look at is each cylinder head's port flow numbers combined with their port cross-sectional area. Evaluating each of these individual sets of numbers give us some insight into how each of these heads would respond on a given engine.

Clearly, there are a ton of variables that can affect overall engine performance. Hopefully by this point in the book, you have deduced that the biggest intake port with the highest peak valve lift flow numbers may not be the best choice for a particular application. Instead, we must take into account how the engine will be used and pay attention to the vehicle in which the engine will be used. Ideally, we want to strike a combination between the short-block, the heads, and the induction system. This helps make outstanding torque, and gives a wide power band between peak torque and peak horsepower that contributes to moving the car down the drag strip or around corners at a road course that will thrill and amaze you.

This chapter also encompasses the widest selection of intake port volumes, so it might be worthwhile to look at displacement in relation to these heads. The smaller the displacement, the less "demand" each cylinder makes on a given port. This can be related directly to velocity since cross-sectional area determines the speed at which the port can deliver the air to

Valve Centerlines

The small-block Chevy was originally designed with inline valves at a 23-degree valve angle. Back in the early 1950s when this head was penned, that was a strong-flowing head. But in 50 years of tweaking on engines, the industry has learned a few things about positioning valves in the combustion chamber. Port flow characteristics are also affected by where the valve is positioned in the combustion chamber. The easiest way to test this is to place a good-flowing cylinder head on a flow bench using a 4-inch bore cylinder adapter. Once those tests are complete, substitute a 4.155-inch bore that would represent a 400 block bored 0.030 inch oversize. We can guarantee that the 0.155-inch larger bore will improve both the intake and exhaust flow numbers. This is because the cylinder walls tend to shroud the movement of air both in and out of the cylinder.

Assuming not everyone is going to be running 4.155-inch bore diameters, the next best thing to a large bore is to move the intake valve in relationship to the bore. When Chevy originally designed the small-block, intake valves at 1.72 inches were barely larger than today's performance exhaust valves. When intake valve sizes began growing, the outside diameter of the valve naturally began moving closer to the cylinder wall. This immediately affects valve flow, especially at higher valve lifts. Some cylinder head manufacturers move the intake and exhaust valves in relation to the bore—the intake valve moves closer to the bore centerline while the exhaust valve moves closer to the opposite wall. The difficulty with this move is that it also directly affects the position of the valve in relation to the rest of the valvetrain, moving the rocker and the rocker stud, which also affects pushrod geometry by placing the pushrod more at an angle.

If the valves have been moved, potential power gains are even greater on large-bore motors. So if you are willing to build a 4.185 to 4.200-inch bore engine, heads with relocated intake valves will really shine. This information is also useful for the engine builder because a relocated intake or exhaust valve directly affects valve-to-piston clearance. This is because most production cast and forged pistons assume a standard location for the valve reliefs. When building a small-block using a head with relocated valve positions, it pays to talk to your piston source to accommodate these changes before the engine is assembled. Then a mock-up of the engine will indicate any valve-to-piston issues that might require machining. This should be finalized before the rotating assembly is balanced.

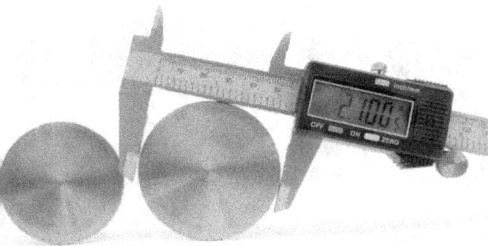

Big intake valves improve flow, but an interesting trick of physics may actually help push the air and fuel mixture into the cylinder at intake closing by virtue of the larger flow curtain area created by the larger valve.

the cylinder. Therefore, a larger cylinder (more displacement) places a greater demand on the intake port, achieving maximum port velocity sooner for a given cross-sectional areas. We would want to feed that larger cylinder with a larger intake port. Basically, we can condense this down to a statement as simple as: A larger-displacement engine can handle a larger intake port volume.

Since velocity plays such a crucial part is this evaluation, it also deserves attention. Consider that a larger port cross-sectional area could be used successfully on a smaller-displacement engine as long as the goal is power at a higher RPM. This would demand a longer-duration camshaft. We get into that in Chapter 12, but the basics behind this is that a longer duration cam adds "time" in degrees to allow the port to fill the cylinder at much higher engine speeds. A larger port cross-sectional area works with this higher engine speed to achieve its maximum port velocity, enhancing peak horsepower. Another way to look at this is that the longer duration camshaft simply moves the torque peak to a higher engine speed. This is assuming that everything else functions normally, the rods don't decide to ventilate the oil pan, and the valvetrain doesn't try to eat itself. Besides requiring a high quality short-block, the heads also must be equipped with some good valvesprings to be able to withstand the rigors of high RPM use.

This means that you can place a larger intake port volume head on a smaller-displacement engine and make it work by spinning the snot out of it to achieve the horsepower goal. This, for example, is the basics behind how naturally aspirated drag race engines are constructed—they just spin 'em faster. Of course, this automatically kills low-end torque and really hampers low-speed driveability since the engine loses much of its low RPM torque through lost volumetric efficiency, a very late-closing intake valve and tons of overlap. Getting back to a specific usage, this also requires a high-stall speed converter (or a manual trans), lots of rear gear, a good suspension, and all the rest that goes with a high RPM package.

Valve Seat Angles

The standard valve seat angle for the most part has always been 45 degrees. But recently, Pro Stock and high-end drag racing engine builders have been experimenting with angles of 50 to 55 degrees with some success. Since this information is reaching the average enthusiast through the performance press and the Internet, it deserves to be more adequately explained. It is true that a seat angle of 50 to 55 degrees will deliver more airflow and, as a result, more power. But there are serious caveats. The first problem is that seat durability is not nearly as good as a 45-degree seat. Taking that one step in the opposite direction, many early performance production engines such as Oldsmobile and Pontiac big-blocks tried 30-degree seats as a way to enhance performance.

The problem with a flatter angle such as 30-degrees is that high-velocity air movement for high RPM use tends to direct the air and fuel more horizontally into the cylinder, directing it toward the cylinder wall from the long side of the port. There is some evidence to suggest that this flatter angle does improve low-lift flow between 0.100 and 0.300-inch, and with production engines that may have been the real reason for its use. Unfortunately, the 30-degree angle also tends to hurt high-lift flow and is perhaps the main reason why the 45-degree seat angle has become an industry standard.

Moving to the 50 to 55-degree seat angle question, in comparison to the 30-degree angle, you can see that the taller angle tends to direct the air and fuel more toward the middle of the cylinder as opposed to the outer walls. One disadvantage is that these taller angles tend to sacrifice lift below 0.400 inch. For street engines with cams with max lift of not much more than 0.500 inch, there's very little reason to go to a 55-degree seat angle. Pro Stock and high-end competition engines employ this 55-degree valve-sealing angle because they are using much taller valve angles that tend to work better with this steeper valve seat angle. All of this is in an attempt to maximize flow when the piston reaches maximum velocity. So while the racers may use it to optimize a pure-bred drag race engine, these trick-of-the-week valve sealing angles are best left to the racers.

Angle milling is a common practice when attempting to reduce the chamber volume. This also has a small affect on the overall valve angle. Keep in mind that this also changes the relationship between the head and the intake manifold sealing surface that must also be rectified.

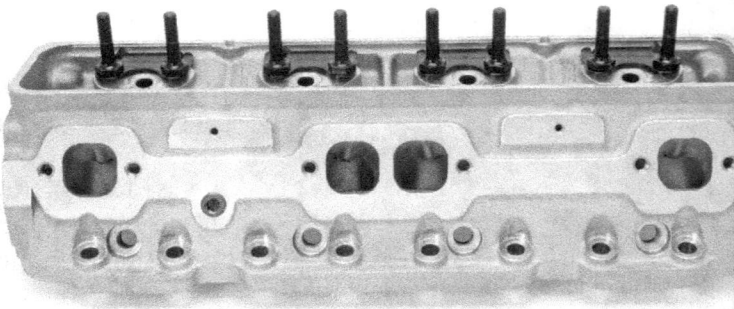

The Edelbrock E-Tec is the Fun Team's 200-cc big-cousin version of the original GM Vortec iron head. This head offers outstanding velocity numbers, which promises great torque in a 355 or 383-ci small-block.

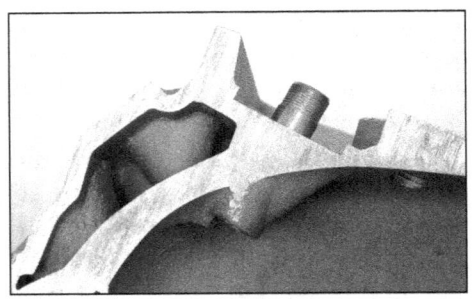

Many head companies warn not to deepen spring pockets when modifying heads. This is mainly because the area between the top of the bowl area and the bottom of the spring seat is often very thin. Sinking the spring pockets to fit a larger valvespring can cause serious problems that you should strive to avoid.

While those high RPM motors are romantic, for the street they are for the most part impractical and not very durable—especially those stiff valvesprings. The more attractive alternative for a hot street engine is to trade RPM for displacement. Instead of a high-winding 355 or 377, let's look at the advantage of a larger cubic inch engine along the order of a 420 or 434-ci bruiser. A small-block of this size can easily take advantage of a 215, 220, or even a 230-cc intake port to create excellent port energy with the combination of good airflow and a reasonable intake port cross-section.

Another point worth emphasizing again is to not ignore the exhaust side of these cylinder heads. It's all too easy to get lost in the evaluation of intake ports and overlook the requirements of the exhaust side. If the cylinder can't push all the bad air out, there won't be as much room for the good air on the next cycle. It's as simple as that. As mentioned in Chapter 3, there is considerable evidence to support enhancing low-lift exhaust port flow to improve cylinder blow-down when the cylinder pressure is the highest. There's also the data from both Duntov and Smokey Yunick that emphasize work in the area of 75 percent of peak valve lift on the exhaust side. So, for a 0.550-inch peak valve lift figure, this means that emphasizing exhaust flow around the 0.410-inch valve lift would be beneficial. These two approaches may appear to be contradicting, but the truth is that enhancing flow at every valve lift point will certainly improve cylinder scavenging.

This is not supposed to be a theory chapter, but it is important to have an idea of how best to apply the different cylinder heads that are offered within this category. Now we take a look at each of these heads a little more closely.

Edelbrock E-Tec 200

This is the larger cousin of the Edelbrock E-Tec 170 and interestingly falls right in the middle between the smaller Edelbrock Performer RPM and the Victor Jr. 23-degree heads. Edelbrock's street cylinder head philosophy has always been to deliver excellent velocity along with decent flow numbers to create strong torque and horsepower for a solid street engine. While the E-Tec's mid-lift intake flow numbers compare favorably to many of the 200 to 215 heads in this category, if we look back at the flow numbers for heads slightly smaller than the E-Tec, there are several smaller heads that out-perform the E-Tec at this level.

However, the Edelbrock head does do well up around 0.500-inch lift with a 253-cfm flow number. Combined with a relatively small cross-sectional number, the E-Tec offers excellent port velocity numbers due to its smaller port cross-section and intake valve, which maintains the energy up through its lift curve. Curiously, the stronger flow velocity numbers are at the top of the curve, with the lowest velocity at 0.300-inch lift. If you buy the concept that 65 percent of maximum valve lift is one area where we

Edelbrock E-Tec 200

Valve Lift (inches)	Intake	Exhaust (flow pipe)	E/I (%)	Intake Port Velocity (cfm/sq.in.)
0.100	64	51	79%	101
0.200	124	106	85%	98
0.300	177	145	82%	93
0.400	221	179	81%	111
0.500	253	195	77%	127
0.600	258	207	80%	129

64-cc Chamber
2.02/1.60 valves
1.99 sq.in. intake port cross-section
200-cc intake port
Tested on a 4.030-inch bore fixture

Dart Iron Eagle 200

Valve Lift (inches)	Intake	Exhaust (flow pipe)	E/I (%)	Intake Port Velocity (cfm/sq.in.)
0.100	62	54	87%	98
0.200	123	106	86%	97
0.300	174	126	72%	91
0.400	213	165	77%	104
0.500	233	174	74%	113
0.600	237	175	74%	115

64-cc Chamber
2.02/1.60 valves
2.05 sq.in. intake port cross-section
200-cc intake port
Tested on a 4.030-inch bore fixture

concentrate our effort, it would appear this head could use some work in the 0.300-inch lift area, even if we have to sacrifice some flow at the top of the curve. From this standpoint, it appears that a minor amount of pocket porting or valve angle enhancements on the E-Tec in the mid-lift flow area could make this head work very well. On the exhaust side, Edelbrock does not back-cut its valves, which is an incredibly easy thing to do to these heads to enhance the exhaust port efficiency. With those couple of changes, the E-Tec is a real player for a mild street engine that enhances the torque on a mid-sized small-block like a 383-ci.

Dart Iron Eagle 200

This is Dart's iron entry in the 200-cc port size market. The flow numbers are respectable, but not outstanding. We won't spend a lot of time on this head since Dart no longer sells it, having replaced it with the Platinum series of iron castings—a far superior head. The flow velocity numbers are acceptable since they come in around 100 cfm/sq.in., but frankly there are several other heads in this same port volume category that offer greater flow rates and velocities.

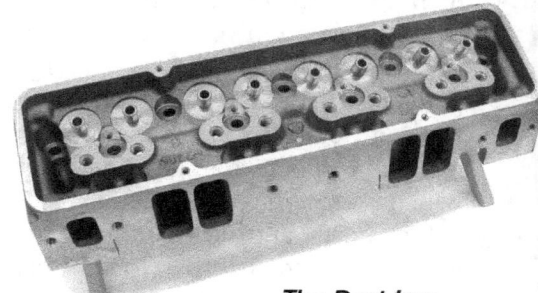

The Dart Iron Eagle 200 is one of Dart's earlier castings that exhibits decent flow potential and respectable low-lift velocity numbers.

Dart Iron Platinum 200

Valve Lift (inches)	Intake	Exhaust (flow pipe)	E/I (%)	Intake Port Velocity (cfm/sq.in.)
0.100	63	60	94%	99
0.200	127	109	85%	100
0.300	177	141	79%	93
0.400	219	169	77%	106
0.500	250	187	75%	121
0.600	260	196	75%	126

64-cc Chamber
2.02/1.60-inches valves
200-cc intake port
2.06 sq.in. intake port cross-section
Tested on a 4.060-inch bore fixture

Dart Pro 1 Aluminum 200

Valve Lift (inches)	Intake	Exhaust (flow pipe)	E/I (%)	Intake Port Velocity (cfm/sq.in.)
0.100	63	60	95%	99
0.200	130	107	82%	102
0.300	175	142	81%	92
0.400	213	172	80%	104
0.500	238	186	78%	116
0.600	248	193	78%	121

64-cc Chamber
2.02/1.60-inches valves
200-cc intake port
2.06 sq.in. intake port cross-section
Tested on a 4.060-inch bore fixture

Dart Platinum 200

As mentioned, the Platinum series has replaced the original Iron Eagles, with an emphasis on Dart's wet flow technology. This focus on the intake side is not necessarily reflected in dry flow-bench testing. This is because the focus with the wet flow technique is to modify the intake port, improving the fuel flow pattern as it exits past the intake valve and into the cylinder. Nevertheless, the Platinum 200 is still an excellent cylinder in terms of intake flow with 250 cfm at 0.500-inch lift. There are other 200-cc heads that flow more in the mid-range, but these heads also rely on much larger port cross-sectional areas. The 200-cc Platinum employs a mere 2.06 sq.in. minimum port cross-sectional area, which is among the smallest of all the 200-cc heads and of this entire category. It's also smaller than the first version AFR 180 and AFR 195 heads. This equates to top five status (within the 200 to 230-cc port volume category) in terms of flow velocity at the higher valve lift numbers.

The Platinum 200 also delivers excellent exhaust flow with average mid-80 percent E/I numbers in the low- to mid-lift range where exhaust flow is especially important. All the new Dart Platinum and Pro 1 heads come equipped with 30-degree back-cut valves as standard equipment on assembled heads, which is one reason for their performance. The cast-iron Platinum heads are excellent castings, with a very nice finish both inside and out. As iron heads go, these are some of the nicest castings we've ever worked with. There is also potential for improvement since there is no additional handwork done to the bowls on either the intake or exhaust sides. While not as rough as production heads, we found a few sharp edges on most of the transitions between the bowl and the deepest throat angle. Be very cautious here since sharp edges are also acknowledged as beneficial to shearing fuel and creating fuel atomization. We recommend making changes only if you have access to a flow bench to evaluate your changes.

Dart Pro 1 200 Aluminum

This is Dart's aluminum version of the iron 200. As you can see from the flow test numbers, this head is similar to the Platinum. In terms of development, this head came after the Iron Eagle, but before the Platinum head. As this book was completed, Dart converted all its Pro 1 heads to Platinum status with wet flow technology, although because of deadlines we did not have access to these heads for testing. This means that, while the Pro 1 is a great head, the newer wet-flow Platinum versions should offer comparable flow and performance to the iron Platinum versions. In fact, an early test of these Pro 1 Platinums indicated that the aluminum heads, with their minor blending of the seat into the throat, were worth as much as 20 hp over the iron Platinum versions. Also keep in mind that all the Pro 1 tests in this book are on as-cast intake and exhaust ports. Only the 227 Dart head is fully CNC ported.

This is the main reason why the Platinum head of the same port volume

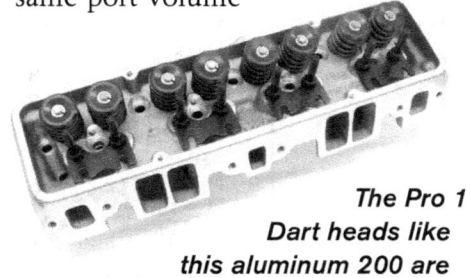

The Pro 1 Dart heads like this aluminum 200 are a step up from the Iron Eagle line both in flow and less weight.

appears to be measurably better than the aluminum Pro 1. The last head to hit the market generally has an advantage. The exhaust flow is very similar to the Platinum 200 and it appears that the two exhaust ports are probably the same. With a decent low-80 percentile E/I, the Pro 1 offers respectable exhaust flow, which may even be good enough to warrant a single pattern instead of a dual-pattern cam when it comes time to select a camshaft. Another worthwhile factoid concerning all the aluminum Dart heads is their excellent pricing. These heads are not the cheapest on the market, but they do represent an excellent performance-per-dollar investment.

World Products Sportsman II

This is one of the original small-block Chevy aftermarket iron cylinder heads. Considering that this is a long-in-the-tooth head, it is still a viable casting with potential. Right off the bat, it offers respectable flow numbers, especially compared to much newer heads in the same category such as the Dart Iron Eagle 200 and the Brodix Race-Rite 200. The intake port velocity numbers are actually better than we anticipated given its 2.19 sq.in. port cross-section. Numbers in the 110 cfm/sq.in. area at the higher valve

The World Products Sportsman II iron head is the oldest of the aftermarket heads and has become outclassed by this latest surge of new 200-cc and larger small-block heads.

LARGE-PORT HEADS

Worlds Products Sportsman II 200

Valve Lift (inches)	Intake	Exhaust (flow pipe)	E/I (%)	Intake Port Velocity (cfm/sq.in.)
0.100	69	58	84%	109
0.200	132	103	78%	104
0.300	188	132	70%	99
0.400	225	151	67%	103
0.500	241	165	68%	110
0.600	243	163	67%	111

72-cc Chamber
2.02/1.60-inch valves
2.19 sq.in. intake port cross-section
200-cc intake port
Tested on a 4.03-inch bore fixture

Brodix Race-Rite 200

Valve Lift (inches)	Intake	Exhaust (flow pipe)	E/I (%)	Intake Port Velocity (cfm/sq.in.)
0.100	64	50	78%	99
0.200	123	80	65%	95
0.300	167	115	69%	86
0.400	210	153	73%	96
0.500	245	176	72%	112
0.600	269	190	70%	123

64-cc Chamber
2.05/1.60 valves
2.18 sq.in. intake port cross-section
200-cc intake port
Tested on a 4.03-inch bore fixture

lifts are actually respectable, although like many heads in this category, the lowest port velocity occurs at 0.300 inch of valve lift, right where a head with a valve lift of 0.500 inch really needs to shine. Like the E-Tec head, this is an area where you could modify the throat area or perhaps fool with valve angles and back-cuts to increase port flow in this mid-lift area without sacrificing too much flow or velocity in the higher areas. The intake velocity curve was one of the surprises after calculating the velocities for all the heads in this category. We expected the Sportsman II to be one of the under achievers, but were pleasantly surprised by its velocity numbers.

On the exhaust side, the Sportsman II starts out strong with an 80 to 75 percent E/I, but this quickly drops off to the high 60 percent range, which indicates that this head is certainly exhaust limited in terms of horsepower. This is probably due to port area restriction, but again, don't overlook simple tricks like a 30-degree back cut on the exhaust valve and some bowl work to increase port flow at the higher valve lifts. Out of the box, this head is not stellar, but with some simple modifications it can still be a player in the small-block market, mainly due to its potential.

Brodix Race-Rite 200

This is the second head along with the Race-Rite 180 recently introduced by Brodix. The RR 200 offers a relatively large 2.18 sq.in. cross-sectional intake port area, which tends to hurt the velocity curve, especially compared to other heads in this area with much smaller cross-sections. The intake flow curve isn't real strong, and that is combined with a slow velocity curve that only begins to shine at the very top of the lift curve at 0.600

The Brodix Race-Rite is the Arkansas-based company's effort at a revised 200-cc intake port head for the street. The smaller port volume is intended for 383 to 400-ci street small-blocks with a decent cam.

inch. Here, this head offers decent flow and velocity, but frankly we don't think there are too many engine builders willing to put a 0.600-inch lift cam in a small-block with only a 200-cc intake port. Adjusting this flow curve to improve the 0.300 and 0.400-inch lift numbers would also pump up the velocity, which could prove to make this head a respectable performer.

The exhaust side is not much better since there are several heads in this category that offer substantially stronger exhaust ports. This leaves the Race-Rite 200 in a bit of a quandary since its high-lift intake port flow numbers can only be questionably supported by the exhaust side since it begins to lay down compared to the intake port's performance. This means the head needs a substantially longer exhaust duration in order to compensate for the exhaust port's performance. Again, there are ways to enhance this head's performance with back-cutting the exhaust valve and pocket porting that would certainly enhance its performance. But when there are several heads on the market that out-perform it right out of the box, the Brodix RR 200 has its work cut out for it.

AFR 210 Version 1

Evaluating the flow and velocity numbers on this head really makes it difficult to look past it to any other head for sheer performance. Before we get started, notice that this head is referenced as Version 1. That's because as this book is written, AFR has just completed work on a revised Eliminator version. It's also important to note that the test on this head represents the full CNC Competition porting effort available from AFR, while most of the heads in this category are as cast. This also makes this AFR 210 head more expensive than most, but you get what you pay for.

First of all, the entire intake flow curve is exceptionally strong. Looking just at intake flow at 0.400 inch of valve lift, the relatively small AFR 210 outperforms most of the heads in this chapter, even ones much larger in port volume and area. The minimum port-cross-section for this head is a relatively compact 2.07 sq.in. By now you should be able to tell that combined with excellent flow numbers, this means outstanding velocity numbers. The 210's minimum velocity number is 100 cfm/sq.in., while the higher valve lift numbers only get better with a peak of 130-plus cfm. If you remember from Chapter 3, an excellent intake port velocity number for any cylinder head is in the neighborhood of 130 cfm/sq.in. The only thing that would make this head better would be higher velocity numbers at the 0.300-inch lift point.

On the exhaust side, the AFR 210 delivers excellent low-lift flow numbers, especially at 0.100 inch of valve lift where it actually exceeds the intake side flow number with a smaller valve. You can guess what that does for exhaust flow velocity. It's possible this head would perform well with a minor amount of additional exhaust event duration, but not much. Overall, with its excellent port velocity and flow numbers, this first version AFR 210 head is tough to beat compared to the other heads in this category.

AFR 210 Eliminator

Before we get into the details, the AFR 210 Eliminator was not released until after this book was sent to the printer, so we had to go with AFR's prototype flow numbers. This is not something we're comfortable with since the production ports tend to be not quite as good, but AFR has consistently delivered on 95 percent of the promise, so we went with their numbers.

The original AFR 210 head combines the awesome power of excellent flow numbers with a relatively conservative port cross-section to deliver tremendous velocity numbers that promises excellent torque and horsepower.

As strong as the original AFR 210 was, the latest version combines improved flow numbers with a slightly smaller cross-section for even more torque potential. That means more power under the curve.

AFR 210 (Version 1)

Valve Lift (inches)	Intake	Exhaust	E/I (%)	Intake Port Velocity (cfm/sq.in.)
0.100	68	74	109%	104
0.200	142	118	83%	109
0.300	196	155	79%	100
0.400	242	182	75%	110
0.500	273	201	73%	124
0.600	279	211	75%	127

76-cc Chamber
2.08/1.60 valves
2.20 sq.in. intake port cross-section
215-cc intake port
Tested on a 4.03-inch bore fixture

AFR 210 Eliminator (Prototype AFR numbers)

Valve Lift (inches)	Intake	Exhaust (flow pipe)	E/I (%)	Intake Port Velocity (cfm/sq.in.)
0.100	--	--	--	--
0.200	147	117	79%	112
0.300	206	166	80%	105
0.400	257	202	78%	111
0.500	290	220	76%	126
0.600	308	230	74%	134
0.700	312	236	75%	135

76-cc Chamber
2.08/1.60-inches valves
210-cc intake port
2.30 sq.in. intake port cross-section
Tested on a 4.125-inch bore fixture

LARGE-PORT HEADS

Dart Iron Eagle 215

Valve Lift (inches)	Intake	Exhaust (flow pipe)	E/I (%)	Intake Port Velocity (cfm/sq.in.)
0.100	65	54	83%	101
0.200	121	105	87%	94
0.300	165	132	80%	85
0.400	213	161	75%	94
0.500	242	176	73%	107
0.600	258	183	71%	114

72-cc Chamber
2.05/1.60 valves
2.26 sq.in. intake port cross-section
215-cc intake port
Tested on a 4.030-inch bore fixture

Dart Platinum Iron 215

Valve Lift (inches)	Intake	Exhaust (flow pipe)	E/I (%)	Intake Port Velocity (cfm/sq.in.)
0.100	64	57	89%	99
0.200	128	111	86%	99
0.300	180	140	78%	93
0.400	221	172	78%	103
0.500	253	189	74%	117
0.600	273	198	72%	127

64-cc Chamber
2.05/1.60-inches valves
215-cc intake port
2.15 sq.in. intake port cross-section
Tested on a 4.060-inch bore fixture

Our initial look at the 210 came at the prototype stage just as head specialist Tony Mamo completed the final tweaks on the port. Again, Air-Flow Research offers this head in the competition mode as a full CNC-ported configuration. Obviously, this offers the most flow potential along with the highest cost. There is also a street configuration as well that compromises the flow a bit, but it is somewhat less expensive. The port cross-sectional area for this head is substantially larger than its predecessor at 2.30 sq.in., but when the flow numbers deliver 308 cfm at 0.600-inch lift, that places the velocity number at 134 cfm/sq.in., which puts this casting at the head of the class.

A close investigation of the Eliminator's intake pocket reveals an increasingly common flow director vane. Interestingly, AFR's version directs the flow in an opposite direction compared to the similar vanes found in the Dart Platinum series heads. While Dart's vanes are dictated by wet flow techniques, AFR has relied instead on the dry flow bench and a wide bowl wall to induce a circular motion to the exiting air and fuel, but in a direction away from the exhaust valve. The mid-lift numbers are also just short of phenomenal in that they also place the velocity curves solidly in the 120-plus range. These are the kind of numbers that push the torque curve up and make a properly cammed engine a strong accelerating engine.

The exhaust ports have also received their share of attention, starting with a 0.250-inch raised centerline, which will no doubt cause a few issues with header fitment. But this is a reasonable price to pay for flow numbers that reinforce why the port is where it is.

Dart Iron Eagle 215

The Dart Iron Eagle 215 head could probably be best described as a mid-pack player. We've included it here even though Dart actually doesn't sell this head any longer. It has now been replaced by the Platinum series of iron heads that all benefit from Dart's growing experience with wet flow technology. We've included the Iron Eagle in this category mainly because they will be around as used heads in the market for quite some time. The Iron Eagle's intake port flow numbers are respectable, but the port velocity numbers are not impressive and begin to fall right from the 0.100-inch valve lift starting point. The exhaust side does a good job of supporting the intake with decent percentages of flow, but keep in mind that with somewhat weak intake flow numbers, the percentages immediately look better. When comparing the exhaust flow to other heads in this category on a pure flow basis, again the Dart Iron Eagle 215 is mid-pack. Our recommendation is that these are decent heads if you find them for a good price, but the Platinum series heads are a better choice if you are going to go with an iron head.

Dart Platinum 215 Iron

In the shuffle of multiple cylinder heads, especially within this category, it's easy to overlook the "middle child" heads because the big guys seem to get all the press. But in the midst of our testing, we ran across some good dry flow numbers for the Dart Platinum 215 head that combine with a decent small port cross-section of 2.15 sq.in. Plus, with the promise of Dart's expertise in wet flow, this head may be the sleeper in this whole

The combustion chamber is a critical part of the entire cylinder head equation, yet it is difficult to evaluate. This is the chamber on the Dart Iron Platinum 215 head. Note how the spark plug is very close to the exhaust valve.

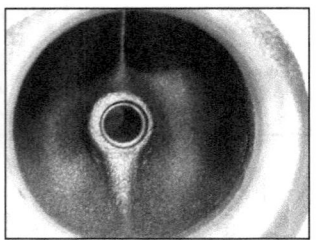

The best way to identify a Dart Platinum intake port (either aluminum or iron) is this vane that is becoming increasingly popular as a way to help direct fuel past the intake valve in a wider, more diffused pattern. This improves combustion efficiency and power. The Platinum also employs a much narrower valvestem boss, which improves flow.

When we get into the larger Dart 215 heads, the company's true abilities begin to come into play. The Dart Pro 1 215 Platinum is an excellent choice for a hot street motor of 383 to 420-ci displacement.

category. The Platinum offers very good velocity and flow numbers on the intake side along with an equally good price if you're willing to add the extra weight of the iron castings. With 253 cfm at 0.500-inch lift combined with a 117 cfm/sq.in. velocity component, this head shapes up to promise excellent torque.

The exhaust port is equally respectable with near-90 percent low-lift E/I numbers that equate to allowing the engine to RPM without backing up the exhaust flow and causing pumping losses at higher engine speeds. Overall, we think this is an excellent choice for either a larger displacement small-block like a 383 or 406, or even a 355 with a larger camshaft where you're willing to spin the engine a little higher to make power.

Dart Pro 1 215 Aluminum

We should probably call the Pro 1 series Dart's "Version 1" as well since the company has upgraded its entire Pro 1 series aluminum heads over to Platinum status. The Pro 1 series is still a solid choice. Again, in comparison to the later Platinum head of the same port size, it's not quite as good and would probably not perform as well on an engine because the Pro 1 has not benefited from the wet flow modifications. As with the previous Pro 1 versions, this is still a front half of the pack head. If you are interested in this size head in aluminum, the Platinum version is an excellent choice.

Edelbrock Victor Jr. 215 Aluminum

Since Edelbrock tends to emphasize small-port velocity numbers over high-lift flow, this approach tends to obscure this head as a decent performance small-block cylinder head. Many performance enthusiasts don't even know that Edelbrock offers an aggressive small-block head. In keeping with Edelbrock's port velocity concept, the Victor Jr. intake port is a comparatively tight 2.05 sq.in., smaller than all the other 215-cc intake port heads, and smaller than a few of the 200-cc intake ports. You can probably guess where this is

Dart Platinum Iron 215

Valve Lift (inches)	Intake	Exhaust (flow pipe)	E/I (%)	Intake Port Velocity (cfm/sq.in.)
0.100	66	60	91%	102
0.200	126	105	83%	98
0.300	170	139	82%	88
0.400	213	174	82%	98
0.500	246	191	77%	113
0.600	268	198	74%	123

72-cc chamber
2.05/1.60-inches valves
215-cc intake port
2.17 sq.in. intake port cross-section
Tested on a 4.060-inch bore fixture

Dart Pro 1 215 Aluminum

Valve Lift (inches)	Intake	Exhaust (flow pipe)	E/I (%)	Intake Port Velocity (cfm/sq.in.)
0.100	70	58	83%	107
0.200	125	112	89%	92
0.300	174	146	84%	89
0.400	220	182	83%	107
0.500	254	197	77%	124
0.600	276	207	75%	134

68-cc Chamber
2.08/1.60 valves
2.05 sq.in. intake port cross-section
215-cc intake port
Tested on a 4.03-inch bore fixture

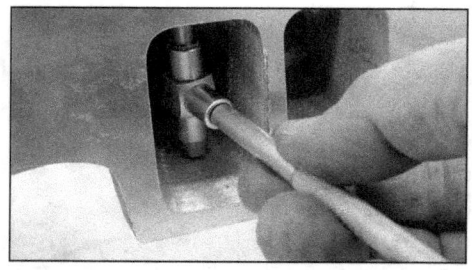

The strength of the Victor Jr. Edelbrock head is its excellent port velocity curve. The flow numbers are decent, but combined with a smaller intake port cross-section, this pumps the velocity, which promises power.

headed. The intake port CFM numbers may not be overly impressive compared to other 215-cc heads, but don't overlook its intake port velocity curve. The low-lift velocity numbers are not as strong as we might have expected, and the head's performance at 0.300-inch lift is especially weak. This means that there is work that could still be accomplished in the throat and valve job area (perhaps with a 30 to 35-degree back angle on the intake valve) that would improve both the flow and the velocity.

Where the Victor Jr. does excel is at the higher lift points, especially at 0.600-inch lift where it actually exceeds the velocity sweet spot of 130 cfm/sq.in. This obviously means it would require a camshaft with 0.600-inch lift or more, which puts it on the ragged edge of a streetable combination. An application where this might work is a larger-displacement small-block in the 410 to 430 ci range. This velocity could contribute to a killer power curve, taking advantage of the small-block's torque based on displacement rather than RPM potential.

On the discharge side, the Victor Jr. exhaust port offers a decent exhaust-to-intake flow relationship, which means it could use a camshaft with a slight amount of additional exhaust duration to be able to deliver maximum horsepower potential. In fact, the Victor Jr. serves up an excellent 80-plus percent E/I average all the way from 0.100 to 0.400 inch of valve lift. This contributes to purging the cylinder of exhaust gas long before the piston reaches BDC, which should reduce pumping losses. Because Edelbrock does not put 30-degree back-cuts on its heads, this is a simple modification that you could do that would probably benefit both the intake and exhaust flow and velocity aspects. Overall, this is a head that offers quite a bit of power potential and should not be overlooked.

TFS 215

Trick Flow Specialties has quietly been building a superb catalog of excellent cylinder heads for the small-block Chevy. To complement the Kenny Duttweiler signature 195-cc head, TFS has come up with a 215-cc intake port casting that offers excellent flow for the port cross-sectional area that makes its velocity curve one of the better ones in this category. With 2.08/1.60-inch valves and a 67 cc combustion chamber, this combination is intended for either a high-RPM smaller-displacement 355 ci small-block, or a larger-displacement 383/406/415-ci small-block that's intended more for torque production than ultimate high RPM horsepower. Another excellent attribute is that these heads are also affordable with prices in the $1,500 to $1,600 range for a complete pair of heads ready to bolt on.

Brodix Track 1 215

This is an aluminum casting from the folks in Mena, Arkansas, that has

Edelbrock Victor Jr. 215

Valve Lift (inches)	Intake	Exhaust (flow pipe)	E/I (%)	Intake Port Velocity (cfm/sq.in.)
0.100	70	58	83%	107
0.200	125	112	89%	92
0.300	174	146	84%	89
0.400	220	182	83%	107
0.500	254	197	77%	124
0.600	276	207	75%	134

68-cc Chamber
2.08/1.60 valves
2.05 sq.in. intake port cross-section
215-cc intake port
Tested on a 4.03-inch bore fixture

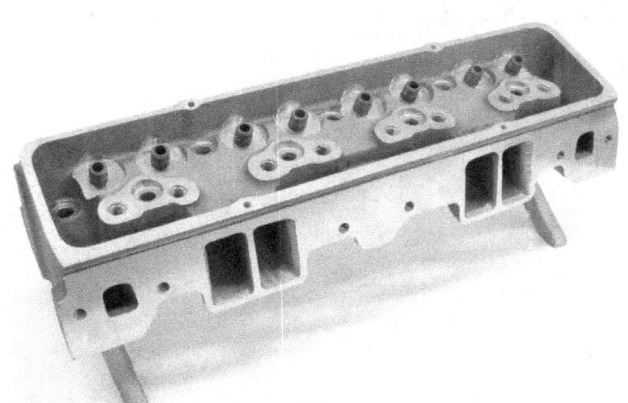

The Brodix Track 1 is another older intake port head that is still popular with some street engine builders, and its numbers indicate it's a mid-pack runner.

CHAPTER 7

been around for quite some time. As a result, its numbers are not quite as impressive as some of the later-developed heads. This places it at somewhat of a disadvantage, but we address it here mainly because you might run across a set at a swap meet or on the Internet for sale, and if the price is right, it could be a real bargain. It does flow well in comparison, for example, to the Dart 215 Iron Eagle and offers better exhaust port flow. Unfortunately, this first design Track 1 relies on a rather large port cross-sectional area in order to accomplish these flow numbers. This creates the slow port velocity numbers you see on our flow chart. For example, the Track 1 suffers from the same low inlet velocities at 0.300 to 0.400-inch lift just as many other heads in this category.

The Track 1 does offer a decent exhaust port, although the E/I numbers are a little deceiving because the intake side is not quite as strong, making the percentage comparison for the exhaust look better. Still, this is not a bad cylinder head and the potential is there. It would be interesting to reduce the port cross-section by a couple of tenths of an inch and see if the port flow would remain the same. This would pump up the velocity and perhaps help this head, especially in the higher valve lift regions.

There is also a Brodix Track 1X, which we have not tested, that uses a 222-cc intake port with a larger 2.100-inch intake valve with a CNC-machined combustion chamber and revised ports. Both this head and the Track 1 are also available through Brodix completely CNC-ported as an option.

Motown 220 Aluminum

World Products builds both Motown 220 and 220 Lite (aluminum) heads for the small-block. Basically, these heads are virtually as close to identical as you can get, except that the aluminum head offers a completely CNC-machined combustion chamber as part of the regular production package while the iron head uses an as-cast chamber. As a 220-cc head, it also relies on a large intake port cross-section to deliver the flow numbers. For example, 245 cfm at 0.400 inch valve lift is a respectable flow number, but with a 2.57 sq.in. port cross-section number, the velocity at the higher valve lifts is lower as a result. The head manages to produce over 100 cfm/sq.in. velocity at several valve lifts, but compared to several heads in this category that can generate velocities of 120 cfm/sq.in. or faster, the Motown 220's velocity numbers are a bit disappointing. But it's hard to ignore an intake port mass flow of 273 cfm at 0.500 inch of valve lift regardless of the velocity. Again, perhaps this is another head that could benefit from downsizing the port cross-sectional area in an attempt to increase velocity without sacrificing flow. The key would be maximizing the speed without sacrificing the flow. If used with a single-plane intake manifold, these heads

The Motown 220 aluminum head is virtually a clone of the iron version except for its CNC-machined combustion chamber that is worth a slight power increase over the standard chamber found in the iron head.

TSF 215				
Valve Lift (inches)	Intake	Exhaust (flow pipe)	E/I (%)	Intake Port Velocity (cfm/sq.in.)
0.100	66	57	86%	101
0.200	141	107	76%	108
0.300	199	145	73%	101
0.400	244	175	72%	111
0.500	273	190	69%	124
0.600	282	198	70%	128

67-cc Chamber
2.08/1.60 valves
2.20 sq.in. intake port cross-section
215-cc intake port
Tested on a 4.155-inch bore fixture

Brodix Track 1 215				
Valve Lift (inches)	Intake	Exhaust (flow pipe)	E/I (%)	Intake Port Velocity (cfm/sq.in.)
0.100	61	49	80%	93
0.200	116	107	92%	89
0.300	168	149	88%	85
0.400	210	178	84%	92
0.500	245	192	78%	107
0.600	269	201	75%	118

68-cc Chamber
2.08/1.60 valves
2.28 sq.in. intake port cross-section
216-cc intake port
Tested on a 4.03-inch bore fixture

LARGE-PORT HEADS

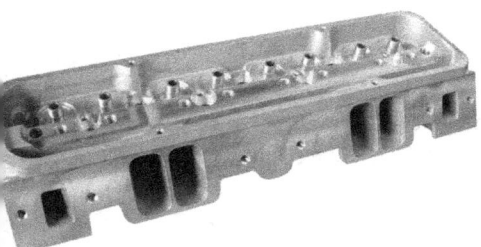

Just before this book went to press, World Products introduced a new 235-cc Motown aluminum 23-degree head to its lineup. The head features both 64-cc and 72-cc chambers along with killer 2.100/1.625-inch valves and is offered either bare or assembled with Manley valves and ARP hardware.

Along with the 235-cc Motown head, World also released a Vortec-style aluminum head, yet the intake bolt pattern remains the same as the original small-block. With generous 2.08/1.60-inch stainless steel valves, the head offers 215-cc intake port volume. According to World, the head uses a Vortec-style "quick burn" combustion chamber design.

The World Motown 220 head offers outstanding CFM numbers on the flow bench, but uses a rather large port cross-section to deliver those numbers, which lowers its intake velocity curve.

would tend to make more peak horsepower, but less mid-range torque than a set of heads with much greater intake port velocity.

The exhaust numbers for this head are also respectable even though the E/I percentages don't reflect that mainly because the intake flow numbers are strong. It's also worth noting that this head would certainly measure better if flow tested on a larger cylinder bore adapter. Since this head was tested on a 4.030-inch bore (as were many of the other heads in this book), there would certainly be a flow improvement across the board if tested on a 4.155-inch bore diameter.

Canfield 220

Much like its smaller brother, the Canfield 220 is another unsung hero in the small-block performance world. This is a large-port head at 220-cc and offers excellent intake flow numbers. The head is equipped with 2.08/1.60-inch valves and despite the rather large intake valve, still creates over 100 cfm/sq.in. velocity numbers, with 112 at 0.200 inch lift particularly good. The Canfield is comparable to even the much vaunted AFR 220 up through 0.500 inch of valve lift with the same size intake valve. If you were looking for a cylinder head for a strong 410 to 430-ci small-block, this would be a good choice with a combination of solid airflow and velocity numbers.

One thing we especially like about the Canfield exhaust is its excellent low-lift flow. This head's low-lift flow between 0.100 to 0.200 inch of valve lift is the best in this category, giving it the ability to blow the cylinder down in the early stages of the exhaust stroke better than any

World Products Motown 220 Lite

Valve Lift (inches)	Intake	Exhaust (flow pipe)	E/I (%)	Intake Port Velocity (cfm/sq.in.)
0.100	59	53	89%	90
0.200	133	107	80%	102
0.300	197	155	78%	100
0.400	245	183	75%	95
0.500	273	193	70%	106
0.600	278	194	70%	108

64-cc Chamber
2.08/1.60 valves
2.57 sq.in. intake port cross-section
220-cc intake port
Tested on a 4.03-inch bore fixture

Canfield 220

Valve Lift (inches)	Intake	Exhaust (flow pipe)	E/I (%)	Intake Port Velocity (cfm/sq.in.)
0.100	70	63	90%	107
0.200	147	116	79%	112
0.300	207	145	70%	105
0.400	243	173	71%	101
0.500	261	184	70%	109
0.600	267	189	71%	111

64-cc Chamber
2.08/1.60 valves
2.40 sq.in. intake port cross-section
220-cc intake port
Tested on a 4.03-inch bore fixture

of the other heads in this category. You don't hear about Canfield in the enthusiast press, so you might have an advantage with this additional knowledge. Again, this head was also tested on a 4.03-inch bore adapter and would probably deliver even higher flow numbers with a larger bore that would tend to unshroud the intake valve.

AFR 220 Version 1

As previously mentioned, these AFR heads will be replaced by the Eliminator by the time you read this, but hundreds are probably in the used market. The intake side offers a best-in-class 0.100-inch intake valve lift, not quite as strong in the 0.300 to 0.400-inches lift curve, but as strong between 0.500 to 0.600-inches of valve lift. We tested this head at 297 cfm at 0.600-inch, which is only exceeded by AFR's Eliminator version. On the exhaust side, the 0.100-inch flow numbers equals the best in the class and between 0.100- and 0.300-inch, the average E/I is a strong 80 percent. Combine those solid flow numbers with a great intake velocity curve, and you have a winning combination. Remember that these larger heads with their 2.08-inch intake valves work best on a 4.125-inch or larger bore size where the intake valve has a chance to take advantage of the larger port and valve area.

AFR 220 Eliminator

The redesign of AFR's entire line of 23-degree heads also includes the 220-cc intake port head. Because production heads have not been released, the information here must rely on AFR's own published numbers. The numbers are generally in line with a slight increase in flow on the intake and exhaust side compared to AFR's original version. The big increase appears to be at 0.400-inch lift on the intake side with a solid 20 cfm bump. Even if the production number is closer to 15 cfm, this is still significant. This head is intended for larger-displacement small-blocks and, like its previous iteration, it works with standard 23 degree valvetrain parts. AFR recommends a shaft system if the engine is run on the street, mainly to ensure the valvetrain remains where it belongs. This also assumes these heads will be used with a mechanical roller cam, which also means some pretty stout valvesprings that have a tendency to beat up valvetrain parts.

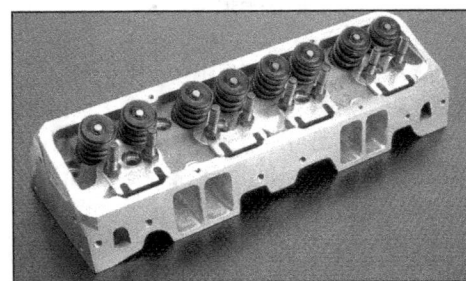

The AFR 220 Eliminator thumps, especially if you were to use it on a larger-displacement small-block in the area of 420 to 434 inches. The combination would make excellent torque and HP without resorting to a monster camshaft.

This new version of the 220 is similar to the first version in that you can order it with either a standard or a spread exhaust port, which is a good idea for endurance engines since it tends to not concentrate as much heat around the four center cylinders. These heads only come in angle plug configuration with a 76-cc combustion chamber. It's also possible to get this head in an as-cast version, as well as the CNC competition package. There's also a race ready version, which pumps the airflow up slightly with finer detail on the CNC porting. Valve sizes are 2.08/1.60 for the intake and exhaust.

Dart CNC 227

This is Dart's fully CNC-machined head that offers the intake, exhaust, and combustion chambers treated to the full boogie effort. The reason that CNC-ported heads—or any ported head for that matter—generally flow better than as-cast heads is because the casting process is somewhat less than completely accurate. Since good sand cast heads can maintain a plus or minus tolerance of 0.030-inch (that's a total potential swing of 0.060-inch), this has a substantial effect on port flow dynamics. The beauty of a CNC-ported head is that the manufacturer can specify the exact port shape with accuracy down to the hundredths of an inch, which offers the most potential for optimal flow.

In the case of the Dart CNC 227 head, the intake and exhaust ports are completely machined, leaving the tell-tale machine tools marks in the intake port. This is also a further advantage since a rough port wall tends to break up liquid fuel that otherwise tends to collect on smooth port walls. This is the main reason why polished intake ports are no longer desirable, making the term "port and polish" outdated.

The CNC-ported Dart Pro 1 227 offers exceptional mid-lift flow numbers, which may not look impressive on the flow bench, but this may be a move toward improving overall power. This head also offers excellent exhaust flow potential.

LARGE-PORT HEADS

AFR 220 Eliminator (Prototype AFR flow numbers)

Valve Lift (inches)	Intake	Exhaust (flow pipe)	E/I (%)	Intake Port Velocity (cfm/sq.in.)
0.100	---	---	---	---
0.200	149	120	80%	114
0.300	208	167	80%	106
0.400	262	214	81%	113
0.500	294	230	78%	127
0.600	313	238	76%	135
0.700	320	243	76%	138

76-cc Chamber
2.08/1.60 valves
220-cc intake port
2.31 sq.in. intake port cross-section
Tested on a 4.155-inch bore fixture

Dart Pro 1 CNC 227

Valve Lift (inches)	Intake	Exhaust (flow pipe)	E/I (%)	Intake Port Velocity (cfm/sq.in.)
0.100	62	57	91%	95
0.200	145	115	79%	111
0.300	195	154	78%	99
0.400	232	182	79%	97
0.500	251	199	79%	104
0.600	265	211	79%	110

64-cc Chamber
2.08/1.60 valves
227-cc intake port
2.40 sq.in. intake port cross-section
Tested on a 4.155-inch bore fixture

At first, since everyone looks at peak flow numbers, it may appear that this port is not very successful. At 265 cfm at 0.600-inch lift, this is hardly a hero number. We also tested this head at 0.700-inch of valve lift, but flow only increased slightly to 267 cfm. But upon closer inspection, this head does reveal where its strengths lie. The CNC head's mid-range flow is substantially better than its Dart cousins, but still not as good as either the Canfield 220 or the larger AFR heads. But as we've seen with other Dart heads, the proof is best left to dyno testing where all the benefits of the head are revealed. We haven't had a chance to put the heat to these particular heads, so it's left to conjecture.

For the exhaust side, the head does deliver outstanding low-lift exhaust flow that generates a phenomenal 91 percent E/I at 0.100 lift and comparable low-80 percentages at 0.200 and 0.300-inches of exhaust lift. This may benefit the engine builder who specs a conservative exhaust lobe that opens later and perhaps closes a little sooner to reduce overlap and add power.

AFR 227 Eliminator

This is the biggest head for the small-block that AFR makes that retains the stock 23-degree valve angle. These heads work best with the new generation of large-displacement small-blocks. It is more ideally suited for 420-, 434-, and 454-ci small-blocks where these larger engines don't have to spin unrealistic engine speeds to generate sufficient intake velocity. This is reinforced by the 2.100/1.60-inch valve layout where the large intake valve would be severely shrouded by any bore size smaller than 4.125-inches. Because of the head's 60/40 valve layout, it's also a good idea to carefully check valve-to-piston clearances to ensure the intake valve will clear the piston.

Again, because this is a new head and we did not have access to test it before this book went to print, we have to go with AFR's numbers. Even if the production numbers are slightly short of what we have listed here, this is a head that can deliver near 300 cfm flow at max lift while still delivering excellent mid-lift numbers. That's impressive considering that the really good GEN III GM heads with a 15-degree valve angle, while better, are not drastically superior.

Another area to carefully consider if you have a set of these heads is the interface between the top of the exhaust port and the exhaust headers. Some street engines no doubt run 1-3/4-inch primary pipe headers, and the exhaust port for most street headers tend to block the top 10 to 15 percent of the exhaust port. At low speeds this is not a big problem. But at wide-open throttle (WOT) at max RPM, this is sure to kill 20 to 30 hp or more if not remedied. The difficulty lies with the relationship between the exhaust bolt-holes and the top of the port, which is roughly 1/4-inch taller. This taller port outlet improves upper valve lift flow, but only if the header does not partially block the outlet.

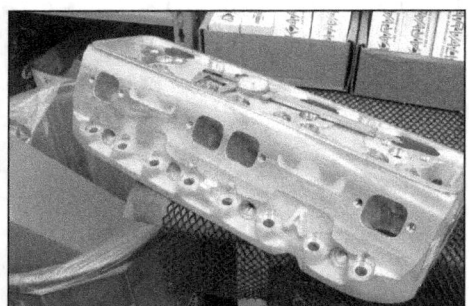

The AFR 227 Eliminator offers flow potential approaching 300 cfm from a head with a standard 23-degree valve angle. Even though it is limited to a near-stock exhaust port location, the exhaust also works.

AFR 227 Eliminator (Prototype AFR numbers)

Valve Lift (inches)	Intake	Exhaust (flow pipe)	E/I (%)	Intake Port Velocity (cfm/sq.in.)
0.100	---	---	---	---
0.200	151	112	81%	114
0.300	210	150	72%	106
0.400	266	190	73%	110
0.500	298	207	70%	123
0.600	313	220	73%	129
0.700	327	243	74%	135

76-cc Chamber
2.10/1.60 valves
227-cc intake port
2.42 sq.in. intake port cross-section
Tested on a 4.125-inch bore fixture

Dart Pro 1 230

Valve Lift (inches)	Intake	Exhaust (flow pipe)	E/I (%)	Intake Port Velocity (cfm/sq.in.)
0.100	62	59	96%	95
0.200	123	105	85%	94
0.300	170	136	80%	87
0.400	215	165	77%	92
0.500	245	180	73%	105
0.600	256	187	73%	110

64-cc Chamber
2.08/1.60-inches valves
230-cc intake port
2.33 sq.in. intake port cross-section
Tested on a 4.155-inch bore fixture

Since most small-block headers rarely offer sizes larger than 1-3/4-inch, you will be forced to either reconfigure the headers with a taller exhaust port outlet, or perhaps go with a set of the Stahl adapter exhaust flanges and also modify the headers slightly.

Dart Pro 1 230

We can clearly call this a bottom-of-the-page cylinder head, as it carries the largest port volume of all of Dart's 23-degree heads. While you might expect this head to really deliver on the CFM, especially considering its 2.3 sq.in. port area, the actual flow numbers are a bit disappointing. In fact, the Platinum 215 iron head bests the Pro 1 230 across the board on the intake side, and the 230 head benefited from a larger test bore diameter of 4.155 versus the 215's 4.060-inch bore diameter. Add in the 230's larger port cross-sectional number and you already know that the port velocities will suffer in comparison to the Platinum 215. Does this mean the Pro 1 230 is lame? Not really, it's just that it is more a situation where the Platinum iron head is, again, benefiting from the most recent technology. There will no doubt be an aluminum 230-cc Pro 1 Platinum head in the future, and you can look for it to make major gains in both CFM and velocity. But for now, if we had a choice, we'd take the extra 40 pounds

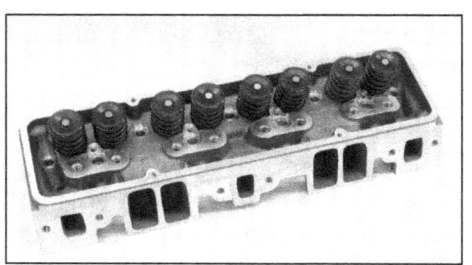

On the huge side of things, Dart also offers a Pro 1 230-cc intake port head that just about maxes out port area for the stock 23-degree valve angle arrangement. This would be for large displacement 430 to 454-ci small-blocks. Several of the larger heads in this category offer cross-sections of around 2.6 sq.in. In an area comparison, that's similar to a production iron oval-port big-block head.

Heads in Review

Description	Intake Port Volume (cc)	Valve Sizes (Int./Exh.)	Intake Cross Section (sq.in.)	Part Number
Edelbrock E-Tec	200	2.02/1.60	1.99	60989
Dart Iron Eagle	200	2.02/1.60	2.05	10311112
Dart Pro 1 Aluminum	200	2.02/1.60	2.06	11411112
Dart Iron Platinum	200	2.02/1.60	2.06	10411112P
World Sportsman II	200	2.02/1.60	2.19	012150-2
Brodix Race-Rite	200	2.05/1.60	2.18	1011008A
AFR 210 (Ver. 1)	210	2.08/1.60	2.21	1050
AFR 210 Eliminator	210	2.08/1.60	2.26	1100
Dart Iron Eagle	215	2.05/1.60	2.26	10511122
Dart Platinum 215	215	2.05/1.60	2.15	10511123P
Dart Pro 1	215	2.05/1.625	2.17	11611133
Edelbrock Vic. Jr.	215	2.08/1.60	2.05	77619
TFS 215	215	2.08/1.60	2.20	32400006
Brodix Track 1	215	2.08/1.60	2.28	STS T1 215
World Motown Lite	220	2.08/1.60	2.57	024150-2
Canfield 220	220	2.08/1.60	2.40	See Canfield
AFR 220 Eliminator	220	2.08/1.60	2.31	1060
Dart Pro 1 CNC 227	227	2.08/1.60	2.40	11711143
AFR 227 Eliminator	227	2.10/1.60	2.42	1120
Dart Pro 1	230	2.08/1.60	2.33	11971143

of nose weight by using the Platinum 215 over the Pro 1 230.

Conclusion

This has turned into a major chapter if for no other reason than there are so many 200 to 230-cc small-block heads on the market. This makes for a confusing mash of different castings to try to navigate through, but it also offers a tremendous selection as long as you can make an intelligent decision relative to your next engine buildup.

Combine velocity with CFM numbers and try to keep the port cross-section small enough to feed your combination and the power will be there.

Heads in Review

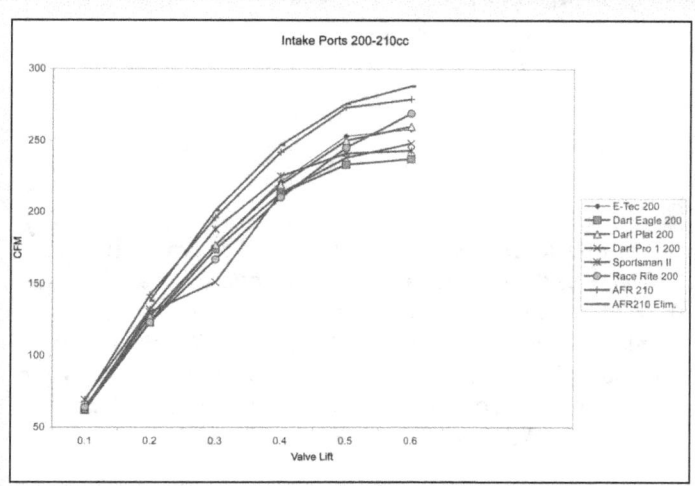

This category of heads is intended for small-blocks larger than 400-ci or engines that are designed to run at engine speeds up to or more than 7,000 rpm. Larger intake ports need either a larger engine or more RPM to create the velocity necessary to make power.

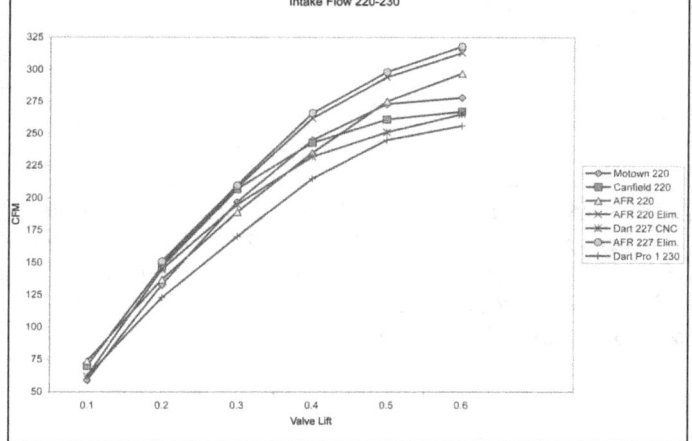

Among the large port castings, AFR takes the top three spots on the graph, closely followed by the surprising Motown 220 head. Note how closely bunched the heads are below 0.300 inch of valve lift.

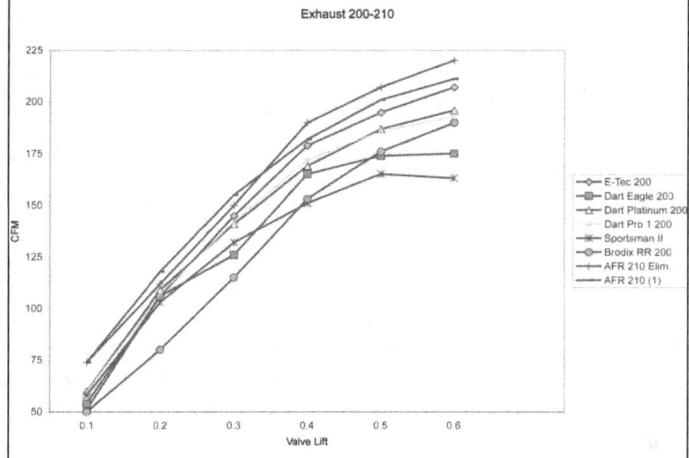

On the exhaust side of the smaller 200 to 210-cc heads, the AFR heads again dominate the graph, followed closely by the Edelbrock E-Tec 200 and the Dart Platinum 200 heads. Note how well the AFR heads flow even at 0.100-inch valve lift. Here is where the non-AFR (and more affordable) heads could really benefit from additional low-lift work.

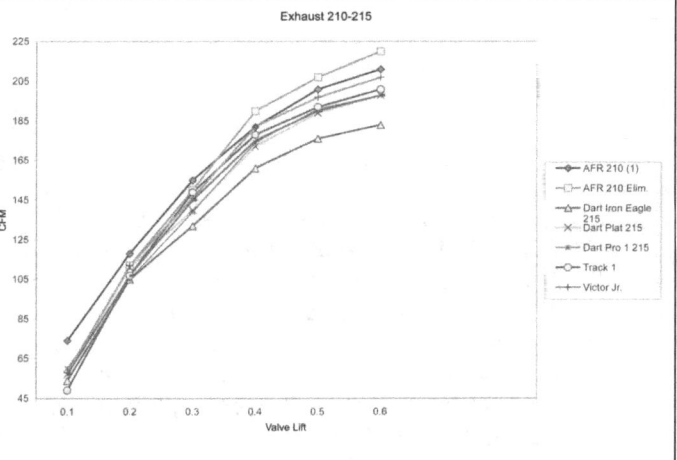

Other than the first version of the AFR 210, most of the rest of the 210 to 215-cc head exhaust ports are very similar. This overlap merely gives the intake flow and velocity considerations more weight since the exhaust flow is so similar.

Heads in Review

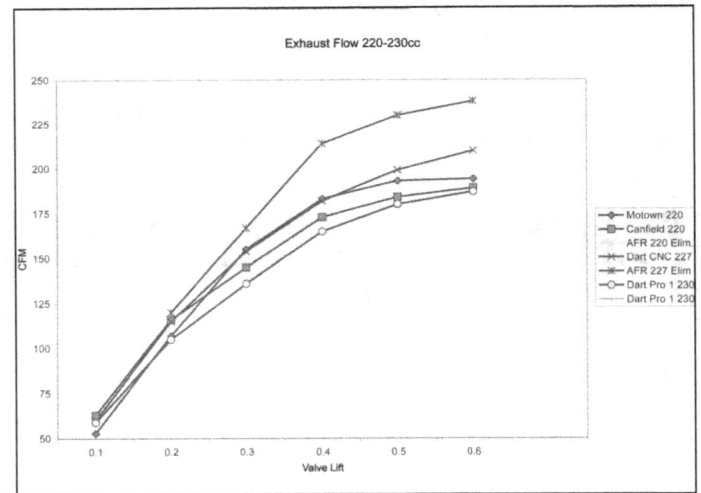

Among the big port heads, the exhaust flow differential is much greater. Note how the AFR 227 Eliminator has the rest of the field covered. Among the remaining exhaust flow plots, the Dart CNC 227 exhaust port indicates solid flow numbers.

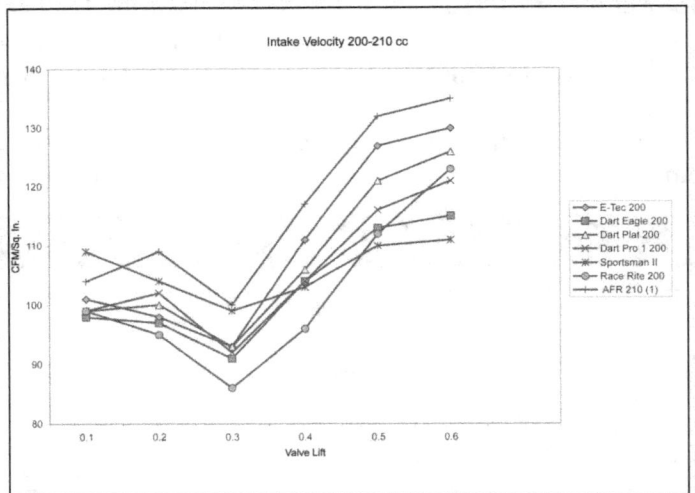

These intake port velocity curves for the small 200- to 210-cc heads indicate that once again, the early version AFR 210 ranks at the top. We didn't plot the AFR Eliminator, but it would have been right there as well. Surprisingly, the Edelbrock E-Tec 200 comes in a strong second in the second half of the curve, followed closely by the Dart Platinum 200 in terms of speed.

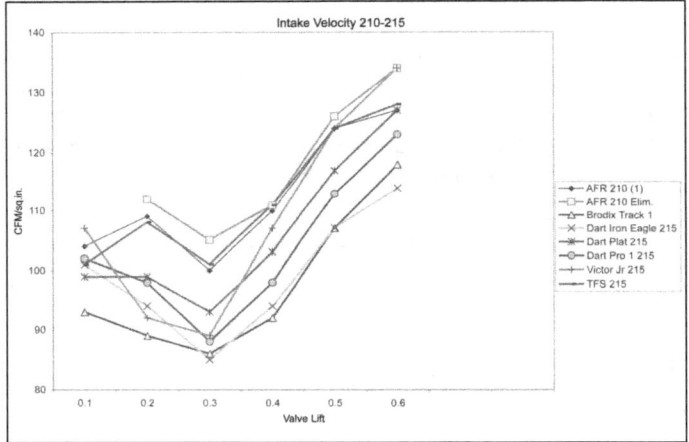

There's plenty to study in this graph. Clearly, both versions of the AFR 210 offer excellent velocity, but note the strength of the Victor Jr. head at the higher valve lifts. The Edelbrock head suffers greatly at both the 0.200 and 0.300 inch of valve lifts, which is where we would concentrate our efforts. Amazingly, this same head has the highest velocity at 0.100 inch of lift. Working on the valve job to raise the 0.200 and 0.300-inch data points up over the 100 cfm/sq.in. level would dramatically improve the Victor Jr.'s overall flow curve and probably result in more power. Here's a situation where plotting each head indicates its shortcomings as well as its strengths. This is useful for indicating the areas where improving a head you already have can be very useful.

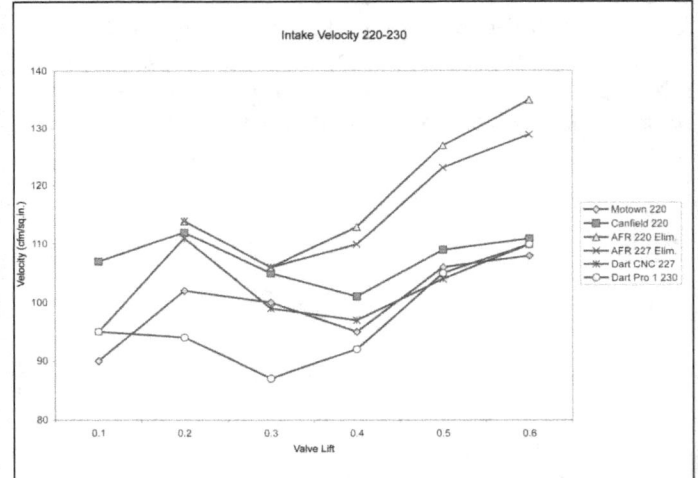

Again, the AFR heads are the velocity kings in this graph, but let's also look at a couple other interesting plots. The Canfield 220 starts out strong, but then the velocity curve flattens out above 0.300. But it is still better than three other heads in this graph. Note how even with poor performances, the overall shape of this graph is still very similar to plots from other small-block heads regardless of size with the 0.300-inch valve lift being the low point of the graph in virtually every case.

CHAPTER 8

SMALL-BLOCK RACE HEADS

There is probably no V-8 pushrod engine in the entire world that has more dedicated cylinder heads designed specifically for racing than the first-generation small-block Chevy. A scant few decades ago, there was basically the iron Bow Tie head cast by GM and a few class-specific aluminum castings, and that was the entire race head buffet menu. Now well into the 21st century, you can't swing a dead camshaft without hitting a new small-block race head. You would think that Brodix damn near owns the race head market with its incredible array of 18, 16, 15, 13.5, and 12-degree valve angle heads aimed at the wild world of drag racing, sprint cars, and dirt track slammers. And as it turns out, valve angles are really the whole point of the race head market.

Rather than get into the details of each cylinder head as we have in the previous chapters, we're instead going to touch the wave tops, if you will, in order to keep this section brief. Frankly, if building race engines occupies your every waking moment, then most of what this book has to offer is of little application. Instead, we look into what makes up a race head and why intake valve angle is such a big deal.

Valve Angle

As we've stated before in various chapters in this book, the stock small-block Chevy valve angle is 23 degrees, but it didn't take engineers long to figure out that a taller, more vertical valve angle offered several advantages to improved flow. In addition to this rather steep valve angle, the stock valves were not located on the cylinder bore centerline. Instead, the OEM valves (and all subsequent versions of the 23-degree small-block head) are located over a quarter of an inch (0.275 inch) away from the bore centerline. At maximum valve lift, this off-center location places the valves closer to the combustion chamber and the cylinder wall, restricting potential airflow.

For the small-block Chevy, the original race heads accepted for use in NASCAR stock car racing that first addressed this valve angle issue were

GM Performance Parts offers a wide range of race heads for the small-block in both 15 and 18-degree versions as well as a splayed valve head. All require custom valve gear and shaft rocker systems.

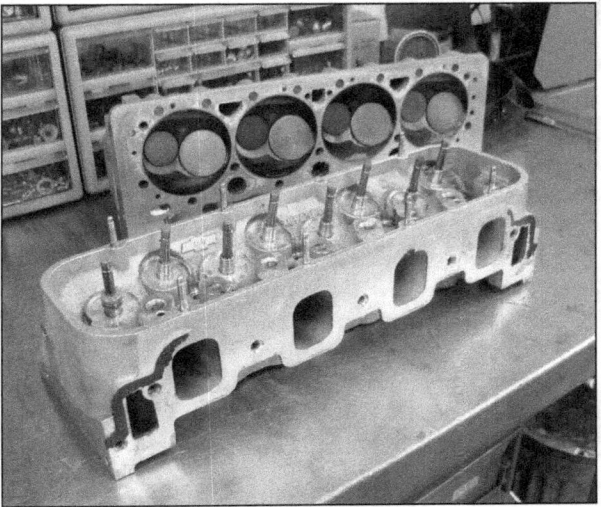

The splayed valve head uses a symmetrical port layout that equally spaces the intake ports by using the intake-exhaust-intake-exhaust valve layout as opposed to the OEM layout that adjoins the two center exhaust ports in the middle of the cylinder head.

the GM 18-degree heads. This move was quickly followed by a set of 15-degree heads, both of which are still available through GM Performance Parts (GMPP) in semi-finished configurations without seats or guides. Since then, several other GMPP heads have appeared that further complicate the issue, requiring us to go much deeper in detail than just a change in valve angles.

Canted Valves

Way back in the 1960s when GM engineers began designing the "Mystery" big-block 427 that would eventually evolve into the Mark IV 396/427/454, cylinder head port designers realized that if they tipped or canted the valves at an angle from

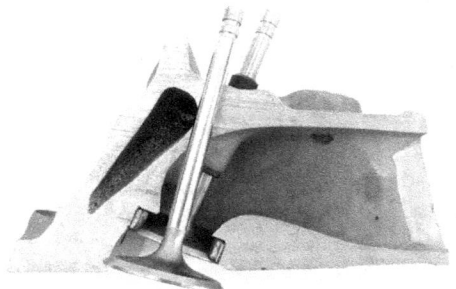

All race heads use a steeper valve angle generally in the 15 to 18-degree range compared to the stock small-block Chevy angle of 23 degrees. This taller angle offers more flow potential, but only when combined with a taller, more efficient intake port.

The Gen IV L-92 Head

This head may seem out of place with these race heads, but if you look at the production-based 15-degree valve angle it makes a little bit more sense. GM has taken the knowledge of the last 50 years of small-block development and incorporated that into this 2007 6.2L GEN IV truck head. At first glance, clearly GM has moved away from the cathedral port of the LS1 GEN III heads and altered the port almost back to what looks like the old big-block Chevy-like rectangle port. Another reason to list this head as more like a race head rather than a production head is this casting's astonishing 320-plus cfm rating and its very large 2.160-inch intake valve. The valve is so large that it cannot be used on a cylinder bore smaller than 4.00 inches in diameter because the valve will hit the edge of the cylinder. The calculated velocity numbers are quite low but not surprising considering the port's large-by-huge cross-sectional area. The intake port's 3.19-sq.in. area is comparable to a large oval port Rat motor cylinder head. What's odd is that this is the OEM port for a 6.2L truck engine.

Another item that makes this head much closer to a race head is its offset intake rocker, required because of the wider intake port. Offset intake rockers used to be the exclusive territory of race engines, but not anymore. Based on current theory, this large intake port will create some serious peak horsepower numbers, but will probably cost a little torque at engine speeds below peak torque due to its large cross-sectional area that reduces velocity. It's entirely possible that this stock L-92 head could support as much as 600 hp on a 400-ci GEN III engine with a good cam spinning in the neighborhood of 6,500 to 6,800 rpm. A large port like this will obviously be excellent with a larger displacement GEN IV street engine in the 400-ci and larger category, especially with a longer duration cam that can take advantage of higher inlet air speeds at the higher engine speeds. If we were going to enhance this head, we would certainly look at the exhaust side as opposed to improving the intake. This is based on the head's rather weak exhaust-to-intake flow percentages at the higher valve lift numbers. Clearly, improving the exhaust flow numbers would help the high engine speed power characteristics of this head. What is curious is why GM would build such a large intake port for a 6.2L truck engine. The best feature of all is that you can buy this head directly from any GM dealership with valves and springs for around $400 each! Compared to the price of some of these other race-oriented cylinder heads with similar flow numbers for a GEN I small-block, it makes you wonder why you would bother with a GEN I motor when a set of stock truck heads will outflow some of the best race heads at half the cost.

L-92 6.2L Truck Engine

Valve Lift (inches)	Intake	Exhaust (flow pipe)	E/I (%)	Intake Port Velocity (cfm/sq.in.)
0.100	72	59	82%	106
0.200	148	116	78%	109
0.300	212	161	76%	104
0.400	264	187	71%	97
0.500	302	203	67%	95
0.600	322	208	65%	101
0.700	316	212	67%	99

70-cc Chamber
2.160/1.58-inches valves
261-cc intake port
3.19 sq.in. intake port cross-section
Tested on a 4.155-inch bore fixture

SMALL-BLOCK RACE HEADS

The symmetrical approach evenly spaces the cylinder head exhaust ports, which prevents concentrating heat on the two center exhaust ports, which is a common problem with production valve layout heads on both drag race and endurance engines.

off-center, the intake flow improved. This created the canted valve head design that made the big-block Chevy famous. This is also the concept that Ford engineers integrated into the Cleveland head design that became famous (or infamous) with the Boss 302 head. The Cleveland and Boss 302 engines may be considered infamous because of their huge port cross-sectional areas. But the concept of the canted valve has not been lost on cylinder head designers. The idea is to cant or tip the valve toward the center of the cylinder bore, which means the valve moves away from the cylinder wall as it opens, unshrouding the air path to move more efficiently around the valve. This not only creates a more efficient air path, but it also allows the engine builder to use a larger intake valve within the same bore size.

As an example, the GM SB 2.2 heads (which will probably be replaced in NASCAR for GM cars by the time you read this) are a symmetrical intake port head that not only stand the valve angle more upright at 11 degrees, but also cant or tilt the intake valve 4 degrees off vertical to improve airflow. To complete the design, the engineers also created an exhaust valve that is not canted, but is angled at a mere 8 degrees. All this contributes to substantial flow improvements over a typical 23-degree valve angle head with inline valves all at the same angle. But there is even more to the story than just a little tilt to the valve.

Head Changes

The moment the designer begins to alter valve angles, this affects all sorts of other cylinder head requirements. For example, the whole idea of moving to a more vertical valve angle is to improve airflow. However, this means the intake port must also move in order to take full advantage of this angle. The port entry at the head must be raised relative to the stock port entry angle. This requires a new intake manifold port entry angle, which means that the old 23-degree intake manifold designs will no longer work, requiring a new intake manifold. But that's just the beginning.

Generally, the exhaust ports also need to be raised to take advantage of the new exhaust valve angle. This also requires a new header design since stock exhaust port location headers won't work. Plus, when it comes to the new symmetrical-port race heads, the entire exhaust flange changes because now the exhaust ports are symmetrical rather than having the two center exhaust valves next to each other as in the stock 23-degree head configuration. This symmetrical port arrangement is far better for endurance engines since this no longer concentrates heat in the middle of the head with the two exhaust valves next to each other. Of course, this new exhaust layout also means custom-built headers.

This different valve angle also means that the OEM valvetrain arrangement with regard to rocker arms, springs, and the entire valvetrain will also be different. Most race heads rely on using an aftermarket rocker shaft system rather than individual rocker arm studs and rockers. This is because most race heads are intended for high-RPM use where the shaft systems excel. With different valve spacing and angles, each new

The latest in trick small-block cylinder heads is the GM Performance Parts SB2.2 ROX that is similar to the SB2.2 design with an 11-degree valve angle that's tipped 4 degrees like a Rat motor. But the trick is that this head is designed for the wider ROX 4.500-inch bore center block. The original small-block bore center distance was 4.400. This allows a larger bore diameter for better flow.

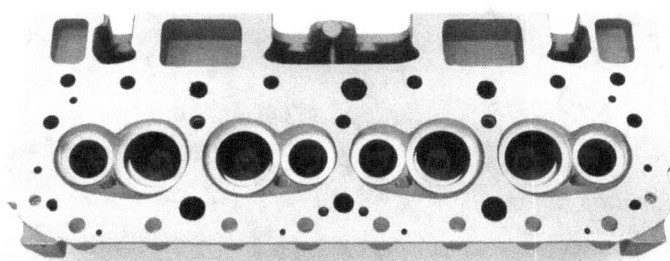

Race heads also create a much more shallow combustion chamber that allows the engine builder to create higher compression ratios without using domed pistons. This is the GM Performance Parts 18-degree head. Most race heads come semi-finished without seat inserts so the cylinder head porting professional can use the inserts of his choice.

All race heads raise the exhaust port exit point on the head in order to improve exhaust flow. Typical 23-degree street heads are generally limited to placing the exhaust port exit in the stock position in order to allow street headers to fit the chassis. Race heads are not restricted to this exhaust port location.

A quick way to identify a race-type head is with its taller intake port location. Note how these heads have much more material under the bottom of the intake port than a typical 23-degree small-block Chevy head.

cylinder head then requires its own specific valvetrain, which comes at a much higher cost than the typical 23-degree small-block Chevy stuff. Part of this is a move to offset intake rocker arms in order to clear the larger intake port. This also requires high-quality pushrods to be able to withstand the rigors of high-RPM use.

Taller valve angles also mean using taller valves, and generally, smaller stem diameters in an attempt to keep weight to a minimum. And don't forget, as soon as we change the valve angle, we also need new pistons to be able to accommodate that differ-ent valve angle. We need custom valve covers for these heads as well. That old 4-bolt perimeter valve cover stuff for stock 23-degree heads just won't do. And let's not even get into titanium valves and their cost. Finally, many of these heads require custom-length head studs or bolts to keep the head glued to the block.

As you can see, there's an incredible pile of details that must be accounted for when swapping to an 18- or 15-degree race head. Chamber size is another variable. Generally, taller valve angles also reduce the depth of the chamber, allowing the chamber to be smaller for higher compression ratios without having to resort to large piston domes to create compression. The GM splayed-valve race head offers as small as a 40-cc combustion chamber. To put that tiny chamber into perspective, on a 420-ci small-block with a 4.155-inch bore and 3.875-inch stroke, a 40-cc combustion chamber would allow the engine builder to create a 15.5:1 compression ratio with a 0.041-inch thick gasket and 10-cc worth of valve reliefs in an otherwise flat-top piston. With this smaller chamber, the engine builder eliminates piston domes that are notorious for reducing combustion efficiency and power.

If you intend to use a set of 18 or 15-degree heads, it doesn't make much sense to bolt them onto a stock production block. If serious horsepower is your goal, then an aftermarket block is also in your future. Besides the inherent strength of these over-the-counter castings, there's also the added bonus of employing a larger bore to take full advantage of the larger valves and higher flow potential. As we've mentioned in Chapter 2 on flow benches, almost any head will deliver better flow numbers when tested on a larger bore. Unless limited by rules on bore size, the goal would be to bolt a set of these high-flow heads on as large a bore as possible.

Advantages

Basically, you can expect to spend a lot of money making a set of 15 or 18-degree heads work on a small-block Chevy. You can also expect to have to perform quite a bit of custom machin-

The wildest part of the Barnes head is how the heads integrate the individual runner ports directly to the intake throttle body, eliminating the need for an intake manifold. All this needs is a cover for the lifter valley.

Race heads also benefit from relocated valve positions that allow the designer to use larger intake valves. It's not uncommon to see 2.155 or 2.200-inch intake valves on a small-block Chevy race head.

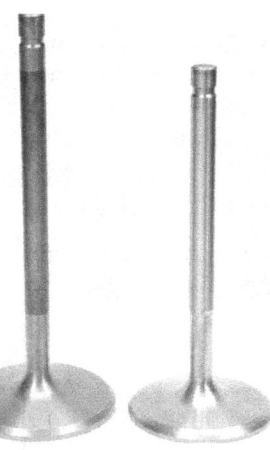

Taller valve angles also require longer intake valves than a typical 23-degree head because of the greater port height and also to create sufficient room for increased valve lift.

Even the bone-stock production LS1 head has a 15-degree valve angle. This came directly from the things that GM learned from building race engines for NASCAR and drag racing. The cathedral port design was driven by the desire to give the injector a straight shot at the back of the intake valve.

While longer valves are required for these taller port heads, they also become heavier as a result of the increased length. This is why many race heads resort to using smaller stem diameters in search of reduced weight.

ing in order to get there. The entire race head market is based upon the fact that there just aren't sufficient numbers to warrant building "kits" you can buy with all the parts you need. With all that said, the advantage to using a set of these is clearly the added flow potential that also adds up to serious power. A fitting example might be a comparison to put this in perspective: The GM SB 2.2 head, for example is capable of as much as 370 cfm at 0.700-inch lift using a 2.19-inch intake valve, while a typical Dart Pro 1 big-block 345-cc rectangle port cylinder head with a 2.30-inch valve flows around 360 cfm at 0.700-inch valve lift. Not only does the race head flow more air, but it does so with a 0.110-inch smaller valve and probably much higher port velocity numbers as well.

The race-head flow numbers are a result of a full CNC custom porting, which isn't really fair to the off-the-shelf Pro 1 head with its cast ports, but it does point out how much potential there is in these heads if you're willing to spend the money to get there.

Conclusion

We hope that this cursory look at race cylinder heads and the exotic world of 15 and 18-degree heads and the baby Rat heads has been interesting. We just touched the surface of

Sprint car racers have long used Barnes heads for these methanol-fuel small-block monster engines. This head reveals an interesting symmetrical port layout and also in-line valves

The Brodix Buffet

If there is a company other than Brodix that makes a wider assortment of race-style aluminum small-block Chevy heads, they must be keeping it a secret. Leafing through the Brodix catalog, there are a staggering number of options once you move into the race head portion of the catalog. We counted 28 different versions of the heads listed to the right, and literally on each page Brodix says there are far more options from which you can choose. If you run across a Brodix head catalog, it's almost worth the time just to look through all the different heads and what they offer. It's astonishing.

Head	Valve Angle (degrees)	Valve Size (inches)	Max CFM
Canted Valve, 330cc	14	2.20/1.60	395
BD Series, 299cc	13.5	2.20/1.60	399
GB 2200, 282cc	13.5	2.20/1.58	396
12x12, 299cc	12	2.20/1.60	388
STS-12, 305cc	15	2.20/1.60	372
WP 15 SP, 267cc	15	2.180/1.625	362
KC 16 STD	16	2.180/1.625	379
WP18SPCAP, 266cc	18	2.180/1.625	395
M218SPX, 254cc	18	2.140/1.600	336

this subject mainly because this book is aimed directly at street-oriented engines. The main reason for including this chapter was to show you what is out there and also to take a closer look at what is required of the rest of the engine, should you find a set of these race heads sitting on your doorstep one fine summer morning. While tempting to use, these heads require a significant investment in other parts in order to make them work. The wise engine builder will construct an entire engine around these specialty heads, rather than try to make these heads work on an existing engine. The latter approach can be both unrewarding and frustrating.

GM SB 2.2 Race Head (GM-supplied data)

Valve Lift (inches)	Intake	Exhaust (flow pipe)	E/I (%)	Intake Port Velocity (cfm/sq.in.)
0.100	–	–	–	–
0.200	154	104	67%	50
0.300	233	149	64%	76
0.400	302	186	61%	98
0.500	349	213	61%	114
0.600	369	231	63%	120
0.700	373	242	65%	122

54-cc Chamber
2.19/1.625-inches valves
287-cc intake port
3.01 sq.in. intake port cross-section
Tested on a 4.125-inch bore fixture

TFS 18 Degree (TFS-supplied data)

Valve Lift (inches)	Intake	Exhaust	E/I (%)	Intake Port Velocity (cfm/sq.in.)
0.100	73	61	83%	108
0.200	144	113	88%	106
0.300	215	158	73%	106
0.400	274	197	72%	101
0.500	313	224	71%	109
0.600	334	230	69%	116
0.700	334	246	73%	116

56-cc Chamber
2.155/1.6250-inches valves
250-cc intake port
2.87 sq.in. intake port cross-section
Tested on a 4.125-inch bore fixture

Brodix -18 STD X (Brodix-supplied data)

Valve Lift (inches)	Intake	Exhaust (flow pipe)	E/I (%)	Intake Port Velocity (cfm/sq.in.)
0.100	–	–	–	–
0.200	157	106	67%	117
0.300	212	145	68%	105
0.400	260	179	69%	96
0.500	303	195	64%	107
	319	205	64%	113
0.700	325	211	65%	115

68-cc Chamber
2.140/1.60-inches valves
244-cc intake port
2.82 sq.in. intake port cross-section
Tested on a 4.155-inch bore fixture

The latest production GEN IV head, the L-92 truck head, looks more like a baby rectangle Rat port and flows almost as well. This head easily cranks out 320-plus cfm at 0.600-inch valve lift numbers using a 2.165-inch intake valve.

Note the use of offset intake rocker shafts on this Brodix –12 race head. The offset rockers are required to move the pushrod over to clear the larger intake ports.

Heads in Review

Description	Intake Port Volume (cc)	Valve Sizes (Int./Exh.)	Intake Cross Section (sq.in.)	Valve Angle	Part Number
Brodix –18X	244	2.140/1.600	18	18	STD X
TFS 18 Degree	250	2.155/1.625	2.87	18	TFS-31800001A
GM L-92	260	2.160/1.88	3.19	12	12582713
GM SB 2.2	287	2.15/1.625	3.01	11	12480021

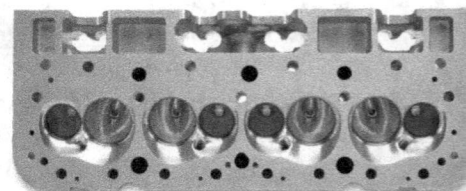

As the valve angle becomes steeper, the exit path from the valve into the chamber increases in importance.

CHAPTER 9

CYLINDER HEAD REBUILDING AND ASSEMBLY

One of the advantages of cylinder heads is that they are relatively easy to work on and don't require a garage full of specialty tools to do simple maintenance and/or assembly work. The work that we do not cover in this chapter is the more specialized procedures such as valve grinding, seat preparation, and installing guides. This should be left to a professional shop with the machines that can deliver this precision work for a decent price. But this still leaves quite a bit of work that you can do yourself in your garage and save yourself some money while also ensuring that the work is performed accurately and to your satisfaction.

Valve Guides

Let's start with a look at important areas that may not necessarily be at the top of your priority list. Let's say that we have a set of used aftermarket aluminum heads that have seen some rough use and will require upgrading. While porting and bigger valves may come to mind first, the initial item on the rebuild agenda should be a new set of valveguides. If you think about the job a valveguide must perform, its primary mission is to maintain the valve at exactly the same location through hundreds of thousands of cycles. This precision is essential because if the guide loses its accuracy, the valve is allowed to move around in relation to the valve seat. This quickly destroys all those precise angles that your machinist spent hours establishing for ideal airflow.

For a small-block Chevy, the generally accepted clearance for valveguides to valves is 0.001-inch for the intake and 0.0015 inch for the exhaust. The exhaust side needs slightly more clearance for additional lubrication since the exhaust valve operates at a much higher overall temperature than the intake valve. This clearance also requires the valvestems to be parallel, straight, and smooth—which is not always the case. In the case of used valves, it's worth the effort to carefully measure the stem diameter at both the top and bottom of the valvestem travel area to check for stem taper. Lateral thrust forces from the rocker arm across the top of the valvestem can easily produce a stem wear that may not be evident if the stem is measured only in the

Most aftermarket heads are equipped with bronze wall guides that are soft enough to embed dirt without damaging the guide while also doing a good job of retaining oil for lubrication.

Assembling heads means more than just bolting everything together. A quality valve job also pays close attention to overall valve tip height to ensure that all the valves are as close to the same height as possible.

middle. If the guides are worn, after cleaning the heads, this should be the first step in the rebuild process. Most aftermarket aluminum heads are fitted with some type of bronze or bronze alloy valveguide material. Iron heads often incorporate iron guides, but bronze inserts are a good way to upgrade the guide material.

Once the guides have been installed and properly honed, this offers a good time to finalize your choice of valves. Often the valve head size is the main consideration, but the selection process is actually far more complicated. As we've seen in the cylinder head flow test comparisons, you often have a choice in terms of valve size with the same size cylinder head. If you are working on a set of iron production heads, there is often room between the intake and exhaust valves to increase the valve size. Many of the earlier 1.94/1.50-inch iron small-block heads offered sufficient room to go up to 2.02/1.60 inches. The most obvious example of this is the test in Chapter 4 on the 492 stock replacement heads. Our flow test on those heads included a change to larger 2.02-inch intake valves to complement the existing 1.60-inch exhaust valves already in place. The larger 2.02 intake valves greatly increased intake flow in comparison to similar sized iron production heads, making this a simple yet effective modification.

Valve spacing is the distance established by the manufacturer and, while it can be changed with significant modifications to a cylinder head, let's assume that very few will attempt it. This means there is a practical limit to the size of the valves. Often, the move to a larger valve pays off in several different areas, not the least of which is a much larger flow curtain area. Combine that with work on maximizing the flow efficiencies of the larger valve and you'd have a great combination. This takes some attention to detail, especially if you are searching for that last ounce of power on your way to horsepower heaven.

Valve Material

A popular phrase when discussing engine parts is "stainless steel" valves. It turns out that this term encompasses an entire range of various materials. We will spare you the crushing boredom of a metallurgy dissertation on the various materials used since we don't understand this stuff either. The important point is that higher quality valves are generally made from better stainless alloys that are far more resilient and able to withstand the rigors of a high-performance application. You'll hear talk about titanium valves and ultra-high temperature resistant alloys like Inconel, but these are completely unnecessary for a street engine. What is important is to invest perhaps a little more money on quality valves both for durability and improved flow reasons.

There are literally dozens of valve manufacturers and most of them produce a reputable product. Companies like Ferrea, Manley, SSI, and many others offer a tremendous selection of materials, shapes, and valve sizes not to mention the ability to custom make valves of almost any size in a reasonable amount of time. We're not here to recommend spending the most money for valves, but rather investing in the right material for your application. A nitromethane-fed Top Fuel engine is going to need a serious exhaust valve for durability at 7,000 horsepower. But a street engine is not going to need that kind of technology. Manley probably has the widest selection of valve materials with six different levels of valves. For a street engine, the selection process gets narrowed to more like four, and this is where price becomes a factor. Manley's Street or Race series of valves are a good example of a good investment in compromise between valve strength combined with a wide selection of styles that best suit your application.

Valves

The simplistic view is that the only real important consideration for a valve is its overall head diameter. But if you spend some time on a flow bench you will learn that subtle nuances and tiny angle changes can have a profound affect on the dry flow and wet flow characteristics of any cylinder head. Let's start with the stem and work our way toward the business end of the valve. Current engine technology is always pushing the envelope toward lighter components, and this extends to valves as well. The GEN III small-block has already moved to an 8-mm (0.313-inch) valvestem, in comparison to the standard small-block 11/32-inch (0.343) valvestem. While this is only a 0.030-inch change, it does contribute to reducing valve weight, which reduces the necessity for higher-load valve springs and produces less abuse on the valve. AFR's Eliminator heads are the first

CYLINDER HEAD REBUILDING AND ASSEMBLY

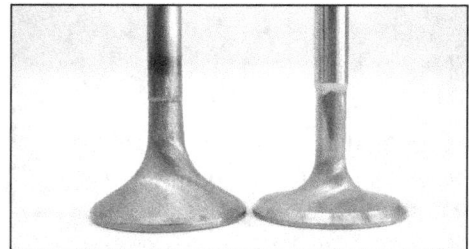

One place where there may be some flow hiding is with a 12-degree back angle on the intake valve. The back angle is the radius between the stem and the valve head and has a direct impact on flow. This is an area of concern for the exhaust side as well.

aftermarket first-generation 23-degree heads that we know of that have made the move to the thinner valvestem diameter to reduce weight.

The back angle on a valve is the transition radius between the valvestem and the head of the valve. This is an area almost universally ignored by enthusiasts, but flow bench testing has shown that cylinder heads become very attuned to this angle. There are no hard and fast rules, but the two most common intake valve back angles offered are 10 and 12 degree. Depending upon the intake port you are working on, the taller 12-degree angle can often offer a slight flow improvement. A taller angle might be better in some instances, but this does add weight to the valve. This is where paying attention to the valves offered by the manufacturer can pay off. For example, Manley offers most of its small-block intake valves with a 10-degree back angle, but there are a few selected 2.02 and 2.055-inch Race Flo valves available with a 12-degree back angle. Again, there's no guarantee that these 12-degree back angle heads are worth more flow. That must be tested in your application in order to make that decision.

A taller angle, tulip-style exhaust valve with a back angle of 15 degrees is actually much more popular with valve manufacturers. This works because of the direction of flow and also because weight is not quite of the same concern since the exhaust valve is substantially smaller. These valves tend to increase mid-range flow while not hurting max lift flow. While back angles are not the magic solution to every application, they represent an area you should pay attention to when investigating flow improvements.

Valve Seat Angles

We can now move on to the actual valve seat itself. While virtually all small-block valves are ground with a 45-degree sealing angle, it's worth noting that some experiments have been done in an attempt to try a less acute angle in hopes of improving flow. For example, the 30-degree seat angle was actually used on production Pontiac engines in the 1960s, but eventually fell out of favor as valve lifts continued to escalate. The 30-degree seat offers some small advantages at valve lifts of 0.300 inch and below, but tends to drastically cut flow at higher valve lifts. On the opposite end of the spectrum, 50 to 55-degree valve seats are now finding favor in Pro Stock and IHRA Pro Mod applications that also see valve lift numbers approaching one inch. This very steep angle promotes high-lift flow and, according to the head specialists we've spoken to, Pro Stock cylinder head specialists rarely concern themselves with flow under 0.400 inch.

While work continues with these taller valve angles, the street small-block is almost universally equipped with 45-degree seats. As evidenced by the work on either side of 45

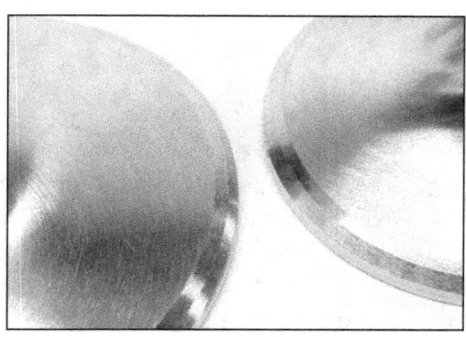

Regardless of which cylinder head you choose, consider a 30-degree back cut on both the intake and exhaust valves to be a requirement. Dart claims that this should be a standard requirement for any performance cylinder head.

degrees, this angle is the best compromise while also serving to act as a very efficient seat-cleaning angle as well for minimizing carbon buildup on the exhaust side. One trick detailed in Chapter 10 is a 30-degree back cut on both the intake and exhaust valves. This small step is almost always worth a few CFM improvement with little or no penalty and is a quick way to improve the airflow on almost any small-block head.

Placement of the seat on the valve is also important. This is one

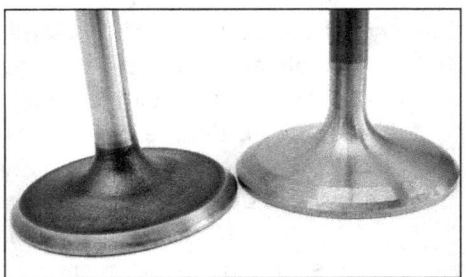

Factory valves generally come with a dip or ditch created directly behind the 45-degree seat angle. This ditch tends to hurt flow in both the intake and exhaust locations. The best solution is to replace them with higher quality aftermarket valves that create a gentler radius.

Valve Angles

There are probably as many different theories on valve seat angles as there are cylinder head specialists working on small-block Chevys. Add in almost every other four-stroke engine with poppet valves and it's surprising that anyone agrees on anything. In the old days, everyone followed what Bill "Grumpy" Jenkins and later what Smokey Yunick expounded on in their books on the small-block Chevy. You could use their numbers today and probably not sacrifice much in the way of flow. The only way to know for sure is to test your changes on a flow bench.

The point of all this is that each intake port design will eventually require its own specific set of valve seat angles in order to maximize flow. This may require only three angles or perhaps five or more. You'll get plenty of opinions on this, but fewer hard facts. What we propose is a standard or typical three-angle valve job that, like the Grumpy Jenkins or Smokey Yunick (and they are similar—what a surprise) will get you started and pointed in the right direction. The more you experiment, the more you will learn what doesn't work and, if you're lucky, a few things that do work.

On the intake side, the standard three-angle valve job is a 35-45-60-degree configuration generally machined on a cutter-style valve machine. For the street, an intake width of 0.050 inch will work well and be durable. To increase flow, you can narrow that down to 0.035 inch, but durability becomes questionable and when the seat pounds out, it is likely to then flow worse than a wider seat dimension. The actual intersection of the seat with the valve should place that contact point as close to the outside diameter of the 45-degree valve face as possible. This will also contribute to improved flow past the valve. As we've mentioned in several other places in this book, a 30-degree back cut angle behind the 45-degree angle should be a part of any high-performance valve job on any small-block.

All valves also have what is called a margin, which is defined as the thickness of the area between the edge of the valve seat face and the chamber side of the valve. Most high-performance intake valves will come with a margin of between 0.050 and 0.065 inch, with a sharp perpendicular edge that helps to reduce reversion or back flow from the cylinder back up the port. Thicker margins only contribute to increased valve weight. On the opposite end of the valve, a good machine shop will also perform a cut across the valve tip to ensure that it is square to the valve centerline. With production valves, even good aftermarket items, it's amazing how much material needs to be removed to square these valve tips. This produces a perpendicular surface for the rocker arm to work against, which limits any kind of side load imparted to the valve.

Exhaust valves, as you might imagine, are completely different animals. The top two valve seat angles are similar at 35 degrees for the top cut leading into the 45-degree seat angle. But then, rather than employ a typical 60 or 70-degree throat angle, many cylinder head specialists like to radius the throat directly into the 45-degree valve seat angle. A cutter can be used to establish this radius, which can then be extended into the port with porting equipment. Remember, on the exhaust side we are working on dry airflow where a radius can improve airflow.

On the valve side, the seat width of 0.060 inch is slightly more than on the intake side since this is the main thermal contact point for the valve that transfers heat out of the valve and into the cylinder head where the coolant can carry this heat away. This also requires a thicker exhaust valve margin mainly for durability reasons. Generally, this margin will be around between 0.070 and 0.090 inch. This thicker margin also offers a chance to place an angle or radius on the chamber side of the valve in order to improve exhaust flow. This is not a guaranteed result with every port, but it clearly does work in some cases. Again, this is a place where individual testing will indicate what this modification is worth.

These basic angles will give you a starting point from which to baseline further experiments that can produce additional flow improvements, or you can use these recommendations as your base valve job and know that cylinder head specialists messing with the small-block Chevy head for the last 50 years have gotten at least this far and you can trust their efforts.

area that separates quality machine work from the also-rans. Perhaps we should take this point to go back to the early style of valve grinding machines that used separate grinding stones to individually cut each angle in a valve seat. If the machinist planned to execute a three-angle valve job, he would first use the 45-degree stone to cut a wide seat angle. Then he might apply a 30-degree top cut that would narrow the seat from the top while adding the flatter angle that exits into the chamber. Then he would use a steep 60-degree stone to transition the lower portion of the 45-degree seat into the throat area of the port. Ideally, the sharp edge left by the bottom portion of the 60-degree stone would blend into the throat area of the port to enhance increased flow. This work required finesse and sharp attention to detail since excessive grinding could easily sink the seat and reduce flow while also changing the overall valve height at the spring. As you can imagine, this was tedious and time-consuming.

There are some who contend that there are certain advantages to grinding a seat to create sharper edges between the seat angles compared to a cutter style that can leave a tiny radius between the cut angles. This may be splitting hairs when it comes to cylinder head flow, although Dart's work with the wet flow bench indicates that a sharp edge between valve angles improves wet flow characteristics. Since we don't know of any back-to-back testing in this area, it sounds like it could go either way, and we're not brave enough to hazard a guess, although if forced to choose, we would side with the valve job with a more pronounced sharp edge between the valve angles.

Most good machine shops now employ a cutter-style machine that uses a specific multi-angle cutting

This is a typical valve seat-cutting tool that was first popularized by the Serdi Company. The machine tool is shaped to cut all seat angles simultaneously. This also ensures that each seat in both heads is machined exactly the same.

blade shaped to create three to five valve angles that are machined simultaneously into the valve seat. The Serdi machine was the first on the market, and since then several other manufacturers have joined this movement. The advantage of this machine is that it cuts a very precise multi-angle valve job in one operation as opposed to using several stones and several steps to create the same result. The latter demands that each different combination of seat angles or seat widths must be accompanied with its own specific cutter. This requires the machine shop to invest in perhaps dozens of cutters to accommodate all the different cylinder heads and multi-angle valve jobs. While the actual machine operation is accomplished much more quickly than the original valve-grinding effort, the cost of the machine is much greater as is the cost of the multiple cutting blades. All of this contributes to a more expensive valve job. But when you consider that the valve seat is considered to be the most flow-critical area in the cylinder head, it makes sense to spend a little more money here in

The more traditional way of creating a multi-angle valve job was with valve grinding tools such as these. Each angle required a dedicated stone that creates that angle in the valve seat. This is a much more time-consuming process.

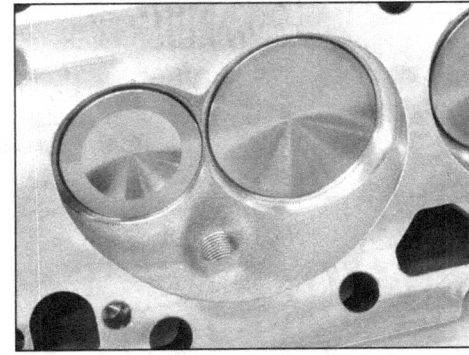

A good machinist knows to cut as little off the seat as possible during machining. As the seat is machined, it sinks into the port, creating a tighter radius that reduces flow. Any seat work also affects the height of the valve on the spring side of the head.

search of more airflow, and therefore more power.

Springs, Seats and Retainers

We touch on just a few highlights on this section since this is covered in much more detail in the *High-Performance Chevy Small-Block Cams & Valvetrains* book, which really should be in your small-block reference library if it isn't already!

CHAPTER 9

Aluminum heads require a steel spring seat to protect the soft aluminum from the valvesprings. The outside diameter style (left) cups the spring around the outside circumference, while the inside diameter style (right) contacts the spring on the inboard side of the spring.

Valvesprings should be carefully matched not only to the camshaft that you've chosen, but also to the entire valvetrain. The classic approach is to choose a very stiff spring in order to control the valvetrain. While this does work, the excessive loads also take a toll on every valvetrain component. For a street engine this is especially harmful and annoying. The majority of small-block Chevy street engines run hydraulic flat tappet camshafts that do not need high valvespring pressures. Seat loads of around 100 to 110 pounds are commonplace and easily achievable with a single spring with a damper. Max valve lift pressures on larger cams may require a dual spring with loads as high as 300 to 310 pounds.

One reason for these conservative pressures is that a hydraulic lifter can withstand only so much valvespring pressure before the load overcomes the piston in the lifter and pushes the oil out (of the lifter). This creates a lost motion device that reduces lift and kills power. Then as the engine returns to idle, the gap created by the pumped down lifter creates a horrific noise from all that clearance. The engine will also run rough, stall, and generally be no fun to drive until the lifters reestablish their proper position. This reinforces why matching the valvespring pressure to the camshaft and the valvetrain is so important. The camshaft companies make this easy for you by offering camshaft kits that come complete with the springs, lifters, retainers, springs, and keepers. If you are relatively new to the art of valvetrain component matching, it's generally a good idea to let the cam company pick out the proper springs.

This also extends to the retainers. It is critical that the retainers be included in the decision-making process and matched to the springs in order to get maximum benefit from each. Improper spring location on a retainer can cause all kinds of dynamic problems that could extend to broken springs and retainers and possibly a dropped valve. None of those situations are something that anyone wants to experience, especially at high RPM. The results are generally expensive.

Weight is another critical factor when choosing valvetrain components. Large-diameter dual springs, monster steel retainers, and big valves all have mass, or weight. At

Bigger is sometimes better, but 10-degree locks are also heavier. Adding weight, especially at the very top of the valve, is not a good idea. Only consider going to larger 10-degree locks if you have had retainer and/or locks problems in the past.

Many aluminum roller rocker arms use a thick arm to create adequate stiffness in the rocker. With larger diameter springs, this can create a clearance problem between the outside diameter of the retainer and the underneath radius of the rocker arm. Always check all 16 rockers for adequate clearance. Steel rocker arms often offer more clearance than aluminum rockers.

A 0.100-inch longer valve produces additional lift clearance, but keep in mind that this additional stem length also increases the valve weight, which is more mass that the valvespring must control. This also gives the retainer more leverage over the guide.

From left to right are a single spring with a damper, a dual spring, and a conical or beehive spring. Conical springs are more difficult to manufacture and more expensive, but offer many advantages including a variable spring rate.

Beehive or conical springs (left) are dramatically lighter than a typical dual spring both in spring mass and also in retainer weight. The spring not only controls the mass of the valve and retainer, but its own mass as well. By reducing spring and retainer weight, the spring can offer more spring pressure to control the valve and the entire valvetrain is happier and more durable.

even a mild 6,000 rpm, these components have to accelerate during the lift cycle, then slow down to change direction at maximum valve lift and then accelerate back toward the closing side and stop again as the valve hits the seat. Anything you can do to lighten this process (without sacrificing strength) will increase durability, making the valvetrain happier. Titanium retainers have become very popular, even with street engines, because they reduce the mass of the retainer without sacrificing strength. Keep in mind that a small-diameter spring, or at least a small spring-wire diameter, also reduces the mass of the spring that must itself accelerate and slow down at very high rates of speed.

The latest generation of conical, or beehive, valvesprings is a move in that reduced mass direction where the small-diameter top of the spring is lighter and uses an exceptionally light retainer. This dramatically reduces the amount of spring/retainer mass that the spring must control. This allows more of the valvespring's pressure to be used to control the valve instead of the spring itself. If there is a disadvantage to these conical or beehive springs, it is that they are more expensive than normal valvesprings, and also that these springs do not need or use a damper. While spring breakage has not been a problem with the high quality of valvespring wire, if the spring should break, there is little short of good luck that would stop the retainer from releasing the valve into the piston. The beehive springs tend to work best in hydraulic roller applications where the lifter contributes additional weight to the valvetrain. We've seen tests in which a Rat motor picked up 20 hp just with the installation of a set of conical valvesprings over a more traditional, large diameter single spring with a damper.

Locks are also important since they are what keep the spring and the valve tied together. Spend the extra money for machined locks rather than stamped ones. They are far better and cost only a few dollars more. It's also important to mention that the small tabs that locate the locks on the valve are not what hold the locks in place. The pressure angle created by the 7 or 10-degree taper between the locks and the retainer are actually what locks the retainer to the valve. The tiny notches on the locks are there only to position the retainer on the valve. The 10-degree locks are not necessary for most street engines. They offer a greater surface area, but are also heavier. Most 10-degree locks also offer a cutout that is used to position a lash cap, which is also something most street engines don't need.

One last component with aluminum heads is a set of valvespring seats. Besides creating a steel barrier between the very hard steel valvespring and the soft aluminum head material, valvespring seats also serve as locators for the springs. There are two basic types, either an inside or outside diameter locator. Spring engineers tell us there is no real difference in terms of performance between the two. It's more a matter of preference, although with large-diameter springs on a small-block Chevy, space comes at a premium so the inside diameter locators are easier to work around.

Often you may have to grind flats on a couple head bolt washers in order to fit them between large diameter valvesprings on a small-block Chevy head. The best way to accomplish this is to place the washers in the bolt-hole recesses before the springs are installed.

Lapping Valves

It's difficult to obtain any kind of agreement when it comes to different cylinder head assembly procedures, and lapping valves is one of those areas. Back when valve grinding tools were less than accurate, one way to ensure that the valve seat and the valve face were completely parallel and would seal properly was to lap the valves using a fine compound and a suction-cup stick. The process is simply to place a small amount of abrasive lapping compound on the valve face, place the valve in the seat, and then spin the valve between your hands with the suction cup stick. The abrasive mildly cuts the seat and valve and evens out any tiny imperfections that might have occurred between the two sealing surfaces.

This was a more common situation when all valve jobs were created using grinding stones. Now with cutter-style machines like the Serdi and others, this situation is far less common. Many engine builders feel that the abrasive tends to radius or erode that sharp edge between the different seat angles and should not be used. This may be true, although perhaps difficult to prove except with a wet flow bench. On the other hand, we've seen good cutter machine seats that indicated a mismatch and a potential poor seal until hit with lapping compound. This doesn't mean that this would occur once the valvespring load is applied to the valve. The majority of cylinder head people we spoke to tend to dismiss valve lapping as archaic, but it might also be that it is a time-consuming technique that they don't want to perform. You decide.

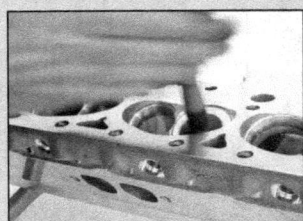

Lapping valves is an ancient art that some still find useful today. A small amount of valve lapping compound placed between the valve and the seat is used to optimize the seat angle by spinning the valve with this wooden handle that connects to the valve with a suction cup.

This light gray line is the machined surface seat width created after lapping the valves. Some contend that lapping takes the sharp edge off the transition between seat angles, which affects wet flow characteristics. Some machinists contend that by using quality seat-machining tools, lapping valves is unnecessary.

Installed Height

Even if you never plan to assemble a set of cylinder heads, it's important to know the procedure and why extra time is spent carefully assembling the cylinder heads so that the valvetrain can perform its tasks efficiently for thousands of trouble-free miles. We've already established the valve-to-guide clearance, so the next step is to measure the valvespring installed height. This is the distance from the spring seat in the head to the bottom side of the retainer where the spring seats. The stock dimension for a small-block Chevy is 1.780 inches. This establishes the starting point, if you will, for the valvespring. This compresses the valvespring slightly, which creates its seated pressure. It's also necessary to measure all 16-valve installed heights because the distance from the spring seat to the retainer will vary by perhaps 0.030 inch or more. This is due to variations in the height of the valve as well as different positions of the valve seat.

Installed height is the actual height of the spring between the retainer and the seat. The easiest way to measure this is with a height mic that quickly reads out the distance.

CYLINDER HEAD REBUILDING AND ASSEMBLY

Retainer-To-Seal Clearance

Next we get into checking retainer-to-seal clearance. Here, our dimension is the distance from the bottom portion of the retainer just underneath the locks to the top of the valveguide seal. We need to have adequate clearance between the retainer and the seal so that valve lift does not push the retainer into the seal. This damages the seal and causes oil control problems, especially on the intake valve side of things. The minimum clearance between the retainer and the seal is 0.050 inch, and even this is tight. The point is that we don't want the retainer smacking the seal at high RPM when perhaps a small amount of valve loft or float kicks the lift up slightly. This can happen in over-rev situations when the spring loses control of the valve for a short period of time.

There are several ways to improve retainer-to-seal clearance should you discover an interference or tight condition. One of the easiest ways to increase the installed height of the spring is by raising the retainer. Crane, for example, offers machined locks in 0.050-inch steps where the retainer can be raised or lowered by 0.050 inch. By raising the retainer this amount, this also reduces the valvespring seat load and overall pressure on the valve. With a 360-pound-per-inch spring, increasing the installed height by 0.050 reduces the load by approximately 18 pounds. Raising the retainer also moves it

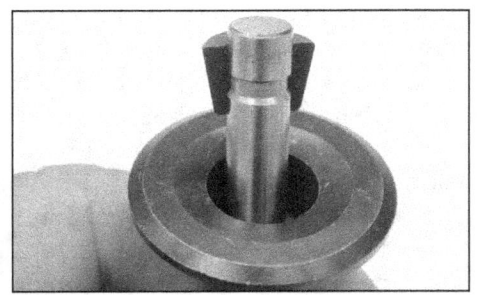

Different manufacturers make retainers that appear to be the same, but in reality create much different installed heights. One trick to tighten or loosen an installed height figure is to try a different manufacturer's retainer.

Another choice for altering installed height is valve locks. Crane offers locks in standard, plus 0.050 and minus 0.050-inch heights that make quick work of tuning the installed height. Ideally, you want to use these same locks on all the valves. If you use them only on selected valves, it is imperative to keep an accurate record of their location so they don't get mixed in with other, standard locks.

The machinist determines the shortest installed height of all 16 valves and uses that dimension as his reference point for the test. Let's say his shortest installed height is 1.760 inches and the tallest is 1.800. The machinist can then install a 0.040-inch thick shim on top of the spring seat for the tallest installed height valve, which reduces that distance to the 1.760-inch height. This creates the exact same load (within perhaps 10 pounds) on each valve. This ensures that the valvespring pressures are equal and each valve has the same control load governing its performance.

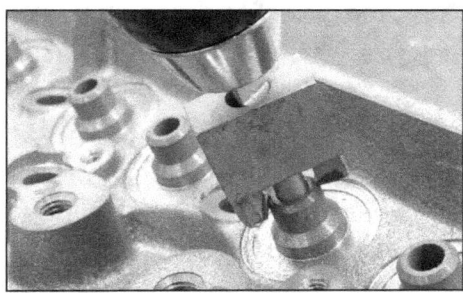

Often, heads like the Vortec iron production head have tall valveguides that must be machined to increase retainer-to-seal clearance. You can purchase these cutting tools from COMP or others and do the work yourself to save some money.

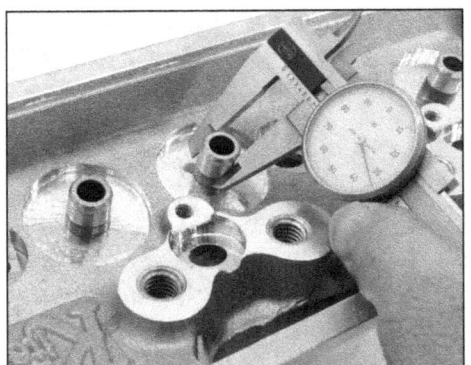

Be sure to measure guide diameter to ensure you get the right positive seal diameter. Positive seals come in two different diameters of 0.500 and 0.531-inch guide diameters.

Always measure retainer-to-seal clearance, as this is often the tightest clearance in the valvetrain. This is very easy to measure with a dial caliper.

Often, the published coil bind figure and the actual measured coil bind are different. Generally, the spring compresses tighter than the published length, which adds to the clearance to bind.

closer to the inside of the rocker arm. Raising the retainer has the same effect as sinking the valvestem tip in the retainer, so you need to be careful to ensure there is adequate clearance between the roller tip and the retainer.

Another alternative, although more expensive, is to increase the length of the valve by 0.100 inch. A longer valve automatically generates an additional 0.100 inch of room between the retainer and the seal. It also allows room for more valve lift. Generally, you want to have all this thought out ahead of time so your engine plan accounts for a 0.650-inch lift camshaft that would quickly overcome a set of stock-length valves. This is why pre-planning your engine on paper first is so important—so you do not have to face purchasing two sets of valves for your engine. Also keep in mind that a longer valve and a taller valvespring both contribute additional weight to the valvetrain, increasing the amount of weight that the valvetrain must control at high engine speeds. Should you decide to go with longer valves, purchase a complete set. Since a small-block Chevy uses a standard valve height for both the intake and exhaust valves, you must use 0.100-inch longer exhaust valves as well, even if they are not needed. This keeps the valvestem heights all the same, which keeps all the pushrods the same length. See how complicated this can get?

Coil Bind

We also need to check for valvespring coil bind. This is the height of the spring fully compressed with the coils stacked solid. This measurement, subtracted from the installed height, is the amount of room the spring will allow for valve lift. As an example, let's say we have a 1.800-inch installed height with a given valvespring that has a coil bind dimension of 1.150 inches: 1.800 – 1.150 = 0.650 inch. With a 0.590-inch valve lift, we have a coil bind clearance of 0.060 inch. Depending upon whose specs you read, either 0.050 or 0.060 inch is the minimum clearance to coil bind. Generally, this clearance will create 0.010 to 0.015 inch of clearance between each of the coils. Running valvesprings near coil bind while still maintaining clearance from coil bind does not seem to affect spring durability.

We've also discovered that published coil bind numbers don't always agree with actual coil bind dimensions. Generally, the cam and valvespring companies will be conservative with their specs, which means that a given spring may have a coil bind spec of 1.210 inches for example, but will actually coil bind at a much lower number, perhaps something like 1.180 inches. This is why you must check all 16 springs for coil bind anytime you are assembling heads. A shorter coil bind number just might give you the extra clearance you need without having to resort to taller valves.

Conclusion

There are many advantages to understanding how to assemble and tune up your own cylinder heads. This requires investing in a specialty spring compressor (both for on and off the engine) and you'll be surprised

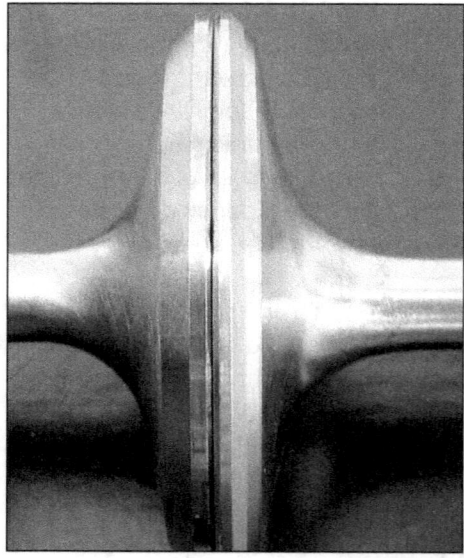

Sharp edges on the intake valve help to shear fuel as it enters the combustion chamber and tend to improve distribution within the combustion chamber. While difficult to see, the valve on the left has a wider margin and no radius to the chamber side face of the intake valve.

Valveguide Seals

You might think this an area that deserves minimal attention, but the reality is that a high quality valveguide seal is essential to making good horsepower. The reason for this is that the seal must be able to withstand serious engine speed and intense heat without failing and must meter a given amount of oil into the guide to lubricate it without allowing too much oil into the guide, which could then find its way into the combustion chamber. The problem with oil in the combustion process is that it contributes to causing serious detonation problems, not to mention the carbon buildup it creates as a result of combustion.

In the early small-block days, stock valvestems had two grooves at the top of the stem, with one used to position a small o-ring between the retainer and the locks. Combined with a thin steel shedder housing over the spring, this worked okay. Later came umbrella seals that fit over the valve and, as their name implies, sheltered the guide from direct oil splash. The ideal seal is a positive seal that is slipped over a machined valveguide. The seal is secured in place by steel rings around the seal to keep it in place. The earliest of these seals was created out of a white hard plastic. Most valvetrain companies still sell these "PC" seals, but they should be avoided for street use. Their advantage is they are small in diameter to clear the inside diameter of a dual or triple spring assembly. The reason they should be avoided is that the hard plastic offers very little ability to follow lateral movement of the valvestem. Several companies now carry Viton rubber seals that offer outstanding sealing capabilities

There are probably a dozen different positive seals to choose from in the aftermarket. Avoid the hard white plastic PC seals—they don't last. Even GM uses positive seals now. Choose the Viton rubber ones; they seem to work the best. Remember, a little more oil down the exhaust guide is a good thing, hence the different seal for the exhaust.

along with excellent durability, which is the ideal combination for a street engine.

There are two variables involved with ordering valveguide seals, valvestem diameter and the outside diameter of the valveguide. The valveguide outside diameter (o.d.) generally comes in either 0.500 or 0.531 inch while most small-block Chevy valves are 0.3415 inch in diameter although some new aftermarket heads like the new version AFR 23-degree heads are coming through with smaller LS1 stem diameter valves of 8-mm (0.31496 inch)

at how often you will use these tools once you own them. Cylinder heads have the greatest potential effect on engine performance, so it just makes sense to have the knowledge and the tools to work on these components yourself. Once you've gone through the procedure a couple of times, assembly and blueprinting your own heads becomes almost second nature.

On the exhaust side, it appears that a slight radius on the face of the valve may also help flow, although this is not a universal truth. You will need to test this on each specific head application since not all exhaust ports respond to this modification.

CHAPTER 10

BASIC PORTING TECHNIQUES

Here is an area where there is a tremendous amount of potential for success and also failure. Cylinder head porting has been an over-used term for the last 20 years, and despite all the words written about this process, you can't go more than 10 minutes with any group of hot rodders before someone uses the term "port and polished," which merely reveals their ignorance on the subject since polishing a port is something that fell out of favor at least 20 years ago.

But the most dangerous part of porting heads is that anyone with a die grinder and a carbide bit thinks of himself as a cylinder head porting master. Nothing could be further from the truth. The reality is that few of these guys have ever seen a real live flow bench, much less had one of their ports honestly evaluated on a flow bench. Worse yet are the Internet boasters who plaster the boards with all kinds of flow number propaganda. Few enough people know how flow benches work, and some of them are more than willing to bogus up numbers to make themselves look good, knowing that perhaps one out of ten customers will actually test these heads before bolting them on an engine.

The point of this little rant is to introduce the concept that there are

It's best to begin by creating an area to work that you don't mind getting really dirty. Grinding on iron or aluminum heads is a messy proposition, so forget about doing it on the kitchen table. Find a spot on a workbench that can be easily cleaned of iron and/or aluminum filings. A head stand would also be a great addition to your tool collection.

plenty of people out there who claim to know how to port cylinder heads. The list of actual accomplished cylinder head porters who actually do know is far shorter. As disconcerting as this may sound, the average enthusiast still has hope. A step in the right direction is reading this book. We don't claim to be porting experts, because if we were, there's much better money to be made making horsepower for people than in sitting behind a computer putting words on a page. Nevertheless, there is basic information out there for the taking that can and will lead to improved power and you can do it. You just have to know a bit about airflow and where to spend your time with the grinder.

This chapter is not about hogging out ports and adding big valves. On the contrary, it's really more about removing only the material that's necessary to increase flow without increasing the overall size of the port. As we learned in Chapter 3, good CFM combined with high velocity creates a very powerful

BASIC PORTING TECHNIQUES

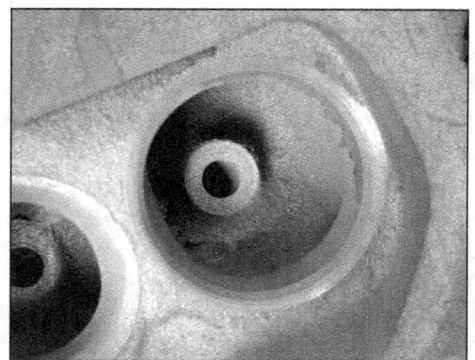

Production valve jobs on the older iron heads for GEN I engines generally leave a ledge directly underneath the valve job that represents a major flow restriction. Removing this to open the throat and blending it into the port is worth 10 percent flow increases or more.

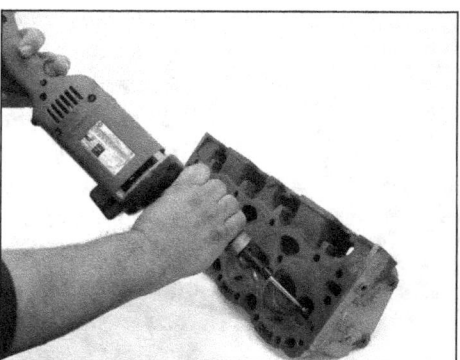

Assuming you are right-handed, hold the main body of the die grinder with your left hand at the top and guide the movement of the business end with your right hand. The key is to always keep the grinder moving across the work surface so you don't dig trenches or holes in the port.

While you might want to jump right in on the intake side, there is actually more power to be had by concentrating on the exhaust side. Increase the exhaust throat to 90 percent of the valve size and do not remove any more material than necessary from the port floor and you will be successful.

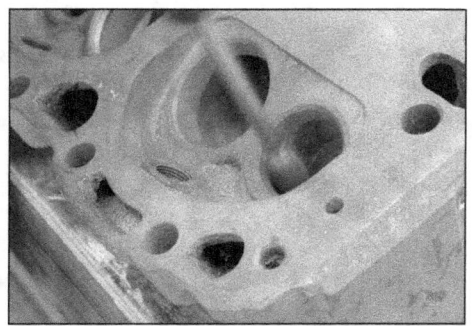

To begin your porting education, you probably want to start on a junk iron head so that if (or when) you screw up, the results are not disastrous. Make sure the head is clean, which makes your porting effort easier.

cylinder head. What we deal with in this chapter is pointing out areas on a small-block Chevy head that respond the most to minor changes. We also offer a few recommendations on how to perform those modifications. Most would also assume that we're going to spend a majority of our time on the intake side. But at least when it comes to production or production-similar heads, there are impressive gains to be had on the exhaust side of the head as well.

We focus our attention in this chapter mainly on production iron and aluminum heads as well as a few of the smaller aftermarket iron castings. These heads offer the greatest potential for improvements. Many of the points made in this chapter apply to other cylinder heads as well, but keep in mind that a good aluminum high-performance aftermarket cylinder head is already the recipient of most of these modifications. This means that major flow improvements require more sophisticated changes that should be left to a porting professional. The beauty of building a street engine is that there are no rules, so any modification you wish to make is fair game.

Even if you have never looked inside an intake port or performed the ritualistic touchy-feely routine of running your fingers inside a high-performance cylinder head port to feel the shape of the port floor, that doesn't mean you can't learn enough to know the difference between a good port and a bad one.

If you are intimidated by the thought of running a grinder inside your precious small-block castings, we recommend starting out by experimenting on a junk set of iron castings. Strip the head of all valves and clean it up so you're not dealing with a greasy monster. Pay attention to the technique rather than trying to create the ultimate intake port. Learn how to control the grinder and how to finesse that carbide bit to get it to do what you desire. Learn the art of never leaving the bit in one spot, but always keeping it moving to create an even surface and a gentle radius. All of these techniques will come to you as you gain experience. But don't be afraid to try this on your own. Some of the best cylinder head people in the business started out just like you, in a dimly lit garage with a cheesy die grinder and a port full of dreams.

Tools of the Trade

Like any good mechanic or tradesman, you can't do a professional job without the right tools. The one big-ticket item that most porters use is an electric grinder. These grinders often feature a variable speed control that

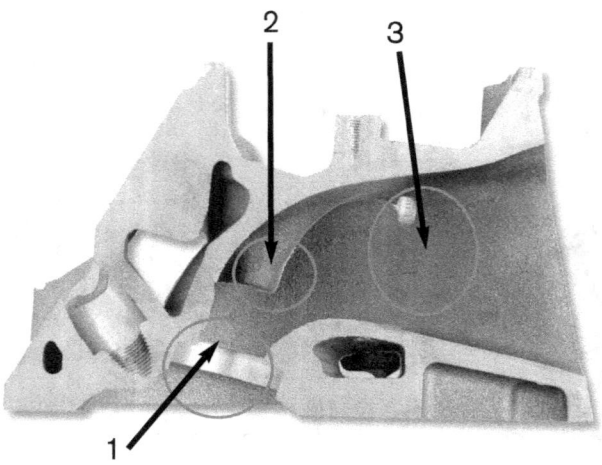

These callouts indicate where typical flow loss occurs in a given port. Maximum flow loss (over 50 percent) occurs at the bowl area, with the next largest restriction in the expansion area at the valve with 30 percent (1). The valveguide also represents a significant flow loss of roughly 10 percent (2). The pushrod restriction and wall friction make up the remainder of a typical flow loss of around 8 percent (3). As you can see, combining the bowl and the expansion area around the valve constitutes over 80 percent of a typical port's flow loss for a given cross-sectional area.

allows the porter to easily control the amount of material he is removing by working more slowly. In other times, there may be a great deal of material to remove, in which case he can maximize the bit speed. Makita makes a good electric rotary grinder, as do several other power tool companies. An electric grinder is preferable since the variable speed is a little easier to control than a pneumatic tool, and an electric grinder doesn't require a massive air compressor to run all day. Plus, most air-powered die grinders are rather short and hard to control compared to the longer electric die grinders. But if an air-powered die grinder is all you have, it certainly works to get started. If you decide later to put more time into porting heads, you can step up to a more professional tool.

For the beginning port artist, the first heads you port will probably be cast iron. Several companies such as Standard Abrasives offer porting kits with different grinders and polishing attachments that are useful, but you should first invest in a few quality carbide cutters. These come in many different shapes and sizes, but a short-shank flame-shaped cutter works for most of what you want to accomplish. A similar-shaped cutter for aluminum has much wider cutter flutes that will not get clogged with aluminum, but even this might not be necessary since most work with aluminum heads removes only minor amounts of aluminum. A high-quality electric die grinder and a couple of carbide bits are all you really need to dive into the world of cylinder head porting. Of course, we also have to offer the usual safety tips that you should already know, including the mandatory eye protection. If nothing else, you don't ever want to experience the pain from a sharp, tiny iron filing thrust into your eye. There are no reasons that justify not wearing safety glasses. It's also a good idea to wear ear protection and some kind of simple breathing mask just to keep out those nasty iron and aluminum filings. Unless you like the idea of black lung disease, it's a good idea anytime you fire up that rotary grinder.

The best porting tool you have, however, is that complex piece of machinery between your ears. Patience and a willingness to finesse the port rather than gouging out huge chunks of material is the key to success. If you've managed to work through this book from the first few chapters, then it should be clear that velocity is an important consideration in port flow. Port shape is the big key to flow on both the intake and exhaust side. The rookie trick is just to push out the shape to make it larger. That may even result in higher flow numbers on the flow bench, but calculating the port

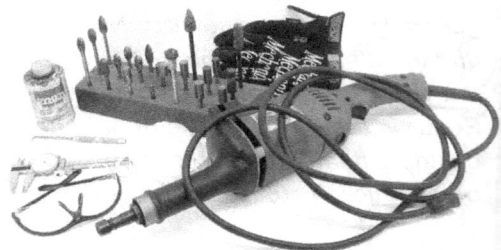

Some of the tools needed include an electric die grinder, an assortment of carbide cutters, sanding rolls (often called tootsie rolls) in a variety of grits, eye protection, a dust mask or respirator, Dykem for creating scribe lines, and a selection of scribes.

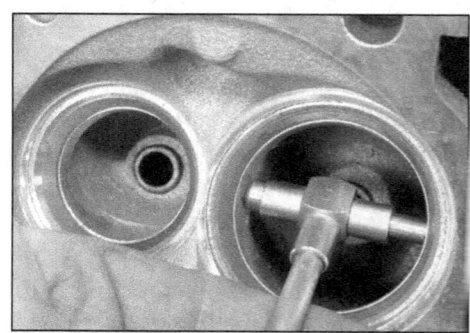

Measure the inside diameter of the port throat, in this case the intake, and use this diameter to determine percentage of the valve diameter by dividing the throat area by the valve diameter. So a 1.77-inch throat diameter divided by a valve diameter of 2.02 equals a throat percentage of 87.6 percent. This only requires a diameter increase out to 1.82 inches to create a 90 percent figure.

velocity numbers may not necessarily result in an improvement. The magic comes when you can increase the CFM along with the port velocity without dramatically increasing the minimum port cross-sectional area. This requires patience and an attention to detail that only comes with lots of experience. Frankly, there's no other way to get there. There is no school on "Thinking Like Air 101" offered at your local high-performance junior college. Here is

30-Degree Back Cut Trick

There is a common trick that many cylinder head modifiers use to improve port flow. It's a simple machine effort that merely places a second angle behind the 45-degree seat angle on the intake or exhaust valve. This back cut simply improves the radius that is created by the seat angles and often increases port flow numbers substantially. The trick comes in that this additional valve angle does not always improve flow where you necessarily desire this change. Port work is as much of an art as it is a science and nowhere is this truer than with back cut angles.

Generally speaking, adding a 30-degree back cut angle on a small-block Chevy intake valve will improve low and mid-lift flow and often will also help or at least not hurt peak flow numbers. Occasionally, this back cut may exact a slight cost to the peak flow numbers. In speaking to cylinder head porters, this is far from what you could even call a rule of thumb. We've seen a 30-degree back cut improve low-lift flow only to kill the upper lift numbers, and we've also seen this same back cut angle improve flow throughout the entire lift curve. To further complicate this concept, this 30-degree angle seems to work better on the exhaust side than it does on the intake. But this is also not a hard and fast rule. An example of how well this back cut can work is with the stock factory iron Vortec head. Initial runs of this head used the typical ditch-cut exhaust valve with a single 45-degree seat. Subsequent production heads began employing a 30-degree back cut on both the intake and exhaust side that generated substantial flow improvements throughout the entire lift curve, but mostly on the exhaust. Despite the costs involved with making this second cut on the exhaust valve, even the factory took the time to make this happen.

This idea should not be limited to just 30 degrees. With so many variables among the dozens of small-block heads available, if you have access to a flow bench where you can perform accurate tests, it's possible that 28 or 31 degrees might be worth even more improvements. One test that one cylinder head developer tried was to add a second, more shallow angle behind the 30-degree back cut with the idea that if one back-cut is good, two should

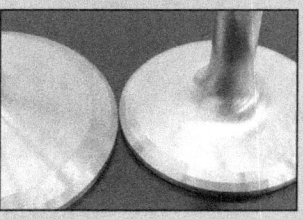

As has been mentioned before, a 30-degree back cut on either or both intake and exhaust valves can improve port flow.

be better. Subsequent testing indicated that this idea, as he put it, "sucked."

Interestingly, only now are the aftermarket manufacturers putting back cuts on the valves in their heads. From a high-volume production standpoint, this extra step is more expensive and adds to the head's ultimate cost. For this reason, most shy away from making this extra step. Lately, with competition increasing, more companies are finding it a necessary step to increase flow. For example, Dart now routinely back-cuts all their valves on the Patinum iron heads and new Platinum Pro 1 series as standard equipment. But this will vary with the heads and the manufacturer. The new AFR 180 Eliminator comes with a back cut intake but not on the exhaust. The only way to know whether this trick will work on your heads is to test each head on both the intake and exhaust sides. If you have access to a flow bench, this is a modification that could be easily accomplished at minimal cost. It's not necessary to flow all 16 ports. Just flow one intake and one exhaust and then add in a new back cut valve in each port and retest. If you have additional time, it would certainly be worth the effort to do tests at a separate angle of 28 and 33 degrees, which might be worthwhile.

Results can be startling. We've seen a stock production exhaust port and valve increase flow by as much as 14 cfm, while in other cases this trick does nothing at all for the mid-range flow and only reduces flow at the higher valve lift points. Also be prepared for the inevitable results that will not make your decision easy. For example, it's possible that a back cut on the intake side may improve low-lift flow only to hurt the high-lift portion of the overall curve. In most cases, the effort will be rewarded. The good news is that the machine work is relatively inexpensive, costing perhaps less than $50 to add the back cut angle on all 16 valves.

CHAPTER 10

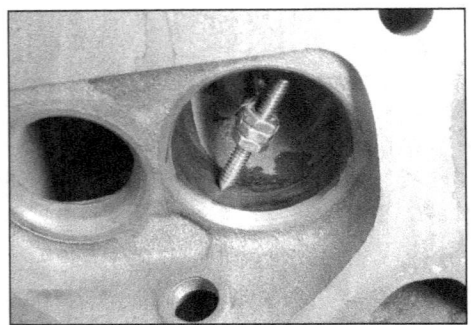

You can use a dial caliper to mark points on a throat area coated with blue Dykem to locate the outer edge of the 90-percent line. In this case, we fashioned a crude scribe by welding two 10-32 nuts to the end of an old valvestem. This throat-marking tool will establish the 90-percent scribe line in the throat area.

where on the job training is really the only way to get there.

The intention of this chapter is not to offer instruction that will make you a professional port expert. All we can do is offer a few ideas, a few airflow basics, and a few corks that are present in many small-block Chevy cylinder heads. We start with a production-style iron head since this is where major flow increases can be obtained while spending perhaps 8 to 10 hours of labor to get there.

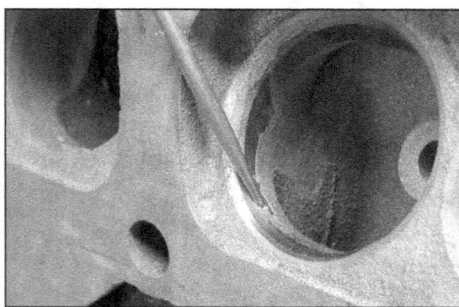

When working on either port, work slowly and carefully to stay away from the seat. Heavy grinding scratches in the seat require machining, which tends to sink the seat into the head, which hurts airflow and also increases chamber volume.

Getting Started

Before you pick up the first tool, let's look at where we will be spending all of our time. There are two basic areas of small-block Chevy heads where the restrictions lie. The easiest one to access is the pushrod restriction area, just downstream of the port opening. If you recall the discussion from the Airflow Basics chapter, this pinch point creates the flow limit that eventually establishes the maximum flow potential of the port. Most entry-level port players think this is a great place to start because it's easy to access. The truth is, this only increases the port cross-sectional area and will deliver a minimal increase in max valve lift flow. It's best to ignore this area and concentrate instead on the area of the port that is the true restriction on a production head.

The place where your effort is most rewarded is actually in the throat area of the port just underneath the valve seat. Careful measurements show that stock heads are often very restricted due to casting variations that the factory ignores. It's this oversight that rewards the intelligent pocket porter if he knows where to grind. That's what we show you in a few short paragraphs. But first, there's more to this story.

One technique that works well for rookie head porters is to always work horizontally. This means rotating the head when you want to work on the sides or the roof of the pocket. Start by placing the head with the intake manifold face down on the bench and working the floor, or short side radius, of the intake pocket. Basically, work the port floor by grinding straight in the pocket following the angle of the valveguide, out to near but not at the 90-degree throat line.

Now rotate the head 90-degrees and do the same straight-in grinding technique. Do this same routine for the other three positions of the head. This leaves a sharp edge or grinding line.

So far, we addressed mainly the intake port because we know that's where the homespun porter will concentrate his efforts. There are certainly rewards to be gained here, but it is the exhaust side where the substantial gains are realized. If you look at the charts on the flow increases based on the combination of the larger valves, pocket porting work, and the 30-degree back cut, the results are amazing on both sides, but the real gains are made on the exhaust side. At

BASIC PORTING TECHNIQUES

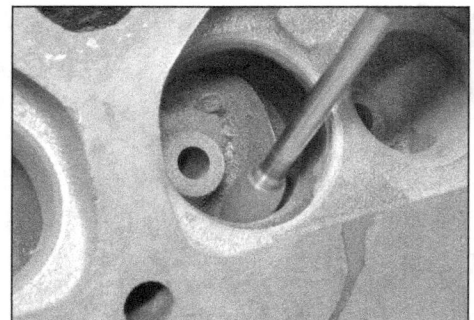

Now with the head back with the intake face down, go deeper into the port and radius the sharp edge into the port throat. Now repeat this same technique for the other three head positions. Remove just enough to blend this sharp edge into the throat.

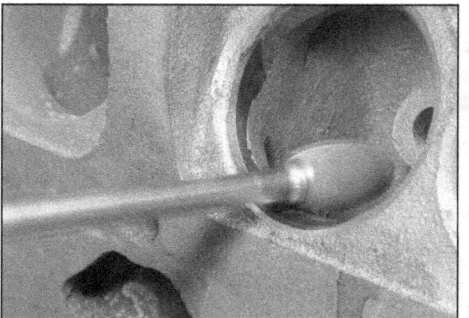

There's also a sharp edge between the bottom of the valve job and where your first cut ended. This also needs to be blended together again by removing only what is needed to do the job. Then repeat this step through the other three head positions.

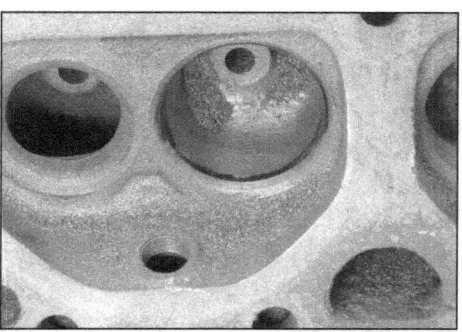

You may be tempted to use a lighter grit sanding-disc to smooth out the grinding marks and make the job look more professional. The reality is that a rougher surface mixes fuel better with the air, so leave it rough.

0.500-inch valve lift there is a 37 cfm gain. We get into the evaluation a little later, but this is a 25 percent gain in flow at max valve lift. For a few hours work, it's tough to beat that kind of return on your investment.

Let's start with a typical iron production head like an 882, 441, or 920 casting number piece. Ideally, you should flow this head first on both the intake and exhaust sides to give us a good solid starting point, but for many enthusiasts that may not be practical. For the purposes of this book, we do it in that order to give you a specific idea of what can be gained by doing this work. We've included flow charts on three steps through the process, starting with enlarging the valve sizes from 1.94/1.50 inches to the typical small-block 2.02/1.60-inch valve size using Manley Street Series stainless steel valves.

While you may feel like you can jump right in and start grinding at this point, there is more homework to do first. If you recall our discussion of throat diameters from earlier chapters, then the 90 percent rule should be familiar. But to refresh your memory, current conventional wisdom holds

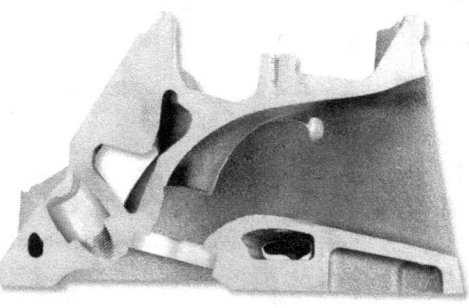

Since all good intake ports enhance mixture velocity, a taller port floor that creates a kind of high ramp leading into the valve pocket area tends to improve airflow by making the radius turn into the bowl less abrupt. This especially helps at lower valve lifts, which is why mid-range flow numbers improve on better heads.

that the throat diameter—the area just below the valve seat—should never be larger than 90 percent of valve diameter. For a 1.94-inch intake valve diameter, this would be a diameter of 1.740 inches, which is slightly larger than the stock throat diameter. So if you were pocket porting a set of stock iron heads with the original valve sizes, this would be the ideal throat diameter.

But since we are adding a 2.02-inch intake valve, this increases the throat dimension out to 1.81 inches.

A poor short-side radius like on older small-block production heads offers a flat floor where the air and fuel shear off the port floor going into the valve bowl, which creates turbulence and reduces airflow, especially at higher valve lifts.

This process also applies to the exhaust side, generating 1.440 inches of exhaust throat diameter dimension. It's critical that this throat diameter not be exceeded. In fact, it's best to be somewhat conservative by 0.010 or 0.015 inch if there is any question, especially since the throat area is not always completely round relative to the valves. This dimension needs to be applied by applying machinist dye to the throat and scribing a line that marks the throat diameter limit. This can be accomplished by making marks using a pair of calipers, or you could

CHAPTER 10

Pocket Work on Aftermarket Heads

We admit it; we took the easy road to showing results based on pocket porting a set of stone stock iron castings. These are not bogus numbers. In fact, there's perhaps another 5 to 10 cfm more that could have been done with those heads, but we purposely kept them conservative to show what's possible. The same cannot be said for applying this effort to aftermarket heads.

Frankly, the factory makes it easy to pump up the flow by doing these simple pocket-porting tricks. Aftermarket heads are not that easy because these companies know all those tricks, so increasing flow is a little tougher to accomplish. There are a few exceptions, however. Basically, the more budget-based iron aftermarket heads generally do not clean up the throat directly underneath the valve seat. There are impressive gains to be made with even some of the larger heads like the World Product Sportsman II head or the Dart Iron Eagles, but by the time you progress up to the Platinum series of Dart iron heads in the 215- and 230-cc heads, this work has already been performed. That's not to say that you cannot improve on what's been done on a production basis, but the rewards are much smaller and you have to spend more time to generate less. When it comes to modifying aftermarket heads, you will also need a flow bench to verify your work. Without a way to evaluate your efforts, you will be wasting your time and probably end up with a head that flows less than it did before you started.

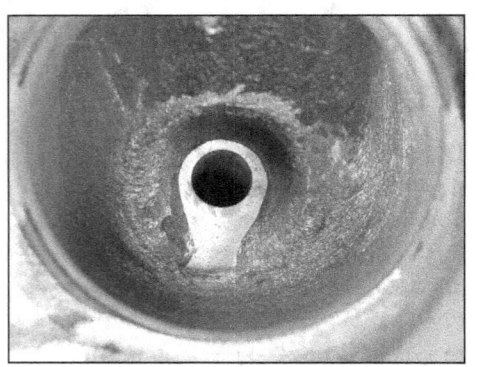

Photos of the latest generation heads reveal directional vanes configured around the guide boss. Attempting this for a bowl job on an iron production head is probably a lot of extra work that may not pay off well in terms of increased airflow.

make a scribe using an adjustable sharp point welded to a valve as in our photos. In the case of our 2.02 inch valve diameter, this scribed line establishes the radius (half the diameter) from the valvestem centerline so the tool would be set at half of the 1.81 inches throat diameter, or 0.905 inch. This tool applies an accurate limit line that is necessary to prevent opening the throat diameter too far.

You can take two different initial approaches to this effort. If you feel you can control the rotary grinder enough to stay away from a new valve seat, you can take the heads to your local machine shop and have them grind the initial intake and exhaust 45-degree seats, leaving about 0.020 inch from completing the seat. This positions the seats and gives you an idea of where your work will progress, but you run the risk of damaging the seat with the grinder, so for the first time around at least, we suggest just doing all the work against the throat diameter limit line.

The captions in this chapter indicate the proper procedure for the actual grinding. We can't emphasize enough the importance of not exceeding the 90-percent diameter and also in working very slowly and carefully. Especially when working with stock iron heads, it is very tempting to get into that port and really start grinding away to make that port look big and flow tons of air. That's the classic backyard hack job that will ruin a set of heads.

Also notice that we avoided reworking the valveguides in this pocket effort. We limited the work here to the area roughly 1 inch below the valve seat location. It is possible to improve flow slightly by narrowing or streamlining the iron guide area, but we wouldn't spend more than a few minutes on this since they don't seem

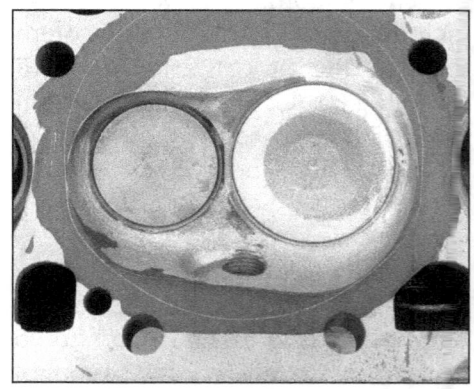

Junk valves can be used to protect the valve job when making combustion chamber modifications with the grinder.

BASIC PORTING TECHNIQUES

Lay the head gasket over the head, line it up with the bolt holes, and tape it down. With the head already coated with Dykem, scribe the outline of the head gasket opening. Do not exceed this line since this can create head gasket sealing problems.

Many rookie head porters think that port matching the intake manifold and cylinder head interface is worth a ton of power. Unless the intake port is smaller than the intake manifold port, there's very little to be gained here.

to respond with increased flow in the same way as other cylinder heads.

Chamber Mods

It's also possible to improve flow beyond just working the pocket area of the intake or exhaust port. Most stock chambers tend to overhang the bore, which creates a step between the top of the intake valve seat, the edge of the chamber, and the actual bore size of the cylinder. This step or ledge is also something that the air must negotiate past on the exhaust side.

The best way to minimize these restrictions is to position a head gasket over the chamber that can be used as a cylinder wall outline. Tracing a line around the inside diameter of the cylinder will indicate where the chamber can be laid back or blended more gently into the cylinder diameter. Again, you need to work carefully here to prevent removing material beyond the scribe line since this may also affect cylinder head gasket sealing integrity. Removing material from the chamber also increases chamber volume, which decreases the compression ratio. The best step is to measure the chamber volume before modifications and then afterward to determine how much volume the modifications have added. Then the head can be milled to compensate for the changes.

It's really beyond the scope of this book to get much beyond this step in terms of improving combustion efficiency with recommendations for chamber modifications since every aftermarket chamber (and many production chambers as well) is designed a little differently and may respond to changes in a different manner. Chapter 11 deals more specifically with combustion chamber design.

Conclusion

If you think about it, this chapter embodies all the basic concepts from this entire book into something that the reader can apply to almost any cylinder head. The proper execution of intake and exhaust porting has less to do with merely hogging out ports to make them large and more with removing as little material as possible while still increasing the flow rate of the port. The concept of port velocity cannot be stressed enough when it comes to improving port flow. Often, it's not what is removed, but rather the resulting shape of the port and its combined flow and velocity curves that make a good port great.

The idea with chamber modifications is to unshroud the intake and exhaust valves to improve flow. Laying the chamber wall back away from the intake accomplishes this.

CHAPTER 10

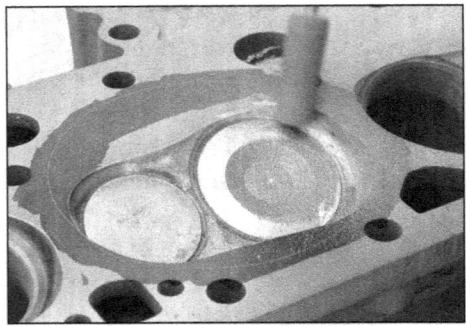

Chamber modifications include removing all sharp edges that might turn into glow plugs in high-RPM applications when the engine is really working. A sharp edge can begin to glow red-hot and cause pre-ignition problems.

Chamber improvements should also include the piston top. This happens to be a big-block Chevy piston, but notice that all the sharp edges of piston machining have been radiused to eliminate hot spots.

Porting is also about restraint and only removing what is necessary to improve flow. Go too far and hitting the water jacket as evidenced by this hole in the bowl area is easily accomplished. Tread carefully here.

Pocket Porting Flow Tests

The following charts illustrate the results of a simple pocket porting effort on a set of small-block Chevy cast iron heads. This also included a valve size increase from 1.94/1.50 to 2.02/1.60 inches using high quality stainless steel Manley Street Series valves. As you can see from the data, the valve size increase alone only marginally improved the flow at certain points. In other places, flow actually decreased. Only after the pocket work was performed did the flow increase. Another important point is that the valves also included a 30-degree back cut on both the intake and exhaust valves. We didn't call out those gains separately, but trust us, this is something you will want to do. It's worth the small expense in machine work.

Stock 920 Iron Castings 1.94/1.50-inch valves

Valve Lift (inches)	Intake	Exhaust	E/I
0.100	63	55	87%
0.200	112	95	85%
0.300	167	130	78%
0.400	202	143	71%
0.500	212	146	69%
0.600	214	148	69%

Stock 920 Casting Added Manley 2.02/1.60-inch stainless valves

Valve Lift (inches)	Intake	Exhaust	E/I
0.100	68	56	82%
0.200	127	99	78%
0.300	180	126	70%
0.400	208	137	66%
0.500	212	138	65%
0.600	213	138	65%

Pocket Ported 920 Castings
2.02/1.60-inch Manley Valves w/30-Degree Back Cut

Valve Lift (inches)	Intake	Exhaust	E/I	Increase Int.	Exh.
0.100	68	60	88%	5	5
0.200	134	112	83%	22	17
0.300	195	145	76%	28	15
0.400	221	169	77%	19	26
0.500	220	183	84%	8	37
0.600	221	186	85%	7	38

The "Increase" column is the total CFM improvement calculated against Test A.

CHAPTER 11

COMBUSTION CHAMBER

The major focus of most cylinder head discussion is flow into and out of the cylinder. While this is certainly an important function, consider that all the tuning efforts directed toward the induction and exhaust system is all aimed at getting air and fuel in or combustion residue out of the cylinder. Ultimately, all this effort is really focused on making cylinder pressure, which becomes torque and horsepower. Since the combustion process is what creates this cylinder pressure, it makes sense that we should pay particular attention to this process. What we're talking about is the combustion space, which consists of the top of the piston and the cylinder head combustion chamber. It is the shape of this entire combustion space, including the top of the piston that helps shape the combustion process.

In the early days of the small-block Chevy and for all engines up to perhaps the mid-1970s, the shape of the combustion chamber was merely a tub or vessel in which to contain the valves. Little attention was given to the early small-block chambers other than the chamber volume's affect on compression ratio. Generally, most performance small-block heads used a 64-cc combustion chamber roughly in the shape of a

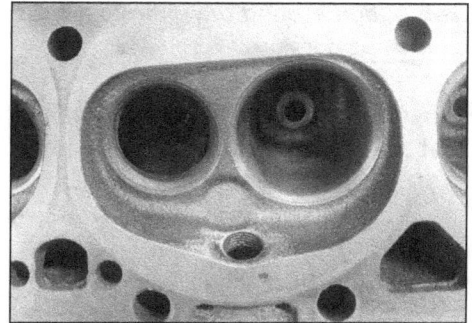

This is an old 64-cc iron chamber from a 461 head—the classic "double hump" head that is still in favor with some small-block enthusiasts. While offering decent intake flow for its port size, this chamber does little to enhance combustion efficiency.

tub. The first major change to chambers came when emissions requirements led to increasing the size of the chamber to reduce compression and attempt to reduce the hydrocarbon count in the exhaust residue. This led to open chambers designed to reduce the quench area of the head, which also reduced oxides of nitrogen (NOx) emissions. This approach did not improve performance, however, especially given the accompanying drop in compression ratio.

Into the '80s and early '90s, combustion chambers began to receive a bit more attention with an attempt to push or move the combustion

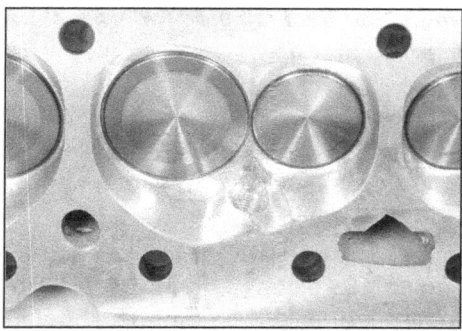

It's difficult to measure how much a chamber is worth, but clearly this new generation of heart-shaped chambers is not as deep and tends to enhance mixture movement across the spark plug and toward the exhaust side. This is the new AFR 210 Eliminator chamber.

A shallower chamber also reduces the height of the chamber wall, which enhances airflow from the port's long side radius. Chamber modifications that lay back this chamber wall also tend to improve port flow as it exits the valve.

HIGH-PERFORMANCE CHEVY SMALL-BLOCK CYLINDER HEADS

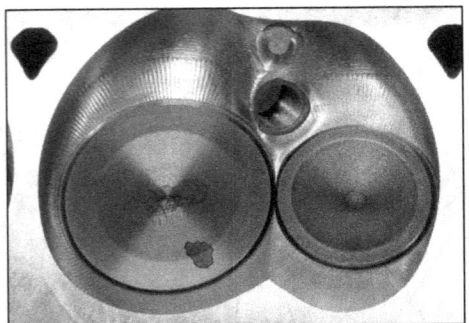

This is a factory LS7 chamber for the GEN IV 505-hp small-block used in the 2006 CZO6 Corvette. Note how the chamber wall is laid away from the valve to mirror the flatter valve angle and the long side radius to improve port flow.

The tighter the radius between the intake valve and the chamber wall on the short or back side of the chamber the less flow that will result. A gentler, smoother radius improves flow and creates more even air-fuel distribution around the entire valve circumference.

Several cylinder companies offer CNC-machined chambers as an option. If the price is right, these precise chamber mods can make more power. This is the new AFR 180 Eliminator chamber. Note the very fine lines created by the CNC machining.

process toward the exhaust side of the chamber. Heart or kidney-shaped chambers began to appear that not only improved flow out of the intake valve, but also attempted to encourage mixture movement toward the exhaust side of the chamber. Angled spark plugs also began to appear with some regularity accompanied by information that suggested that the spark plug could improve combustion by beginning the event from a more advantageous position.

It's only been since the 1990s that serious OEM work has begun on attempting to improve power by evaluating the combustion event using in-cylinder pressure analysis and more accurate dyno testing to evaluate what really occurs in the cylinder during combustion. A big revelation was that the shape of the combustion chamber does have an immediate and worthwhile affect on combustion efficiency. This is one reason why late-model GEN III and GEN IV engines are capable of running 11:1 static compression ratios with relatively short intake duration numbers on 91-octane fuel and still survive a 100,000-mile durability test. These engines also enjoy the benefit of electronic spark control that pulls timing out of the engine as soon as detonation is detected, but there are still many things that we can learn from these combinations.

Combustion chamber shape is actually dictated by several conditions. First is the valve angle, which for a production-based GEN I small-block Chevy is 23 degrees. As we saw in Chapter 9, a shallower angle is beneficial from a flow standpoint, and this also creates a shallower combustion chamber, which aids in creating compression. The standard small-block 23-degree angle dictates a somewhat deeper chamber. You may have also heard of angle-milling heads. This "roll-over" technique changes the deck angle relative to the valves, but at best this is worth only a degree or so. The main reason for angle-milling heads is to remove more material from the deep side of the chamber in order to reduce chamber volume to increase compression. The chamber must also accommodate the valve sizes. With the small-block now capable of 454 ci or more of displacement with tall-deck versions, valve sizes have had to grow as well—well surpassing the 2.02/1.60-inch standard. In fact, it's possible now to get as big as a 2.250-inch intake valve for larger small-block race heads.

Squeezing in the spark plug location is another critical component of combustion chamber design. Ideally, the spark plug should be in the geometric center of the combustion chamber where the flame front is required to travel the shortest distance

According to Darin Morgan, the engine specialist at Reher-Morrison Racing Engines, the slight depression in the face of most intake and exhaust valves can create small vortices that are capable of disrupting the combustion process. This may be the case with tight chamber volumes in Pro Stock engines, but probably not worth the effort in a street engine. The recesses in the valves are there to reduce valve weight.

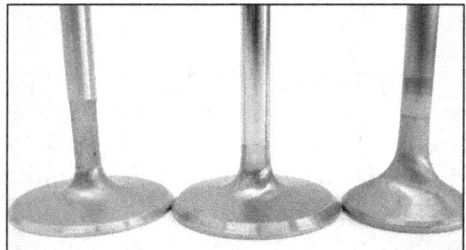
The back radius of an intake valve is an area that gets little attention. Always use 12-degree back angle valves. The 10-degree valves are lighter, but offer a flatter angle that doesn't flow as well. On the exhaust side, sometimes a tulip-style valve can enhance flow, but you should flow test this before using these valves.

There is some evidence to show that a radius on the face of the exhaust valve offers some exhaust flow improvements. This becomes a situation where individual exhaust ports or applications will dictate its use. Don't be afraid to try this to see if it works.

Jim McFarland championed the use of strategically placed dimples in combustion chambers and on piston tops as small vortex-generators. The theory is that these dimples tend to create more chamber activity before combustion starts.

in any direction to complete combustion. With a 4-valve per cylinder chamber or a Hemi, this is very easy to achieve. With a wedge-type chamber, the valves occupy this real estate, requiring the designer to move the spark plug over to the exhaust side of the chamber. In the 1970s, one of the first racers to discover that an angled spark plug was worth a little power was the late Smokey Yunick. Angling the spark plug toward the exhaust valve not only places the plug closer to the center of the cylinder, but also directs more of the combustion process toward the exhaust side of the chamber. Most newer aftermarket heads also use long-reach plugs not only to increase thread engagement in aluminum heads, but also use this longer reach to place the business end of the spark plug closer to the center of the cylinder.

Chamber Shape and Wet Flow

While it may seem that the chamber shape is dictated by some mystical attempt to direct the combustion event, most cylinder head designers will tell you that the chamber design is actually dictated by the ports. Let's take a look at what occurs here, which should give you a better understanding of combustion chamber design and their functional requirements. As mentioned earlier, early chambers were mere deep tubs. As the chambers became shallower, this unshrouded the valves, improving flow. Taking this one step further is the concept of thinking of the chamber wall that continues the long side radius of the port as a continuation of the valve angle. As we mentioned in Chapter 9, with flatter valve angles, this becomes even more relevant. Laying the chamber wall back in an attempt to continue the flow out of the valve only improves flow. This is why even slight chamber modifications on production heads can improve flow even after the air has moved past the intake valve into the chamber. If the chamber wall does not pinch off or impede flow coming out of the valve, airflow generally improves at all valve lifts, but especially at the higher valve lifts.

Chamber shape is also critical as it relates to the wet flow aspects of chamber dynamics. Most of the discussions about intake ports and chamber shape tend to be concerned only with the effect of changes on dry airflow because that's been the predominate method of testing until now. But with the advent of wet flow testing, the effect of the intake port and chamber design on the wet flow aspects can no longer be ignored. Chamber shape and the exit of the air and fuel out of the port and into the cylinder have a big impact on power and efficiency. We've included photos of this effect from Dart's wet flow bench on how the liquid fuel enters the cylinder. Currently this evaluation, by design, does not take into account the effect of the piston moving up or down in the cylinder, but these rudimentary first steps still reveal a startling picture of what happens to the fuel as it enters the cylinder.

We've stated in this book that high-end racers and cylinder head developers often acknowledge and have experienced multiple examples of where their dry flow test bench has "lied" to them. Some use their flow bench only occasionally to help in development. In talking with the

Clues to Combustion

We have included some photos of combustion chambers that have been colored by use and there is a time-honored tradition of attempting to evaluate combustion efficiency by "reading" the tracks in the snow, if you will, left over from the combustion process. This usually takes extensive experience and more than a little bit of art combined with a small amount of science. The first and easiest areas to identify are the clean portions of the chamber. Generally, these appear most frequently adjacent to the intake valve against the steep chamber wall. This is most often the result of fuel wash, where liquid or semi-liquid fuel merely washes clean any combustion residue. One attendant theory about clean areas of a chamber (or areas with the lightest deposits) is that this is where combustion efficiency is highest. There is certainly evidence to support this, often found in the simplest of places. If you look closely into a wood-burning fireplace, notice that the bricks nearest the

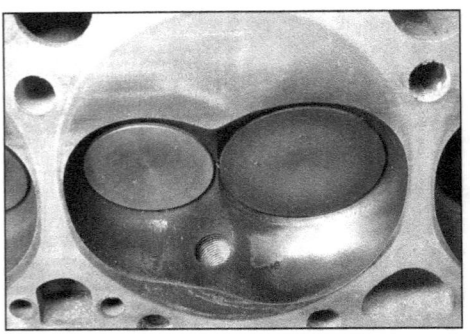

Reading combustion chambers in an effort to evaluate combustion activity and efficiency is an art form that is elusive at best. Fuel wash creates clean areas, as does complete combustion efficiency. Fuel wash is evident with most cylinder heads near the intake valve where liquid fuel tends to keep that portion of the chamber clean. Look for an even grayish-brown residue as an indication of good combustion activity. Greasy, black smudges generally indicate rich air-fuel ratio concentrations that slow the combustion process.

This photo reveals very poor combustion activity on the piston top where we have both clean areas as well as rather greasy and inconsistent results of combustion. This engine would not respond to tuning and was down on power mainly due to an improper match of pistons and combustion chamber.

guys at Dart, and specifically to cylinder head specialist Tony McAfee, it's very possible that changes to the port that contribute to dry airflow improvements actually make the dynamic wet flow picture worse. Then, when the cylinder heads are actually tested on the engine, the results are disappointing, or as one wag put it: "We're suffering from improvement, again." The Dart guys were less than forthcoming in terms of specifics as to where or how this happens, perhaps because we were knocking on a door they have just recently opened themselves. Clearly, this is an area that offers tremendous opportunities that are only now beginning to be explored.

There are other cylinder head designers and port specialists who are still professionally skeptical and prefer to design their ports based only on what they see on the dry flow bench along with the results they see on the dyno. While the wet flow controversy will continue to flourish in the coming years, so will evidence that proves to be either a colossal waste of effort, time, and resources, or the next new frontier in which numerous revelations in newfound power will emerge.

It's essential to always match the correct spark plug with the right cylinder head. Most aluminum heads use 3/4-inch long-reach threaded plugs to engage more threads in the softer metal. Iron heads use the shorter-reach plugs. The long-reach plugs use a gasket for sealing while the short-reach plugs generally use a tapered seat.

Extended tip spark plugs are great for everyday driving, but with higher engine speeds, more compression, and/or higher cylinder temperatures like with nitrous you better be using a short nose plug. The shorter tip uses a shorter ground strap path to the head. A longer ground strap can act like a glow plug if it overheats. This can cause serious pre-ignition damage.

COMBUSTION CHAMBER

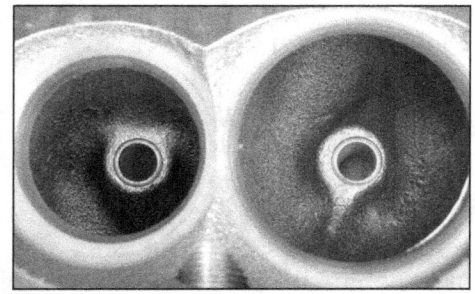

Dart's Platinum iron heads have relocated the spark plug deeper into the chamber and closer to the exhaust valve in an attempt to improve combustion activity. The closer the plug is to the geometric center of the combustion space, the quicker and more complete the combustion process.

flame tend to be clean and without residue, while farther away from the hottest pat of the flame, black combustion residue begins to form on the brick surfaces. The theory here is that the intense heat of the combustion process burns away the carbon while father away from the flame, this carbon has a chance to deposit.

The same kind of evaluation can be made in the combustion chamber. What we're looking for is a chamber

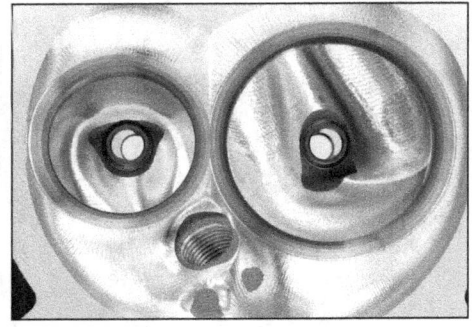

Angled spark plugs have been around for a long time. Few enthusiasts know that the idea is to move the plug closer to the exhaust side to help push the combustion process to that side of the chamber. This outstanding example is the fully CNC-machined LS7 combustion chamber.

with an even pattern of combustion across the entire chamber: with an even coating on the piston top, chamber floor, and walls as we get closer to the exhaust valve area of the chamber. Ideally, the combustion space will be evenly colored, but in reality that rarely occurs. Each cylinder exhibits its only special "footprint" that, if evaluated closely, can offer clues as to the combustion space's efficiency. Large areas of fuel wash are not good, neither are centralized areas of heavy, sooty-black carbon deposits. These are signs of poor combustion activity where the flame front either fails to travel or offers very little heat to eliminate the carbon deposits. Small, clean spots along one side of the spark plug boss are also commonplace, but this also indicates fuel movement across the spark plug. A well thought-out chamber will attempt to push the fuel in a circular motion exiting the intake port, moving the air/fuel mixture across the spark plug and toward the exhaust side of the chamber.

It's also common to see the exhaust valve a slightly lighter color than the rest of the combustion chamber. This can be attributed to the exhaust valve's higher operation temperature. An exhaust valve with carbon deposits is clearly not running at its peak temperature, which indicates the cylinder is not running anywhere near its peak potential. All of this information can also be used to help evaluate the piston top as well since it constitutes the "floor" of the combustion space. Because the small-block is a wedge engine, the quench area is generally clean since little combustion occurs in that area, but the rest of the piston should reveal evidence of equal heat if the chamber space is efficient.

We have included a couple photos of a small-block dyno test where the

Along with all the other spark plug data, colder plugs are essential for a high-RPM street engine to keep the engine out of trouble. Colder plugs transfer more heat away from the plug so it doesn't overheat. On long, high-speed runs the plug can overheat and turn into a glow plug that can take out pistons, ring lands, and even whole engines if the problem is severe enough.

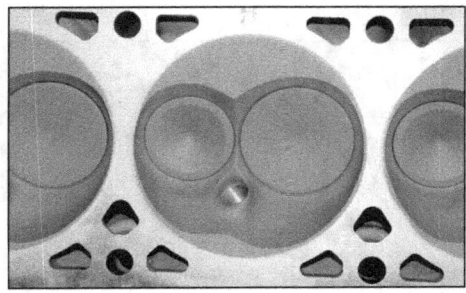

Combustion chamber and piston coatings are becoming more popular and more durable. They do offer protection from damage during lean mixture runs or heat damage from a too-hot spark plug. Dart now has an in-house coatings department that can coat chambers or valves right from the factory.

cylinder head modifications were not positive, resulting in an engine that did not respond well to changes (oftentimes not responding at all), while also requiring more ignition timing and much more fuel than a comparable engine package where the combustion space was far more efficient. Once we removed the cylinder heads, the residual burn patterns on

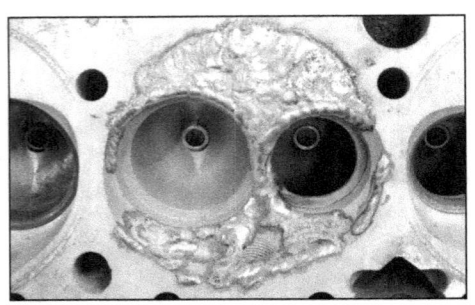

One advantage to aluminum heads is it is easy to repair or modify ports, or in this case the combustion chamber. Here, aluminum weld has been added to repair a combustion chamber. This puts a bunch of heat into the chamber, which will require heat-treating the head and all new seats and guides.

the top of each piston clearly indicated that the engine was not performing the combustion process efficiently. There were large clean spaces on the pistons tops where there was no combustion activity present, matched by a center area of the piston evidenced with irregularly shaped areas of greasy black, sooty combustion residue. It was obvious very quickly that this engine was just not happy and the chamber modifications we had tried did not work.

The point of this is that during disassembly, there are many clues to how well the engine is running, far beyond just the power numbers displayed on the dyno curve. So the next time you tear that small-block apart, take some time to look at what the piston tops and combustion chambers are telling you. It may even be worth it to take some digital photos that you can later evaluate on your computer in more detail.

Conclusion

There are few areas in the internal combustion engine that are more shrouded in mystery, yet offer the most potential for gain than the combustion space. We are learning more every day about not only how air and fuel enter the cylinder, but also what happens to that mixture after it has been oxidized and the clues that the combustion process leaves behind. It's up to the detail-oriented hot rodder and engine builder to decipher these hieroglyphics using a little bit of common sense and a keen eye for the smallest of combustion clues. It's fun. You ought to try it.

Swirl and Tumble

If you are a serious fan of high-performance engines and especially of cylinder heads, then you may have heard or even read a little bit about promoting in-cylinder swirl and tumble. Swirl can be defined as the circular movement of the mixture entering the cylinder which tends to follow the radius of the bore, while tumble is the vertical movement of the incoming air downward but also in a circular fashion. The concept suggests that swirl and (to a lesser degree) tumble help to promote greater mixture motion, creating a more homogenous mixture for more complete combustion. For low-speed production engines such as trucks and commuter cars, there is some data to suggest that inducing swirl does improve combustion efficiency, mostly in terms of reduced hydrocarbon emissions and improved fuel economy. Several OEM have gone so far as to create swirl-inducing ports that direct intake flow in a circular direction as it enters the cylinder.

This concept has been applied to high-performance engines as well, including several small companies that sell electronic meters that can be adapted to a dry flow bench such as a SuperFlow 600 to measure the amount of swirl and tumble in the cylinder. From the limited information we've gathered, tumble seems to be relatively non-existent in a two-valve engine like a small-block Chevy. Four-valve engines seem to generate quite a bit of tumble based on the natural tendency of the inlet mixture to roll as it exits the intake valve. Two-valve engine airflow exhibits no such tendencies, and the direct effect that tumble has on combustion efficiency in a two-valve head is questionable.

Swirl is somewhat more measurable in two-valve engines, but again mainly with regards to low-speed, part-throttle operation. Studying several different cylinder heads on a couple of different wet flow benches at both 28 and 55 inches of water test depression, we saw very little natural tendency for swirl and Dart Machinery's Tony McAfee feels that neither swirl nor tumble exist in a cylinder at least in terms of the industry standard for development of wide-open-throttle performance. This is the reason we feel that any further discussion of swirl or tumble would be counter-productive.

Compression Ratio Calulating

One of the first topics to spin out of a discussion of combustion chambers is compression ratio. Since chamber size does play a big part in determining compression, it might be helpful to go through all of the variables involved with determining compression ratio. We show you how to compute compression ratio the old fashioned way so you understand the concepts, then we give you a source for a free compression ratio computer program that does the math for you in microseconds.

Computers are wonderful things, as are free computer programs that save the hassle of time-wasting longhand math. The Performance Trends compression ratio program is a free download from the www.performancetrends.com website that makes doing the math as easy as a few mouse clicks.

The compression ratio can be defined as the ratio of the volume of the cylinder with the piston at BDC versus the volume of the cylinder with the piston at TDC. This ratio can be mathematically determined rather easily, but actually measuring the volumes does take a little time. For the purposes of discussion, the following are the variables involved in determining compression:

- Piston bore
- Piston stroke
- Combustion chamber volume
- Piston top volume
- Piston deck height volume
- Head gasket thickness volume

Each of these variables affects the actual compression ratio. To calculate the ratio, you must first measure each volume, which also requires using the same values. For example, combustion chamber volume is generally measured in cubic centimeters (cc), but when we calculate cylinder volume, we generally work in inches to create cubic inches. In any math formula, we must always use the same values. The easiest way to do that is to convert cubic inches into cubic centimeters by multiplying cubic inches by 16.387. This means that one cylinder from a 350-ci small-block Chevy engine is 43.73-ci, which equals 716.6-cc. You could also go the other route and convert cubic centimeters to cubic inches by multiplying cubic centimeters by 0.061, which makes a 64-cc chamber equal to 3.90-ci.

Swept Volume: This is the actual volume of the cylinder taking into account the variables of bore and stroke. The formula is:

Swept Volume = Bore x Bore x Stroke x 0.7854 (constant)

For a 350-ci engagement:

Cylinder Volume = 4.00 x 4.00 x 3.48 x .7854 = 43.73-ci

Combustion Chamber Volume: Next let's say that the cylinder head we're using measures out with a 64-cc chamber. Given our above example, we know that this converts to 3.90 cubic inches.

Deck Height Volume: We determine this volume using the same formula, replacing the stroke with the deck height figure. Let's stick with our 350-ci engine example using a 0.010-inch deck height figure:

Deck Height Volume =
4.00 x 4.00 x 0.010 x 0.7854 = 0.1256-ci

Head Gasket Volume: We take the easy route with the head gasket volume and use either the manufacturer's compressed thickness number for a typical composite head gasket or the actual compressed volume. Generally, compressed thickness is between 0.039 and 0.41 inches while Fel-Pro's 1034 composite gasket volume is 9 cc. We also must convert that to cubic inches (9 x 0.061 = 0.549-ci).

Piston Top Volume: We also need to know the volume of the piston. This gets a little more complicated because the piston top design has a direct effect on compression ratio. The simplest example is a pure flat top piston with no valve reliefs. This rarely occurs in real life. Generally, a "flat top" piston employs between two and four valve reliefs that measure between 3 and 6-cc. If the piston has a dish, then we can measure this vol-

Compression Ratio Calulating *Continued*

ume and add that amount to the volume of the combustion chamber. If the piston has a dome, we can measure that and then subtract that volume from the combustion chamber. We do this to make the math simpler since the direct effect of either a dished or domed piston is effectively changing the volume of the combustion chamber. Let's say we're dealing with a 10-cc domed piston. Using our conversion factor: 10 x 0.061 = 0.610-ci.

Now that we have measured and calculated all our variables, we can create our formula, which looks like this:

$$\text{Compression Ratio} = \frac{\text{Swept Vol.} + \text{Chamber Vol.} + \text{Deck Vol.} + \text{Gasket Vol.} + \text{Piston Vol.}}{\text{Chamber Vol.} + \text{Deck Vol.} + \text{Gasket Vol.} + \text{Piston Vol.}}$$

Using our above examples, remember that we have a domed piston, so we need to subtract the piston volume rather than add it. With that slight change, the equation looks like this:

$$\frac{43.73 + 3.90 + 0.125 + 0.549 + (-0.610)}{3.90 + 0.125 + 0.549 + (-0.610)}$$

$$\frac{47.694}{3.964}$$

Compression Ratio = 12.03:1

We went through this whole procedure so you could get an appreciation of how compression ratio is calculated and how each variable contributes to the equation. But rather than wade through that lengthy equation each time, you can take the shortcut and use Performance Trends' free downloadable compression ratio calculator that does the math for you in as much time as it takes to input the variables. All you have to do is access the website (www.performancetrends.com) and click on the compression ratio calculator button and follow the directions. Performance Trends does this in hopes that you like what you see and purchase either the full-featured version of this program, or one of their other programs. Either way, you win.

In plugging our numbers into the Performance Trends calculator, it came up with a figure of 12.1:1, which is probably due to calculating the volume of a true circle with the head gasket. We used the Fel-Pro measured volume that is slightly larger, which accounts for the minor difference in the two figures. Frankly, 0.07 of a ratio isn't anything to quibble over, so we won't.

The beauty of the Performance Trends calculator is that it gives you the freedom to experiment with all the different variables to help you achieve the static compression ratio you need for your engine.

Angle Milling

It may appear that a quick way to improve the valve angle would be to angle mill the head by three or four degrees, but it's actually not that easy. The original idea behind angle milling was to increase the amount of chamber volume removed for each 0.001-inch milled from the head. A side benefit of this process is that it produces a minor change in the valve angle. According to Judson Massingill, who owns and runs the School of Automotive Machinists (SAM) in Houston, Texas, 0.017-inch removed from the head for every inch of head width reduces the valve angle by one degree. For a small-block Chevy head that is roughly 7.750 inches in width that represents an angle mill of roughly 0.130 inch, which anyone will agree is a tremendous amount.

Angle milling removes the most material from the exhaust side of the head and the least from the intake side. The most you could change the valve angle on a small-block Chevy head is perhaps 1.5 degrees, which would take the stock 23-degree angle to 21.5. Another benefit from this process is a slight increase in airflow by raising the runners and tends to unshroud the valves slightly by moving them closer to the geometric center of the combustion space. Of course, the other side of this equation is that angle milling also causes a serious mismatch at the intake manifold sealing surface. This can be rectified with an additional milling operation.

COMBUSTION CHAMBER

Quench Effects

The small-block Chevy is designed as a wedge engine. This means that a portion of the combustion chamber above the cylinder is flat and even with the deck surface of the head. This design creates a very tight area between the piston (which features a matching flat area) and the head. The idea is to create what is called a quench or squish area between the piston and the head. As the piston approaches TDC, the piston squishes the air and fuel mixture in this area out into the combustion chamber. This creates a tremendous mixture motion in the combustion chamber, which both more thoroughly mixes the air and fuel, and also compacts this mixture into a tighter area from which combustion can result.

The key to how well this squish or quench area works is directly related to the clearance between the piston and the cylinder head. The tighter the piston-to-head clearance, the greater effect this quench area has on combustion efficiency. Obviously, there is a limit since bearing clearance, rod length stretch, and piston rock all contribute to requiring a clearance of some sort to prevent piston-to-cylinder-head contact. For steel connecting rod street type engines, the ideal figure is around 0.040 inch, which also happens to be the thickness of most composition head gaskets. If you're really aggressive, some professional engine builders suggest going down to 0.039 or perhaps 0.037 inch of piston-to-head clearance as an absolute minimum. Minimizing piston-to-wall clearance and using a longer connecting rod helps with this minimum clearance figure since both of these variables reduce piston rock, which is a big variable in piston-to-head clearance.

The net result of tightening the quench clearance is more dramatic mixture motion, as we mentioned before. This tends to mix the air and fuel much more thoroughly, which results in better combustion efficiency. This is evidenced when the engine responds with improved power with less ignition timing. A tighter quench area is a great way to minimize timing requirements in higher-compression engines. This means you can run less timing and not have detonation problems that typically plague higher static compression ratios. If this tight quench area is combined with a fairly efficient combustion chamber design, the combination can be worth significant power increases. This is an area definitely worth making changes to on your next street engine.

The quench area is created when the rising piston squeezes the mixture out from between the flat portion of the chamber and the piston top. This creates intense mixture motion in the cylinder, which reduces timing requirements and more complete combustion of the air-fuel mixture. A tight piston-to-head clearance of 0.039 inch for a steel connecting rod small-block tends to improve that mixture motion.

With tighter, smaller chambers now in vogue, D-shaped dished pistons are necessary to create the quench area yet reduce the static compression ratio to a manageable level to work with 91 to 93-octane premium fuel.

HIGH-PERFORMANCE CHEVY SMALL-BLOCK CYLINDER HEADS

CHAPTER 11

The Big Event

As we discussed in the beginning of this chapter, everything that we do to create power all ends up in the cylinder lit by the spark plug, so it's worth looking at exactly what happens at this point in the four-stroke cycle. As soon as the spark event occurs, a small, roughly circular-shaped kernel of flame begins to form in a jagged pattern working outward away from the spark plug. This is why the ideal placement for the spark plug is in the geometric center of the chamber in order to minimize the distance this flame front must travel in order to complete the combustion process. It's important to mention that the combustion event is not the explosion that your eighth-grade science teacher probably used as an explanation of what happens when the spark is lit. A better description would be that the flame travels across the chamber more like a classic west-to-east weather pattern if you were looking at a map of the United States. Or another analogy might be something like a wildfire burning across a wide expanse of grass growing in a field. A small spark is all that is needed to begin the combustion process, but the dry grass doesn't explode. Instead, it burns at a somewhat even rate away from the fire's origination point with the fire constantly looking for more grass to oxidize. In areas where the grass is evenly distributed, the fire burns rather quickly. If there is a denser portion, the fire will tend to reside there and not move nearly as quickly. Using this same analogy, if the grass is less dense with larger patches of earth between the grasses, the fire will move in fits and starts and may even extinguish in places.

The same is true in the combustion chamber since combustion requires fuel to be oxidized with the air molecules distributed in an equal or homogeneous fashion. Ideally, if the fuel enters the combustion space in equally sized and spaced fuel droplets and is mixed uniformly with the air, the combustion process is smooth and moves rather quickly. However, if the fuel tends to enter the cylinder more like a stream of liquid rather than an atomized mist, then the combustion process will be less than optimal. Large droplets of fuel require more time to burn than smaller droplets, and more of these larger fuel droplets end up leaving the cylinder unburned because of insufficient time to complete the combustion process. This is what contributes to less efficient BSFC numbers since less of the fuel is oxidized before the exhaust valve opens. Also keep in mind that even with excellent combustion not all the fuel is burned at wide-open throttle because the engine is purposefully jetted rich to ensure that all the air is used to burn the fuel, since air is the limitation in building more power. Otherwise, part-throttle air/fuel ratios tend to be closer to "ideal" (stoichiometric) ratio of 14.7:1, which is the chemically "correct" or most efficient air-fuel ratio.

Detonation, by definition, is uncontrolled combustion where a portion of the air/fuel mixture (called end gases) spontaneously ignites before the flame front arrives. End gases are generally located the greatest distance from the spark plug and therefore are subjected to increasing high pressure and temperature environment. This occurs because the pressure and heat in the cylinder is rising as the flame front moves across the combustion space. When the end gases ignite, this creates a second flame front that travels in the opposite direction from the original. The combination of these two high-pressure flame fronts is a pressure spike that generally occurs before the piston arrives at TDC. As a result, this pressure spike, combined with the piston moving upwards, creates enormous pressure that attempts to push the piston downward. This collision of pressure tends to violently hammer the piston against the cylinder wall because the piston has nowhere else to go! This rattle is extremely hard on the piston and can often break cast or hypereutectic pistons and at least bend a good set of forged pistons. The classic euphemism for detonation is, "the pistons are trying to swap holes," which creates a wonderful visual that isn't far from the truth!

The other form of uncontrolled combustion is pre-ignition, which is somewhat easier to understand since this is traced to an unwanted ignition source. High-performance engines often suffer from pre-ignition if combustion creates some type of localized hot spot within the combustion space that can act as an uncontrolled ignition source. The most common source of pre-ignition is a long ground strap on an extended nose spark plug. The longer porcelain portion of the spark plug requires an equally lengthy ground strap. In high cylinder pressure applications, especially with nitrous or supercharged engines, the high cylinder temperatures quickly concentrate a great amount of heat in this little ground strap, turning it into a very efficient glow plug. This glowing spark plug end then quickly ignites the incoming air/fuel charge on the inlet stroke. This unintended ignition can spike the cylinder pressure as the

The Big Event *Continued*

piston comes up on the compression stroke and can very quickly destroy a piston and/or connecting rod with very little warning. As such, you must take every step possible to avoid pre-ignition problems.

It's important to understand the difference between these two types of uncontrolled combustion since solving these problems will require completely different solutions. We've included a small chart that lists several of the more common sources of difficulty with detonation and pre-ignition:

Causes of Detonation
- High engine temperature
- High inlet air temperature
- Excessive dynamic cylinder pressure
- Excessive cylinder temperature
- Excessive static compression ratio
- Excessive coolant temperature
- Low octane fuel
- Air/fuel ratio too lean
- Poor or non-existent quench area
- Hot spots in chamber from nucleate boiling

Causes of Pre-Ignition
- Spark plug heat range too hot
- Spark plug ground strap too long
- Exhaust valve too hot - glowing
- Thin exhaust valve margin - glowing
- Excessive carbon deposits - glowing
- Localized hot spot - cooling system

Brake Specific Fuel Consumption

One of the best ways to evaluate an engine's efficiency is to look at how well that engine converts fuel into torque and horsepower. The basic formula simply divides the amount of fuel used in pounds per hour (lbs/hr) consumption at wide-open throttle by the observed (uncorrected) horsepower. This creates a decimal equivalent that until recently was generally accepted to be around 0.50 expressed in pounds of fuel per horsepower-hour (lbs/hp-hr), or the number of pounds of fuel used in one hour to produce the observed horsepower. As an example, if the engine burns 200 pounds of fuel in one hour and produces 500 hp, then at that hp level, the BSFC would be 0.40. With continued research and creation of much more efficient intake ports, combustion space, and better ways of atomizing fuel as it enters the combustion chamber, race engine BSFC numbers have continued to fall over the years to the point now where it is not uncommon to see these ratings as amazing as 0.32 or even lower. By doing the math, it's easy to see that if the engine is able to burn less fuel for the same amount (or more) horsepower, the BSFC number will become smaller, which is what you're looking to accomplish.

This is an efficiency evaluation and should not be used (although it often is) as an indication of the air-fuel ratio being rich or lean. An engine suffering from a larger BSFC number may not necessarily respond to reducing a jet size in an attempt to improve the BSFC by leaning out the air-fuel ratio. Engines that produce a poor (high) BSFC number generally require more timing and more jet in order to make maximum power. This is because of poor mixture motion in the cylinder, poor atomization, a bad chamber configuration, or any combination of the above.

Improved wet flow development of aftermarket (and production) cylinder heads continues to push the BSFC number continually lower as a result of increased efficiency. While BSFC is not a big concern for street engine builders or users, it is a classic indication of how well the engine is transforming fuel into heat and how responsive the engine will be to tuning changes. A well-designed combustion space requires less fuel and less ignition timing to generate peak power to the point that additional timing or fuel will only reduce power. This type of cylinder head can also often respond to a much leaner air-fuel ratio. We've been told that current Pro Stock technology points the air-fuel ratio at or around 13.5:1, which is much leaner than most street engines only because these carbureted engines not only employ excellent mixture distribution in the intake manifold, but also a well-designed combustion space that maximizes in-cylinder mixture motion. When it all works, this is when the BSFC numbers tumble toward greater efficiency while the power continues to climb. That may be a gross oversimplification, but that's how it works.

CHAPTER 12

MATCHING CAMS AND CYLINDER HEADS

"Hey, cam selection is simple. I'll just pick the biggest cam in the catalog and that'll make the most horsepower and I'll be a hero." This is the "bigger is better" theory—simple, easy, and rarely the right answer. Frankly, when it comes to building performance engines, if bigger was the only answer, everybody would be an engine builder, making power would be easy, and books like this would not be necessary. The reality of a performance engine is far more complex, and not nearly as easily understood. Today there is far more information out there, it's easier to access, and as a result there are many more people who have a handle on what it takes to build a strong performance engine. All we do here is add to that information base.

While building a high-output race engine is very complex and expensive, engine builders face a much less challenging requirement than street engine builders. Race engine builders are usually not as encumbered by budget constraints and only have to worry about making power within a relatively narrow RPM range. Let's take a road-race engine for a Trans Am car as an example. Road-race engines are required to operate in a much wider RPM band than drag-race engines and also must do so for perhaps as long as 24 hours. Let's say that engine must make power between 5,500 and 8,000 rpm. That's a fairly wide power bandwidth of 2,500. One way to evaluate an engine is to look at the RPM spread between peak torque and peak horsepower. A well-designed engine may have a peak torque of 5,500 and a peak horsepower point of

Assuming that the short block can seal the cylinder pressure, the key components to making HP and torque are an excellent set of cylinder heads and a camshaft that offers suitable valve timing that can take full advantage of what the cylinder heads can deliver.

Street performance involves a much wider RPM spread than a typical race engine because a street engine should perform well from idle all the way through to the peak HP level. This is a very tall order. Typically, many street engines sacrifice low-end power for more top-end power, but it is possible to have both with the right combination of components.

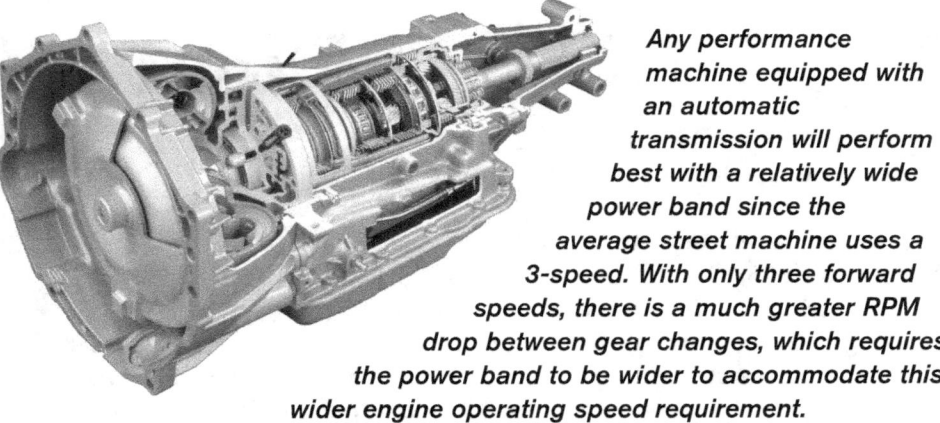
Any performance machine equipped with an automatic transmission will perform best with a relatively wide power band since the average street machine uses a 3-speed. With only three forward speeds, there is a much greater RPM drop between gear changes, which requires the power band to be wider to accommodate this wider engine operating speed requirement.

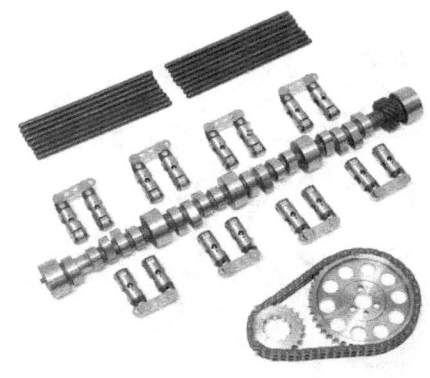
Currently, hydraulic roller cams are very popular for the street set, but we suggest not overlooking the possibility of a mechanical roller cam. A street mechanical roller grind offers outstanding power potential for the money. Stay away from drag race oriented lobe profiles, however, since they are abusive on valvetrain parts when used on the street.

If the world of camshafts is still a bit baffling to you, we suggest investing in the High-Performance Chevy Small-Block Cams & Valvetrains book as an excellent introduction. That book goes into far more detail than can be covered in this short chapter.

The most popular cam design for street small-blocks is the flat tappet hydraulic version. Flat tappet cams are extremely affordable and can produce excellent power. There are literally dozens of cam companies offering hundreds of grinds for the small-block Chevy, which actually makes the selection process more difficult. The horsepower-per-dollar value is the greatest with a flat tappet cam.

7,000 rpm. That creates a power band of 1,500 rpm. Most engines tend to create power bands that are closer to 1,000 to 1,200 rpm.

Now let's look at a medium output street engine in a 3,500-lb car with a 2,400 rpm stall speed torque converter and a peak horsepower point of 6,000. That's a power band requirement of 3,600 rpm, which is far greater than a typical race engine's power band. Street operation requires (and often demands) that the engine be tractable at idle, light throttle opening cruise speeds, and then be instantly capable of wide-open-throttle operation with strong acceleration from that low engine speed range. This is not intended to trivialize race engine building, but race engines generally are not faced with such a wide RPM band requirement.

Ultimately, this means concentrating on peak horsepower is not even close to the best approach for a street engine. Let's take a more broad-minded approach and consider something called power under the curve. Let's say that our street car candidate for a new motor has a 3,000-rpm torque converter, a 3.73:1 gear, and weighs 3,600 pounds. We inputted a virtual 383 for the Racing Systems Analysis drag strip simulation program called Quarter Pro (www.quarterjr.com). Not only does this program give us a complete rundown of the engine with an ET and speed and breakdown of the run through each gear, but it also offers an interesting look at the amount of time the engine resides at certain engine speeds. During the 11.45-second run down the quarter mile, the program breaks down the amount of time in seconds in each of the RPM areas. Between 5,500 and 6,200 rpm, by adding the time in seconds for each of these bands, the engine spends roughly 5.2 seconds of the total of the quarter-mile run in this RPM range. But if we add the 5,000 and 5,500 rpm bands together, we get a total of 6.0 seconds. This means that if we try to improve the car's ET, it is best to put our efforts toward improving power in the 5,000 to 5,500 rpm area. This generates the maximum benefit from the effort. Of course, this assumes the car is launching properly and not suffering from tire spin or one of hundreds of

If you want to immerse yourself a little deeper into the theory of how cams and cylinder heads contribute to the whole HP game, the S-A Design book DeskTop Dynos *that accompanies the DeskTop Dyno engine simulation program is an excellent resource for furthering your understanding of the whole induction/exhaust process. (Editor's Note: the book has recently gone out of print, but might be available from certain online sources and vendors.)*

other potential problems that tend to plague any car running down the quarter mile. The point here is that since this car runs through the lights at only 5,875 rpm, it's not even hitting peak horsepower RPM at the finish line. This means that the engine only achieves peak horsepower RPM at the top of first and second gears. This limits the maximum benefit the car will see from that peak horsepower.

What does all this mean? That you should spend resources improving power in the mid-range area of the engine because of the limited time the engine spends at peak horsepower. This would also tend to be true of a road-race car, although gear selection and track course layout would affect this. If we change just the rear gear ratio to a 3.30:1 rear gear, the results alter dramatically. Now, because the engine doesn't accelerate as quickly in each gear (because we've effectively shortened the leverage the engine has over the car), the car barely pulls through the quarter mile at 5,100 rpm and resides between 4,600 and 5,500 rpm for an amazing 7.2 seconds of the total 11.65-second quarter-mile pass. You can see how just changing the rear gear affects where you should approach building power within the RPM band. If you were limited to a tall gear like this as a compromise for the street, it becomes obvious why larger-displacement engines perform better: because they make more torque and accelerate more efficiently because of their greater torque. The whole point of this is how you target an engine for a particular car configuration. The classic blunder for a car limited to a 3.30:1 to 3.50:1 geared would be a high-horsepower small-block that operates at 6,500 rpm or higher to make power. This combination would be a pooch of epic proportions even though the engine might really make decent power.

Heads and Cams

That may seem like a long introduction to matching camshafts and cylinder heads, but the brutal reality is that massive mismatching is something that happens almost on a daily basis. On the surface, it may seem easy enough to merely match up big intake ports with a big cam and you're in business. While this is certainly better than matching a big intake port with a stock-duration cam, the truth is that matching cams takes a little more finesse. This book is full of the incredible diversity of the small-block Chevy cylinder head

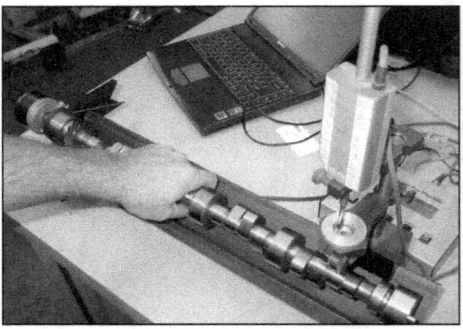

While most cam companies are very good at grinding cams, the more meticulous engine builder checks the cam profiles to ensure they are installing a cam that is actually what they ordered. This minimizes confusion when there are problems to diagnose on an engine that does not perform up to expectations.

Most aftermarket heads respond positively to increases in valve lift. One of the easiest ways to bump the lift curve is with higher ratio rocker arms. Keep in mind that this is no free ride. Greater valve lift using rocker ratio also imparts much higher valve acceleration values. This can cause valve float and other valve control issues at higher engine speeds if not carefully controlled.

array, but with that wide selection, it's also easy to make a mistake. In the days before computer simulation programs, the only way to know which cam was a best fit with a given range of camshaft profiles was to either test the combinations on the dyno or rely on information from trustworthy

MATCHING CAMS AND CYLINDER HEADS

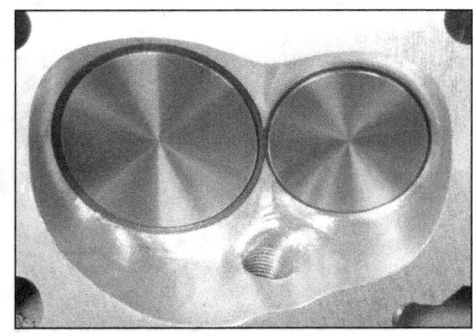

This book talks mainly about the processes of induction and exhaust, but those processes only contribute to the ultimate goal of combustion within the cylinder. A properly designed combustion chamber improves airflow into and out of the cylinder, while also reducing negative work by requiring less initial advance to produce maximum power.

If your goal is a low ET at the drag strip, carefully matching the camshaft to the torque converter puts you well on your way to improving the 60-foot times. Other variables that affect this cam and converter selection are stall speed, the engine's torque curve, vehicle weight, rear and transmission gear ratios, chassis tuning, and about a hundred other variables.

Today, there are so many excellent engine simulation programs that it just doesn't make sense not to start experimenting with engine combinations on the computer long before you lay down your hard-earned dollars or turn that first wrench. Among the programs that we have experience with the COMP Cams' CamQuest6 camshaft selection software, the ProRacing Sim Dynomation program, the ProRacing Sim DeskTop Dyno, and the Performance Trends Engine Analyzer. The Dynomation program is the only one that uses wave propagation techniques to simulate engine power. The other programs are more closely associated with what have been called "empty and fill" models that use sophisticated math models that are then combined with actual engine dyno testing data to bring the estimates more closely in line with actual engine performance. Not surprisingly, the Dynomation program is much more expensive and is probably not going to be the first choice for an entry-level enthusiast. For the typical street enthusiast, the Desk-Top Dyno program does an excellent job and is very easy to use.

The real strength associated with these simulation programs is not necessarily the actual horsepower number that the program spits out, but rather in the several variations of cylinder head and camshaft combinations that allow you to narrow your choice down to the best combination for your intended application. The pitfall with these programs is to dial in a combination of cylinder head and cam and then shoot for the biggest horsepower number you can create. If the engine is intended for street use, an engine like this may be impressive, but for a street car with a compromised rear gear ratio and a stall speed converter that's not

sources. While this is a time-honored technique, and ultimately dyno testing is the only way to know for sure, it is an expensive, time-consuming procedure that is especially out of reach for the entry-level enthusiast.

A quick way to evaluate how well you've balanced the cam timing and static compression ratio game is with cranking compression. A good number to shoot for with a pump gas engine is between 185 and 195 psi of cranking compression. Less than 180 makes the engine lazy, while pressure in excess of 200 psi causes detonation problems on pump gas, especially on a warm day.

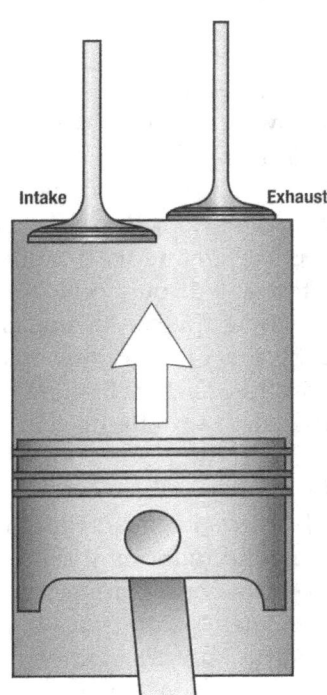

The intake closing point is by far the most important of the four basic intake and exhaust valve events. Intake closing establishes not only when peak HP occurs within the RPM band, but also peak torque and the shape of the power curve.

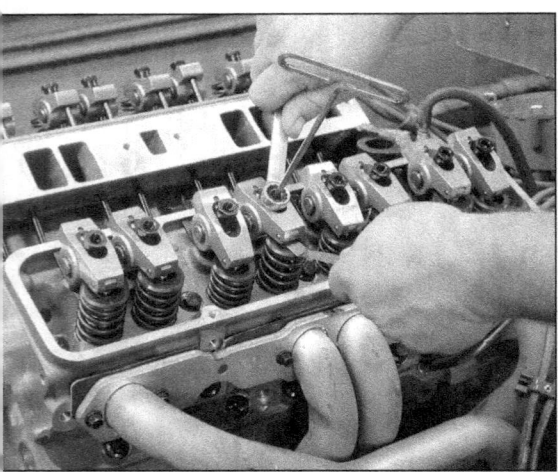

Mechanical lifter camshafts require a lash setting, which is easy to accomplish once you know the trick. Bump the engine until the exhaust valve begins to open and set the intake lash. Then bump the engine again until the intake valve is on the closing side and then set the exhaust lash.

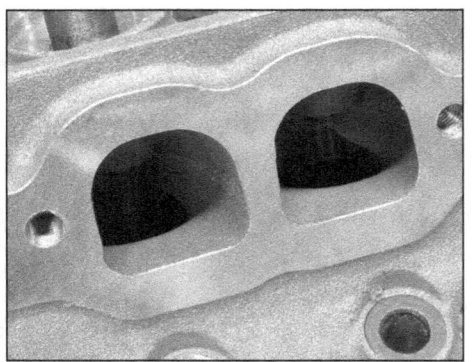

It's important to consider exhaust port flow when choosing a cam for a given engine combination. A poor exhaust port requires more exhaust duration in order to give the exhaust more time to blow down the cylinder. Conversely, a very good exhaust port requires less exhaust duration to accomplish the same job.

An engine will never make good power if the valvesprings are not properly matched to the camshaft and valvetrain. We've seen an engine lose power at engine speeds as low as 4,000 rpm suffering from weak valvesprings long before the engine goes into valve float. Often, stiffer valvesprings also require much stronger pushrods to prevent deflection.

nearly idealized, then a great peak horsepower number may not be what you want. While this next statement is certainly redundant within the covers of this book, it bears repeating: A street-car engine with higher average torque throughout the RPM range where the car spends all of its time in the quarter mile will push the car to quicker ETs and speeds compared to an engine with strong peak horsepower but a softer torque curve.

This doesn't mean that all street engine combinations should be limited to ultra-conservative cam timing figures. There's a place for aggressive camshafts, and we address that in the sidebar "Camshaft Duration and the Power Curve." But certainly, there is limited application for bottom-of-the-page cam timing figures that are so often recommended by armchair "experts" who don't take into account that the engine will be run in a street car that is riddled with compromises. What we're really after in this situation is to maximize cylinder pressure. Every four-stroke engine has one point in its RPM curve where the cylinder pressure is at its peak. This is peak torque and, logically, it's also where maximum volumetric efficiency (VE) occurs. One way to increase cylinder pressure is to bump up the compression.

Here is where the ideal situation of optimizing (not just maximizing) compression is a balancing act between combustion chamber design, octane rating of the fuel, and camshaft timing can really help tweak the power curve. This is certainly a careful balancing act. Many enthusiasts assume that a street engine has to run 9:1 compression in order to stay out of detonation with an aggressive timing curve. Octane rating on premium pump fuel varies between 91 and 93 octane depending upon geographic location. While this is certainly not as good as it used to be, this still leaves sufficient detonation resistance to build a strong street engine. One key to improved efficiency is the shape and design of the combustion chamber.

While Chapter 11 deals specifically with chamber variables, here we look at how best to take advantage of those specific advances as it relates to ignition timing, octane rating, and power. As we mentioned in Chapter 11, a well-designed chamber lays the groundwork for more horsepower and torque in several ways. A good chamber does not need as much ignition timing in order to promote rapid combustion of the air-fuel mixture. This means, that maximum ignition lead might only be 32 to 34 degrees of timing as opposed to a sub-par chamber that needs 36 to perhaps 38 degrees of timing. The better quality chambers are usually slightly smaller, which when combined with a flat-top piston offer excellent flame travel opportunities across the combustion space while also increasing the compression ratio slightly. Tie this in with a tight

Camshaft Duration and the Power Curve

When it comes to camshafts, there are some basic relationships that, while simple, are often overlooked when it comes to choosing a camshaft for a given engine combination. The first and easiest variable to consider is lift. The best way to generate lift is by using a longer-duration camshaft, which gives the lobe designer time (in degrees of duration) to generate this lift. Flat tappet camshafts (either hydraulic or mechanical) are, by design, limited to a given amount of lift per degree of camshaft rotation. Otherwise, a too-steep lobe merely grinds the edge of the lifter right into the side of the lobe. Roller cams use a wheel follower that can offer much more lift-per-degree, but is limited by acceleration rate of the lifter. If you look closely as the specs of similar flat tappet and roller cam lobes for the small-block Chevy, you see that for a similar number of degree of duration at 0.050 inch of tappet lift, the roller lobe generates much more lift than the flat tappet. Break down the lift curves of each lobe however, and you'll discover that the flat tappet lobe generates much more lift-per-degree from the base circle through 0.100-inch lobe lift than the hydraulic roller. After that, the roller, which is not velocity limited like the flat tappet cam, will generate much more overall lift.

The second variable in cam design is lobe duration. Here is where many engine builders can get tripped up. Let's start with an OEM production flat tappet hydraulic camshaft of 200 degrees of duration at 0.050-inch tappet lift. Combined with the rest of the engine package, it generates let's say 300 hp at 5,000 rpm in a 350-ci engine. The usual choice for a budding engine builder is to choose a much larger camshaft in search of much more horsepower. Adding duration to the intake lobe, for example, means initiating the intake opening point sooner, in degrees before Top Dead Center (BTDC) and closing the intake valve later, after Bottom Dead Center (ABDC). The idea with longer intake duration is to give the engine more time (in degrees of crankshaft rotation) at high RPM to fill the cylinder. This is most important since at 6,000 rpm, the intake portion of the entire cycle takes place 50 times per second. This leaves little time to fill the cylinder, so we add degrees of duration to the intake lobe to offer more time.

By adding duration, we also close the intake valve later as the piston is rising toward the compression cycle. The net effect of this later closing intake is to push the point at which the engine achieves peak VE later in the RPM curve. This makes sense based on our description of why we choose a later closing intake valve. Since the point of peak VE also coincides with peak torque, by choosing a longer duration intake lobe camshaft, we also raise the peak torque point. The rest of the engine design also effects the engine's power curve (such as intake runner size and length and header primary pipe size and length) but we won't get into how all those parts interrelate for the sake of brevity.

The key to all this is that a longer duration camshaft pushes the torque peak higher in the engine speed curve. Assuming the rest of the engine can support this increase in engine speed and breathing capability, this increases horsepower because now our torque peak occurs at a higher engine speed. This is all based on the formula for horsepower, which is simply HP = Torque x RPM / 5252. From this simple formula you can see that merely by raising the RPM level at which you design the engine to make peak torque, it will automatically make more horsepower. Let's drive this home with a couple of examples.

Small-block 1 uses a short duration cam and mild head to create a peak torque value of 400 ft-lbs at 4,000 rpm. That figure also creates 304 hp at that same RPM. But if we add a longer cam and a smattering of other engine pieces to support creating those same 400 ft-lbs of torque in small-block 2 at 5,000 rpm, this computes out to 380 hp.

While making horsepower can be viewed as simply as that, the reality is that by raising the peak torque point from 4,000 to 5,000 rpm, this radically changes and engine's entire operating characteristics. Without getting into too many details, small-block 2 would exhibit a much lower idle vacuum, its low-speed, part-throttle torque would be substantially reduced, along with lower fuel economy and much greater emissions. For a street engine in a bad-attitude muscle car, these are certainly operating characteristics that might in fact be viewed with favor. But not all engines can, or should, be built this way. It comes down to a realistic evaluation of how the engine will be used and then choosing a camshaft that best fits that operating envelope. For example, a longer-duration cam requires a looser stall speed converter, and because of its lack of low RPM torque, it also needs a more aggressive rear axle ratio to help with acceleration and also to push the overall engine operating range into a higher-RPM band where the camshaft makes more average power. As an example of this, why would you build an engine that makes peak horsepower at 6,800 rpm, for example, and then put that engine in a car with a rear gear that only allows the engine to turn barely 6,000 at the end of the quarter mile. You now have a situation where the vehicle specs can't take maximum advantage of the engine's potential. So then why build an engine that doesn't fit the car if you do not intend to build the car? This leads us to the decision point of whether to build an engine to match the rest of the car, or to build the engine to make maximum power and then building the transmission, rear axle assembly, and suspension to support that power level. While the second position ultimately creates a quicker car, it will also be more expensive.

CHAPTER 12

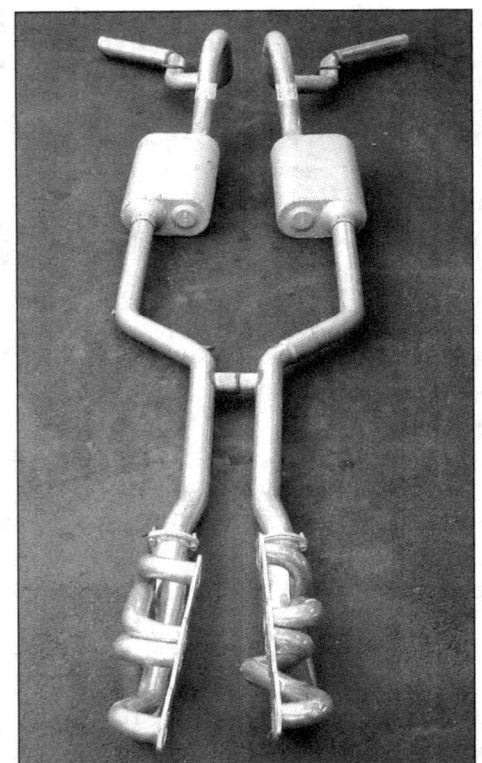

Of course, the most powerful small-block ever built will fall on its face if handicapped with a restrictive exhaust system. A well-designed, mandrel-bent system reduces backpressure while ensuring adequate exhaust flow. Backpressure levels in excess of 2 psi should be considered excessive.

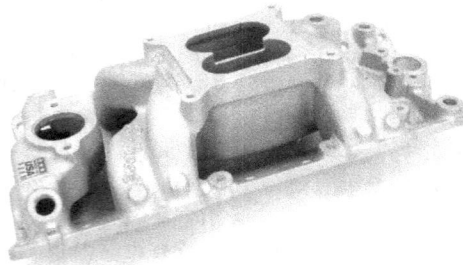

Intake manifolds also directly affect the torque curve and peak HP engine potential. The best dual plane we've found for the small-block Chevy is the Edelbrock Performer RPM Air Gap. It offers the outstanding combination of excellent torque and good peak HP numbers.

piston-to-head clearance for a more active quench area (which also reduces detonation sensitivity) and you can see how it might be possible to run a street engine with a good-sized cam at 10 to perhaps 10.5:1 compression and not suffer from detonation problems on pump gasoline.

This whole combination comes down to how well you balance the cylinder head package with the camshaft to make horsepower. If, for example, you want to build a strong torquey engine that pulls real strong in the low-to-mid RPM range with less emphasis on peak horsepower, then you might want to be a little more conservative with the static compression ratio compared to a combination designed to really make some peak horsepower numbers. This is because the peak horsepower combo must rely on a longer-duration camshaft that tends to bleed off cylinder pressure in the midrange due to its greater overlap. This allows the builder to squeeze the static compression a little tighter, knowing that some of that pressure will bleed off by the effect of overlap. A torquey engine often uses a slightly wider lobe separation angle and less duration. Both of these situations tend to improve torque, which increases cylinder pressure.

As a rough rule of thumb, you can look at this combination from the standpoint that as duration on the camshaft increases, you can also squeeze the static compression ratio a little tighter. Conversely, if the duration is only slightly above stock, it's going to be dangerous to squeeze much more than a typical 9:1 compression ratio without running into detonation problems. This is a fine line that must be walked with care in order to get as much out of your engine as possible.

Larger small-blocks like the 434 and 454-ci heavy-breathers may also require larger 1-7/8-inch headers to really make power at higher RPM. This larger primary exhaust pipe diameter is best created using what is called the Stahl header adapter pipe that moves the mounting bolts outboard to accommodate the larger pipe diameters.

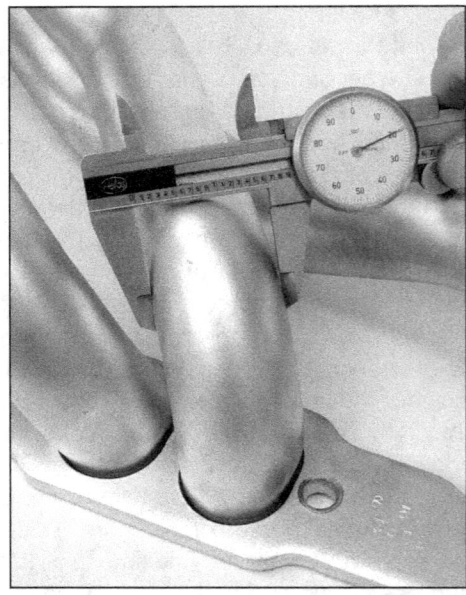

Smaller primary pipe diameters tend to improve torque at and below-peak torque, while larger pipe diameters push the peak torque RPM point higher in the engine speed curve. For a mild street engine, a 1-5/8-inch primary pipe diameter is an excellent choice to enhance torque. Long tube headers, in the range of 34 to 36 inches in length, also improve torque with very little cost at higher engine speeds.

Power Comes From The Combos

It should be no secret that a powerful street small-block Chevy will come as much from the proper combination of parts as much as it will originate from even the best small-block heads. Stated another way, even the best heads like a set of AFR, Canfield, or TFS 195s would be wasted on an engine choked with a set of stock cast-iron exhaust manifolds or a stock, low-rise intake manifold. The better the intake and exhaust ports are on a set of cylinder heads, the better the intake manifold needs to be in order to take maximum advantage of the heads.

Owners planning on a milder engine combination probably won't spend the big money on the best heads in the mix, so we'll take the high road here and take a look at a couple of engine combinations that would work very well for a stout street engine. Let's assume we're going to build a 383-ci small-block and our goal is 475 to 500 hp on pump gas. That's a pretty tall order since 500 hp requires 1.3 hp/ci. We plugged this into our DeskTop Dyno program just to get an idea of a cam combo that would deliver.

Using a virtual set of AFR 195 CNC-ported Version 1 heads, a 475-hp combo requires a relatively conservative 268 cam that specs out around 224/236 degrees of duration at 0.050-inch tappet lift and probably with a set of 1.6:1 roller rockers. The rest of the specs use a Performer RPM Air Gap intake, a 750-cfm carburetor, 1-3/4-inch headers, and a good mandrel-bent exhaust system measuring no less than 2-1/2 inches. Compression can be as much as 10:1 because the AFR chamber is pretty good. This will also require a tight piston-to-head clearance of 0.040 inch to help prevent detonation. This is a relatively mild combination that would actually be very streetable.

Pushing the horsepower bar past 500 will require a bigger camshaft. That's not necessarily bad, but what a longer-duration cam does is push the engine's general torque curve higher in the engine speed range. Where the previous cam's peak torque might occur at 4,300 to 4,500 rpm, a bigger cam like a 280 advertised cam will push the torque peak up to around 5,000 rpm. The 280 cam specs out at 236/241 degrees of duration at 0.050-inch tappet lift with a slightly wider lobe separation angle of 112 degrees or so. This will help the mid-range a little, but this cam will still push the torque peak to almost 5,000 rpm. It will certainly work, but here's where you start building the car around the engine. A motor like this sounds really cool with all that power, but in order to make it work well in the car, this will require a 4,000-rpm torque converter, deep gears like a 4.10 or so, and this will also demand a somewhat lighter car to get it moving.

For a heavier car around 3,800 pounds with driver, you would be much better off with the shorter duration, more conservative camshaft with its lower peak torque point so that the car doesn't need a deep gear or a high-stall speed converter. Those components are okay as long as this isn't your daily driver. Deep gears and a loose converter are no fun in heavy traffic and you will quickly lose your enthusiasm for driving a sluggish converter. All this comes back to being honest about the way your engine will be used and how that application has an affect on cam and cylinder head choice.

A Matter of Timing

Even though a good combustion chamber does not need as much advance, anytime you increase static compression, there is the risk of detonation. One way to improve your chances of staying away from that dreaded cylinder rattling is with a slower advance curve. This helps the engine stay out of detonation at lower engine speeds where perhaps a shorter duration cam combined with marginally high compression can cause the engine to rattle. This is accomplished by merely running a slower advance curve so that total ignition timing isn't achieved until perhaps 3,000 rpm rather than the more common 2,400 to 2,500 rpm. There are a bunch of other ideas that can reduce detonation sensitivity that we outline in Chapter 13.

One of the most overlooked and yet critical aspects of ignition timing is attempting to improve timing accuracy as the engine goes through its entire RPM band. Higher quality timing lights often reveal that the timing can vary by 4 to 6 degrees as

Cam & Heads Chart

The problem with rules of thumb or charts is that they are, by design, dangerously oversimplified. For most enthusiasts with a little bit of experience or at least years of reading the car magazines, this chart will appear simplistic and not very useful. But for those new to the game, this chart is intended to give you a range of options as far as small-block Chevy intake port volumes versus cam timing, combined with a static compression ratio with the emphasis on premium pump gasoline. The cam timing figures assume a flat-tappet hydraulic camshaft with degrees of duration at 0.050-inch tappet lift. This should get you close, but there are certainly options that could really be dangerous, so tread carefully. Before you start buying parts, take some time to do your homework and we'd recommend trying several combinations on a computer engine simulation. Keep in mind that these computer simulations will not tell you if the engine goes into detonation. Most simulations assume that you will use a fuel that has sufficient octane to prevent detonation. This means you should talk to engine builders with previous experience before settling on a combination that may cause major detonation problems.

Heads (Intake Port Volume)	Compression Ratio	Camshaft (Degrees of Duration @ 0.050)
170 – 180cc	9.0:1	210 – 220
180 – 195cc	9.0 – 9.5:1	224 – 230
195 – 210cc	10.0 – 10.5:1	230 – 240

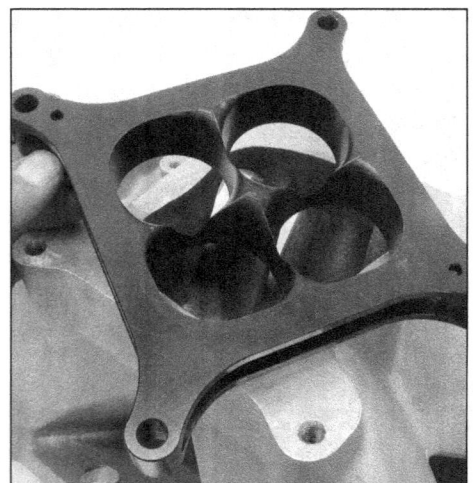

Carburetor spacers like the HVH or Wilson tapered four-hole spacers can often be used with great success in conjunction with larger plenum, single plane intake manifolds with larger carburetors. We've seen these spacers easily make 10 hp on an otherwise properly tuned small-block.

the engine goes through the entire RPM band due to a multitude of variables that are not limited to a loose timing chain, clearance in the distributor, harmonics between the crank and the cam, and any number of other variables. The only real way to eliminate this spark scatter is the use of a crank trigger ignition, but we've not performed any A-B tests to confirm how much power this is worth.

Another interesting result of high valvespring pressures and high engine speed is the reality that camshafts will twist. It's not unusual for a small-block cam in a high-RPM application to retard several degrees between the front and rear of the camshaft. This is of little concern for

A larger carburetor will always make more peak horsepower, and if tuned properly (which is somewhat of a black art in itself) can be used on the street with great success. But you won't find that kind of low-speed performance from a cheap, off-the-shelf carburetor. Custom carburetor tuners get big bucks for their expertise, but often this can be worth the money.

Cam Lobe Prospecting

Throughout this chapter and others in this book, we reference camshafts with duration specifications at 0.050-inch tappet lift along with the lift numbers. What these specs don't take into account is the profile of the lobe. We've never done this, but if you were to canvas all the cam lobes from all the different manufacturers it's feasible that there might be dozens of profiles for the same given duration at 0.050 inch of tappet lift. The search for the ideal cam lobe has driven the creation of tools like the Cam Pro by Audie Technology that allows anyone to trace a lobe and not only check the quality control of the original cam grinder, but more importantly to get a look at lobe design.

It's beyond the scope of this sidebar to even begin to get into cam design. A good move would be to invest in this author's *High-Performance Chevy Small-Block Cams & Valvetrains* book that goes into far more detail. But it is worth mentioning a couple of clues that can help even the least experienced of rookie enthusiasts in identifying a newer lobe design from an older version.

Hydraulic flat tappet camshafts are the staple of the street performance market, so we'll limit our discussion to this type of cam. For a typical hydraulic camshaft, the important numbers to look at are the advertised duration and duration at 0.050-inch tappet lift numbers. As a gross oversimplification, older camshafts tended to use a less aggressive approach to lobe lift between the base circle and the 0.050-inch tappet lift position. Newer camshafts are far more radical in their acceleration of the lifter off the lobe's base circle. Cam designer and original owner of Crane Cams, Harvey Crane, coined the term "hydraulic intensity" to describe the number of degrees between these two data points. Basically, older cam lobes use 50 to as much as 60 degrees of duration to achieve the 0.050-inch tappet lift point. Newer cam lobe designs have tightened this envelope so that now it is common to see hydraulic intensity numbers of 44 degrees or perhaps even tighter.

One caveat that must be employed when comparing lobes of different manufacturers is that not all cam companies spec their advertised duration numbers at the same checking height. For example, Crane chooses to spec its advertised duration figures at 0.004 inch of tappet lift, while COMP Cams uses 0.006 inch. This means an apples-to-oranges comparison of looking at Crane versus COMP hydraulic intensity numbers because the Crane numbers will always be longer because of a total lifter travel difference of 0.002 inch, which could easily represent several degrees of duration. If, however, research indicates that the hydraulic intensity numbers are still roughly 6 or 8 degrees apart, you can bet that the shorter number is, in fact, shorter.

Of course, there's no guarantee that just because the hydraulic intensity of a given lobe indicates a faster ramp that this means the lobe is a superior design or that it is the best choice for your application. But it's worth noting that older lobe designs tend to inhabit the realms of less expensive camshafts. Many of these lobe designs can be as much as 40 or 50 years old, designed back in the dark ages of the 1950s when a more radical flat tappet lobe merely bumped the duration up to generate more lift. It's best to avoid these bargain basement style cams since they really won't deliver anywhere near the kind of power and torque that later lobe designs can generate.

---

most street engine builders, but it is of serious note to drag race engine builders. This is one big reason for the move to larger cam cores for drag race engines. The larger cam core is actually a benefit for several reasons. While reducing twist, it also allows the cam grinder to start with a larger base circle diameter, which is beneficial for a multitude of reasons that all have to do with high-speed valvetrain stability.

Conclusion

This chapter could probably go on for half this book if we attempted to include all the variables that go into combining camshafts and cylinder heads. The big key is making power in a realistic engine speed range that makes sense for your application. The big variable is sizing the cylinder head to maximize the power within the engine speed you've chosen. Do that, and your street engine will be a ton of fun to drive.

CHAPTER 13

POWER PACKAGES

The best way to evaluate any engine is by its entire power curve. Basing a performance purchase decision strictly on peak HP alone is just not a good idea. All engines tend to compromise their overall power curves based on the components used. It pays to know as much as you can about an engine before laying down your money.

One thing that has changed recently is the lower level of an anti-wear agent called ZDDP, or zinc phosphate, in virtually all oils intended for street use. This additive is what helps reduce wear on sliding flat tappet cam followers. One way to hedge your bet is to use oils like Shell's Rotella T, which is intended for diesel engines, but also has much higher levels of ZDDP and can be successfully used in gasoline-fed engines.

While studying flow data sheets, cfm-per-square-inch velocity charts, and obscure flow window area information is fun, the whole reason for doing all this research is to pick the best cylinder head and camshaft combination to ultimately make a bunch of power. It seems crazy, but a lot of people have put a ton of time into this avocation. So it makes sense to look at a few engine combinations to see how these cylinder heads, cams, compression, induction, and exhaust systems all combine to make power.

The previous chapter dealt with matching cams and heads, and these two components have the greatest impact on the power curve, but that assumes that the rest of the engine is properly configured. We've used this small sampling of engines here mainly because we know the dyno numbers are accurate and that they've not been "enhanced" in search of hero horsepower numbers that unfortunately dominate bench racing sessions and Internet chat room discussions on small-block Chevy engines.

It's also important to point out that these engines are not introduced here as the ultimate combinations for torque or horsepower. In fact, in every one of these examples, we could go back and change the cam, heads, carburetor, or some other significant component and perhaps gain a little power. One point worth mentioning is that often these attempts at making more power merely cost the designer power at some other RPM point. Generally, a bigger cam will push the torque curve up, which does a great job of improving peak horsepower, but this comes at the cost of a significant loss of torque below peak torque. That is the

POWER PACKAGES

While cooling system details may not sound like glamorous HP components, the truth is that a big fiberglass or aluminum flex fan can eat 10 to 15 hp! A much smarter approach is a large aluminum radiator and a pair of electric fans.

This whole book has been about the proper selection of cylinder heads, with attention paid to camshafts and the induction system as well. Even with a small camshaft, a decent short block with a good set of heads still makes good power.

compromise of engine development. Ideally, what we'd like to do is make a change that pumps the entire torque curve up over the previous combination with no penalty anywhere. When you can do that, you're a hero, but it happens less frequently.

More realistically, making changes to the power curve is a little more sophisticated than just shooting for more peak horsepower. Sure, big horsepower numbers are important and even make for great bragging rights. But if we are talking about street engines here, then we should also be realistic enough to acknowledge that the average street car is probably not set up to take advantage of an effort aimed at only increasing peak horsepower. What does this mean? Let's take a closer look at the overall power curve and what it means to a typical street-driven car.

The Detonation Zone

One key to maximizing engine performance is to dial in the ideal ignition timing at each RPM point to make peak power. Often this may require more timing than pump gas can withstand. While the easiest way around this is to increase octane rating by using race gas or mixing a combination of race and pump gas, there are other tricks you can employ to keep your engine out of detonation.

We've created a short list of little tricks that can help prevent both pre-ignition and detonation. Pre-ignition is actually initiation of combustion before the spark plug fires. This is most often caused by a hot spot in the combustion space that starts combustion long before the spark plug fires, in which detonation is almost always the result. Detonation is uncontrolled combustion where, instead of a slow, steady combustion event, increased cylinder temperature and pressure combine to ignite unburned fuel and air in the combustion space, which creates a pressure spike. None of that is good for power. In order to prevent detonation or pre-ignition from occurring, there are several things an engine builder/tuner can do to keep his engine out of the detonation zone.

Techniques to Reduce Detonation Sensitivity
- Lower inlet air temperature
- Slower, optimized ignition curve
- Accurate ignition timing throughout RPM band
- Mixing a small amount of race gas with pump gas
- Colder heat range spark plugs
- Tighter piston-to-head clearance—improve quench
- Lower engine operating temperature
- Piston and combustion chamber coatings
- Improved/smaller fuel droplet size into the combustion chamber
- Balanced air-fuel ratio between all 8 cylinders
- Improve oil control to minimize oil contamination in the combustion space
- Optimized air-fuel ratio for all cylinders

HIGH-PERFORMANCE CHEVY SMALL-BLOCK CYLINDER HEADS

CHAPTER 13

Most medium displacement street engines respond to a good dual-plane intake, but larger displacement small-blocks like 420- and 434-ci engines respond to a well-designed single plane if peak HP is an important part of the equation.

Let's take the situation of a stout street engine, making an honest 500 hp at 6,500 rpm. A dedicated drag racer who is interested in building the quickest automatic possible would immediately plug in a 5,000 rpm stall speed converter and a 4.56:1 gear with a 29-inch tall rear tire to spin this engine at about 6,600 rpm through the lights. This combination in a 3,700-lb car would push it to 10.99 at 121 mph. Taking a more conservative approach to the same car with a taller 3.73:1 rear gear, 26-inch tall tires, and a more streetable 3,000-rpm stall speed converter slows this combination down to a 11.43 at around 119 mph. Note that we did not change the power

Don't forget that headers can have a big impact on the power curve. Look for headers with a primary tube length of at least 34 inches. While it's not readily apparent, we've seen 10 to 15 ft-lbs of torque and an equal amount of HP difference between a budget set of headers with unequal tube lengths compared to a quality set of headers that are closer to equal length.

Engine 1: 355-ci Mild Street Package

RPM	TQ	HP
3000	396	226
3500	426	284
4000	438*	334
4500	436	374
5000	419	399
5500	399	418
6000	371	424*

Displacement: 355ci
Bore and Stroke: 4.030 x 3.48
Power: 438 ft-lbs @ 4,000
424 hp @ 6,000
Power/ci: 1.23 ft-lbs/ci, 1.19 hp/ci
Compression: 9.2:1
Camshaft: COMP Cams Dual Energy 278
219/220 degrees duration @ 0.050
0.462/0.482-inches of lift, 110 degrees lobe separation angle
Cylinder Heads: Edelbrock Performer RPM
Valve Sizes: 2.02/1.60
Intake Manifold: Performer RPM
Carburetor: Holley 750 cfm
Headers: DynoMax 1-5/8-inch headers

This is a conservative small-block consisting of a 0.030-over set of flat-top forged pistons with stock rods and a stock iron 3.48-inch stroke crank. The cam is a slightly dated COMP Cams 278 Dual Energy cam. A better choice that would make more torque would be a COMP Xtreme Energy 268 flat tappet hydraulic, which offers a little more duration at 0.050-inch tappet lift. This mild cam, however, matched nicely with the set of Edelbrock Performer RPM aluminum 170-cc intake port cylinder heads, which offered excellent flow velocity, which is one reason for the engine's decent torque. This test was performed with a Performer RPM intake manifold and a 750-cfm Holley carburetor. A newer choice for this engine would also be an upgrade to the Edelbrock Performer RPM Air Gap.

This would make a good street engine even in a 3,400-lb Camaro since it has a broad power band of 2,000 rpm between peak torque and peak horsepower. High inlet velocity from the conservative intake ports is the main reason for this good torque. If these heads were used on a larger displacement engine like a 383, you would expect the torque to improve at the cost of reduced peak horsepower, as the undersized ports (on a 383, for example) would limit total airflow. This makes these Edelbrock Performer RPM heads an excellent choice for a wide range of mild street engines ranging in displacement from 327 to 383-ci engines.

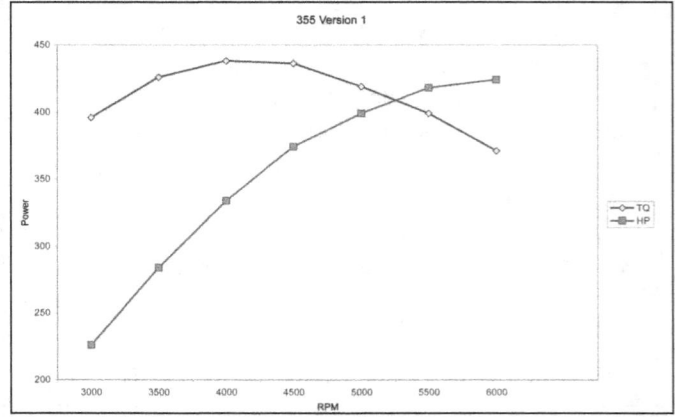

POWER PACKAGES

It's hard to beat the combination of a 750-cfm mechanical secondary Holley carburetor on top of an Edelbrock Performer RPM Air Gap intake for most mild performance small-block Chevys. This is a great combination that just seems to work on almost any street engine package.

curve, but changed the gears and made the car more conservative for the street and also used more of the engine's torque curve. Note that the trap speed changed much less than the ET. The biggest change was the launch RPM with a higher stall speed converter to take advantage of launching the car at its peak torque. This clearly makes the car more ET-efficient since the MPH only changed 1 mph compared to an ET differential of over 0.40 second. Another big

Engine 2: Mild 355 Street Package II

RPM	TQ	HP
2500	394	189
3000	411	234
3500	434	288
4000	469	356
4500	470*	403
5000	446	424
5500	410	430*
6000	356	407

Displacement:	355ci
Bore and Stroke:	4.03 x 3.48
Power:	470 @ 4,500
	430 @ 5,500
Power/ci:	1.32 ft-lbs/ci, 1.21 hp/ci
Compression:	9.5:1
Camshaft:	COMP Cams Magnum 270 flat tappet hydraulic
	224/224 degrees duration @ 0.050
	0.470/0.470 lift, 110 degrees lobe separation angle
Cylinder Heads:	AFR 180 Version 1
Valve Sizes:	2.02/1.60
Intake Manifold:	AFR dual plane
Carburetor:	Holley 750 cfm
Headers:	Hooker 1-5/8-inch

We decided to include this combination, because it is very similar to the previous one and because it illustrates some interesting comparisons worth evaluating. At first glance, these two engines produce within 6 hp of the same peak power. But upon closer examination, it's clear that this second combination with the AFR 180 heads produces significantly more torque throughout the entire engine speed range. The overall average for the AFR heads is slightly higher, but the real difference is between 4,000 and 5,000 rpm where this 355 makes an average of 32 more ft-lbs of torque than the previous combination. The camshaft numbers are somewhat similar, with this engine's Magnum 270 single pattern cam slightly longer in duration. Both engines used a 750-cfm Holley carb while this engine employed an AFR dual-plane intake manifold that is also comparable. One additional variable that may make a difference is that the Magnum cam is a single-pattern cam, meaning it dials in the same degrees of duration on the exhaust side as on the intake. The previous combination uses a dual-pattern COMP cam with additional exhaust duration and lift that might possibly be over-scavenging the exhaust side and costing some torque in the middle RPM band. An even better choice for this AFR engine would be a custom grind COMP Xtreme Energy XE268 lobe for the intake with its same 224 at 0.050 duration, but this is a shorter cam that is a bit more aggressive. Then we'd choose an XE 262 exhaust lobe that is also 225 degrees at 0.050 to make this a single pattern cam. Torque might improve even more with no loss of top-end power.

The major point here is that it's important to look at more than just peak power when evaluating an engine's performance. We guarantee that if both engines were tested in the same car, this second combination with its enhanced torque curve would both be more fun to drive as well as quicker in the quarter mile with all other factors being equal.

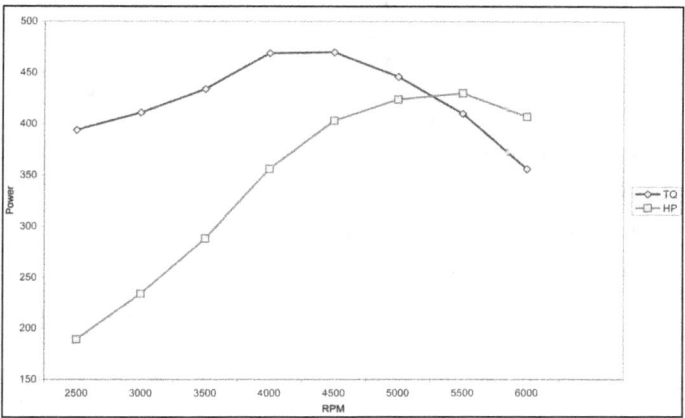

CHAPTER 13

As power increases past the 500-hp mark, keep in mind that the engine is making a bunch more heat. In our experience, this is where spark plug heat range plays a greater role even on a naturally aspirated engine. While projected nose plugs are good for better emissions, that long ground strap can often turn into a heat sink and a source of pre-ignition if it gets hot enough.

change was the deeper rear gear ratio that both launched the car harder and also carried more RPM through the lights. The deeper gear mostly compensated for the taller rear tire, but this also plants more tire on the track for a better 60-foot time.

The deeper geared combination spends more time in the RPM band between 5,500 and 6,500 rpm, while the taller 3.73:1-gear combo spends the majority of its time between 5,000 and 5,500 rpm. The point here is that if you're unwilling to drive a street car with 4.10:1 or perhaps 4.56:1 gears, it doesn't make much sense to build an engine where you rely on the power it makes above 5,500 rpm since your engine will spend very little time in this power band. Turning this situation around, the smart engine builder would then work on enhancing the power his engine makes within the RPM band where the car will spend a majority of its time. It just makes sense to do it that way.

What this really comes down to is whether you are going to build an engine and then configure the car around the engine, or build an engine that will take maximum advantage of the combination the car has at the time. With most street cars not optimally geared or equipped with high stall speed converters, this means enhancing the torque curve in the 4,000 to 5,000 rpm area where

Engine 3: The 383 Power Deal

RPM	TQ	HP
2500	430	205
3000	454	259
3500	481	320
4000	489	372
4500	501*	429
5000	488	464
5500	459	480
6000	436	498*
6500	375	464

Displacement: 383ci
Bore and Stroke: 4.030 x 3.75
Power: 501 ft-lbs torque @ 4,500
498 hp @ 6,000
Power/ci: 1.31 ft-lbs/ci, 1.30 hp/ci
Compression: 10.0:1
Camshaft: Crane PowerMax 296 hydraulic roller 234/242 degrees duration @ 0.050 0.539/0.558-inches lift, 112 degrees lobe separation angle
Cylinder Heads: TFS 215cc
Valve Sizes: 2.08/1.60
Intake Manifold: Edelbrock Performer RPM Air Gap
Carburetor: 800 cfm Holley
Headers: Hooker 1-3/4-inch

The most popular Gen I small-block Chevy on the planet has to be the 383. This is a typical strong street engine with a relatively mild hydraulic roller, which contributes to its great torque. At 10:1 compression, this particular short-block relies on forged flat-top pistons, which are a perfect fit for the cam. The cam timing is tied directly to the good flow and velocity numbers from the Trick Flow Specialties 215-cc aluminum heads that offer excellent flow for the cross-sectional area. Combined with the an Edelbrock Performer RPM Air Gap dual-plane intake and the 800-cfm Holley mechanical secondary carburetor, the induction system does a great job of delivering the magical 501 ft-lbs at 4,500 rpm. This combination would have made more peak horsepower with a single plane intake, but it also would have sacrificed some torque in order to achieve this goal. The Performer RPM Air Gap is one of the great overall torque manifolds on the market today for the small-block Chevy. Rounding out this combination is a set of 1-3/4-inch street headers combined with a complete 2-1/2-inch Walker DynoMax muffler exhaust system.

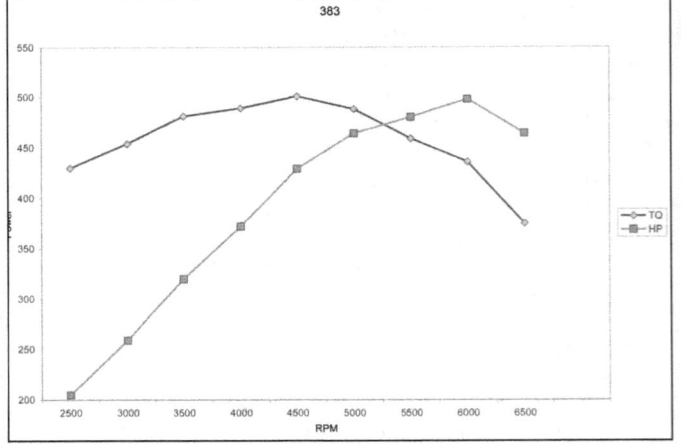

POWER PACKAGES

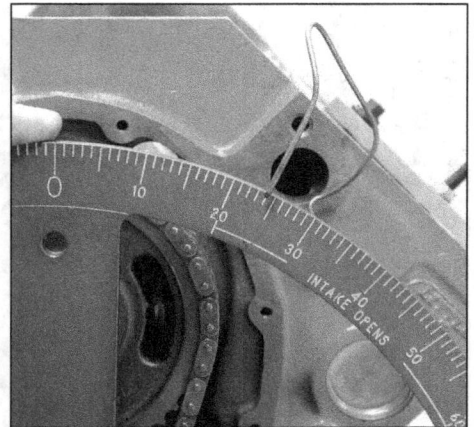

Details are what separate a professional engine builder from the backyard wanna-be. Degreeing the cam is a step that may seem time consuming, but it serves an important function to ensure accurate engine assembly.

this power has a dramatic affect on vehicle acceleration. If you think about it, this is why even a mild 150-hp nitrous system has such a dramatic impact on acceleration. That 150-hp at peak horsepower is really only used at the top of first and second gears because the car clears the lights in third gear at a much lower RPM. This jump in horsepower helps, but the reality is that the major torque gain created by the nitrous (along the lines of 200 ft lbs of torque at 4,000 rpm) is the major reason the car accelerates so strongly and pulls off those one-second ET improvements. It's not the horsepower gain, but the massive infusion of torque that is the reason for the quicker ET and speed. It's that simple.

With mechanical camshafts, there is also the option of changing the lash on either the intake or exhaust lobes (or to both) to make small tuning changes to the engine that could increase power. Basically, a 0.001-inch change on the lash will change the duration by one degree. Increasing lash shortens the effective duration while tightening lash lengthens duration.

Engine 4: The 406 Burner

RPM	TQ	HP
4000	447	349
4500	509	436
5000	536*	510
5500	523	547
6000	500	572
6500	463	573*
7000	419	558

Displacement: 406ci
Bore and Stroke: 4.155 x 3.75
Power: 536 ft-lbs @ 5,000
573 hp @ 6,500
Power/ci: 1.19 ft-lbs/ci, 1.41 hp/ci
Compression: 10.0:1
Camshaft: Lunati hydraulic roller
242/252 degrees @ 0.050
0.560/0.572-inches lift, 112 degrees lobe separation
Cylinder Heads: AFR 210cc (Ver. 1) Competition Package
Valve Sizes: 2.08/1.60
Intake Manifold: Victor Jr.
Carburetor: 750 Holley
Headers: Hedman 1-7/8-inch

If this test had been pulled below 3,000 rpm, this engine would probably still have produced over 400 ft-lbs of torque. Given its 1,500-rpm power band between peak torque and peak HP, this would make an excellent street engine. Hydraulic roller cams offer excellent lift that is put to powerful use by the AFR 210 Version 1 heads. The longer duration puts the peak horsepower point up rather high in RPM, which means that close attention to low inertia weights in the valvetrain, such as using titanium retainers and not overly-aggressive spring rates, is necessary to prevent valve float at 7,000 rpm. Here's a case where a mechanical roller cam would be a better choice for overall durability since it is difficult to add too much valvespring pressure because of running the risk of pumping the lifters down with excessive pressure at high engine speeds. One trick for using hydraulic roller tappets is to maintain a somewhat high oil pressure, since this helps prevent the spring pressure from pumping oil out of the lifter cavity, especially at high engine speeds.

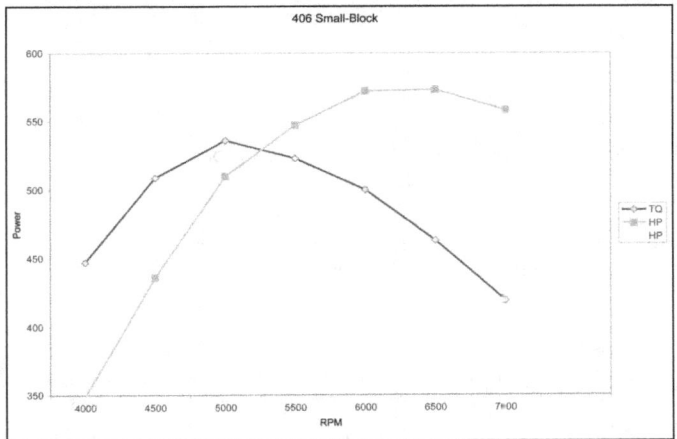

HIGH-PERFORMANCE CHEVY SMALL-BLOCK CYLINDER HEADS

Don't get us wrong; horsepower still plays an important part in a quick ET and an impressive trap speed. The torque versus horsepower controversy will no doubt rage on long after these pages have turned to dust, but we contend that maximizing overall useable power always results in a quicker car with all other variables being the same. In other words, if we have two engines that make the same peak horsepower at the same RPM, but one makes more torque than the other, the more powerful torque curve engine will out-accelerate its opponent every time. And as long as we can stick those tires to the pavement on our street-driven car, we'll always choose to give up a little bit of top-end power for a bigger boost in torque right around peak torque. Torque and traction will beat that other guy to the next stoplight every time. You can bank on that.

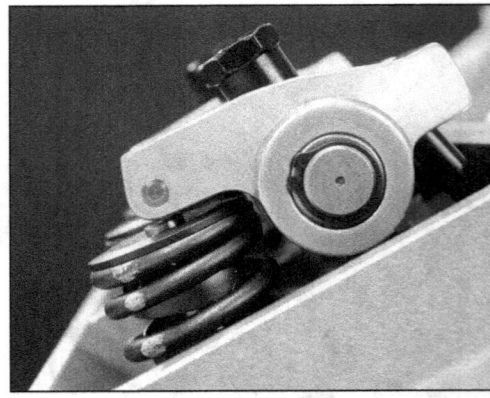

One way to experiment with an engine package is to add a steeper rocker ratio independently to either the intake or the exhaust side to see if additional lift might make a difference in power.

Engine 5: 434-ci Small-Black Street Heater

RPM	TQ	HP
4600	588	515
4800	589*	538
5000	584	556
5200	575	570
5400	564	580
5600	558	595
5800	548	605
6000	535	611
6200	520	614
6400	507	618*

Displacement:	434ci
Bore and Stroke:	4.155 x 4.00
Power:	589 ft-lbs @ 4,800
	618 hp @ 6,400
Power/ci:	1.36 ft-lbs/ci, 1.42 hp/ci
Compression:	11.0:1
Camshaft:	COMP Cams mechanical roller 264/269 degrees duration @ 0.050 0.631/0.631-inches lift, 108 degrees lobe separation
Cylinder Heads:	AFR CNC 227, Version 1
Valve Sizes:	2.08/1.60
Intake Manifold:	Edelbrock Super Victor
Carburetor:	Holley 950 hp
Headers:	Hooker 1-7/8-inch headers w/ 3.00-inch collector

This is a hot street small-block with a relatively mild 11.0:1 compression ratio, in the sense that with a long duration cam, the late-closing intake valve bleeds off cylinder pressure, especially at engine speeds below peak torque. As a result, this engine made over 600 hp on 91-octane pump gas by working with its relatively lumpy COMP Cams mechanical roller cam. If you've read this author's matching book on camshafts and valvetrains, we discuss big camshafts in relationship to displacement. This cam appears very large, but the peak RPM horsepower point reveals that the duration is not overly excessive for this displacement. An interesting test would be to see how much HP the engine would trade for torque by opting for a slightly shorter duration camshaft.

The SuperFlow 901 dyno used a set of 1-7/8-inches primary pipe diameter headers with a 3-inch exhaust system using Flowmaster mufflers. The most exotic component in this entire engine (besides the stroker rotating assembly) is the AFR 227-cc aluminum cylinder heads, which are the largest intake port volume heads from AFR that still retain the stock 23-degree valve angle. With a 1,600-rpm spread between peak torque and peak HP, this engine offers excellent utility and would not necessarily require a real deep gear. Plus, peak HP is only 6,400 rpm, which is a relatively low engine speed for this much duration. This happens because of the larger displacement per cylinder, which makes the camshaft "appear" smaller.

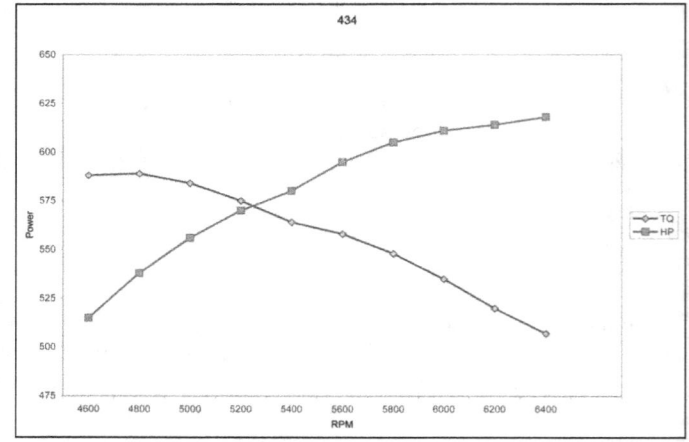

Engine 6: Monster 454

RPM	TQ	HP
4000	559	426
4200	574	459
4400	582*	487
4600	582	510
4800	581	531
5000	575	547
5200	572	566
5400	565	581
5600	544	580
5800	527	582
6000	516	590
6200	510	602
6400	501	610*

Displacement: 454ci
Bore and Stroke: 4.250 x 4.00
Power: 584 ft-lbs @ 4,500
610 hp @ 6,400
Power/ci: 1.28 ft-lbs/ci, 1.34 hp/ci
Compression: 9.1:1
Camshaft: Crane flat tappet hydraulic
244/252 degrees @ 0.050
0.516/0.525 inches lift, 106 degrees lobe separation angle
Cylinder Heads: Motown iron 220cc
Valve Sizes: 2.135/1.60
Intake Manifold: World Products dual plane
Carburetor: Bill Mitchell modified 870 cfm Holley
Headers: Hooker 1-3/4-inch

The ultimate displacement small-block in a stock deck height block is the 454-ci. World Products builds this as a crate engine with a scant 0.150-inch between the cylinder walls on this large-bore motor. With this much size, a more aggressive camshaft will make excellent power. While a large displacement small-block is probably more expensive than its Rat motor counterpart, the power numbers are surprisingly similar. The advantage then goes to the small-block with much less static weight than a big-block.

This engine could actually really benefit from not only a longer-duration mechanical roller cam with more lift, but would also really charge with a great set of heads. Bolt on a set of AFR or TFS heads on this beast along with a roller cam to take advantage of the increased valve lift capacity and this combo would really rock. The Motown 220 heads are certainly large enough, but they lack the excellent flow numbers to really pump up the power numbers. Bolt the AFR 227 heads used in the previous 434-ci engine on this motor with its extra 20 cubic inches, and both the HP and the torque would increase appreciably. This is evidenced by the fact that the 434-ci engine actually made more power than its large cousin. This 454 could probably pick up an additional 15 to perhaps 20 hp with better cylinder heads. To be fair, this 454 also was somewhat hamstrung by its flat tappet hydraulic camshaft that is down in lift compared to the 434-ci engine's roller by almost 0.100 inch. Bolt a solid roller into this 454 and it would really stomp.

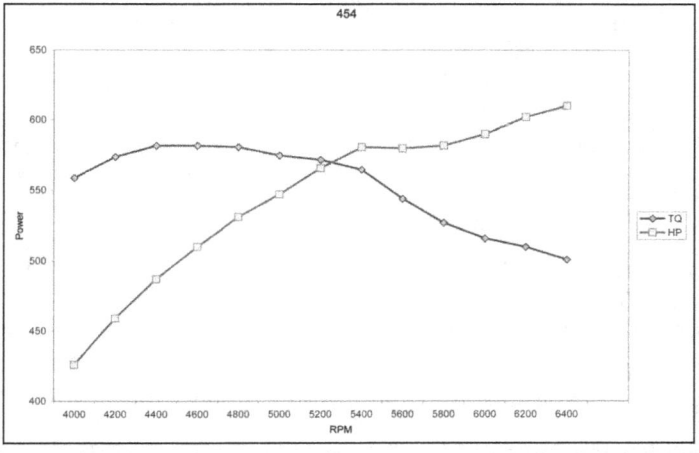

SOURCE GUIDE

AirFlow Research (AFR)
28611 W. Industry Dr.
Valencia, CA 91355
661/ 257-8124
www.airflowresearch.com

Automotive Racing Products (ARP)
531 Spectrum Circle
Oxnard, CA 93030
800/ 826-3045
www.arp-bolts.com

Brodix, Inc.
301 Maple St.
Mena, AR 71953
479/ 394-1075
www.brodix.com

Canfield Heads
580 W. Main St.
Canfield, OH 44406
330/ 533-7092
www.canfieldheads.com

CarTech Books
39966 Grand Ave.
North Branch, MN 55056
651-277-1200
www.cartechbooks.com

COMP Cams
3406 Democrat Rd.
Memphis, TN 38118
901/ 795-2400
800/ 999-0853 Cam Help
www.compcams.com

Crane Cams
530 Fentress Blvd.
Daytona Beach, FL 32114
386/ 258-6174 Tech
www.cranecams.com

Crower Cams & Equipment
3333 Main St.
Chula Vista, CA 91911
619/ 661-6477
www.crower.com

Dart Machinery
353 Oliver Dr.
Troy, MI 48084
248/ 362-1188
www.dartheads.com

Edelbrock
2700 California St.
Torrance, CA 90503
800/ 416-8628 Tech
www.edelbrock.com

Ferrea Racing Components
2600 NW 55th Court, Ste. 238
Ft. Lauderdale, FL 33309
954/ 733-2505
www.ferrea.com

GM Performance Parts
800/ 577-6888 nearest GMPP dealer
www.goodwrench.com

High Velocity Heads
710 John Sevier Highway
Knoxville, TN 37920
865/ 573-9151
www.highvelocityheads.com

Holley Performance Products
1801 Russellville Road
Bowling Green, KY 42101
270/ 781-9741
www.holley.com

Manley Performance Products
1960 Swarthmore Ave.
Lakewood, NJ 08701
732/ 905-3366
www.manleyperformance.com

Motion Software
535 W. Lambert Unit E
Brea, CA 92621-3911
714/ 255-2931 W
www.mrgasket.com

Performance Trends, Inc.
Box 530164
Livonia, MI 48153
248/ 473-9230
www.performancetrends.com

Powerhouse Products
3402 Democrat Rd.
Memphis, TN 38118
901/ 795-7600
www.powerhouseproducts.com

RHS
34316 Democrat Rd.
Memphis, TN 38118
901/ 259-1134
www.racingheadservice.com

Scoggin-Dickey Parts Center
5901 Spur 327
Lubbock, TX 79424
800/ 456-0211 Parts Center
806/ 798-4013 Parts
806/ 798-4108 Tech Line
www.sdpc2000.com

SI Valves
2175-A Agate Court
Simi Valley, CA 93065
800/ 564-8258
805/ 582-0085
www.sivalves.com

Summit Racing Equipment
P.O. Box 909
Akron, OH 44309-0909
800/ 230-3030
www.summitracing.com

SuperFlow Corporation
3512 North Tejon
Colorado Springs, CO 80907-5299
719/ 471-1746
www.superflow.com

Trick Flow Specialties (TFS)
1248 Southeast Ave.
Tallmadge, OH 44278
330/ 630-1555
www.trickflow.com

World Products
35 Trade Zone Dr.
Ronkonkoma, NY 11779
631/ 737-0372
www.worldcastings.com

More great titles available from CarTech®...

S-A DESIGN

Ford Performance — Practical building tips, for all Ford V-8 engines. (SA05)

Smokey Yunick's Power Secrets — Smokey explains race-engine prep from carbs to shop tools. (SA06)

Super Tuning & Modifying Holley Carburetors — Perf, street and off-road applications. (SA08)

Custom Painting — The Do-It-Yourself Guide to – Advice on choosing paint, prep and touch-up. (SA10)

Street Supercharging, The Complete Guide to — Bolt-on buying, installing and tuning blowers. (SA17)

Engine Blueprinting — Using tools, block selection & prep, crank mods, pistons, heads, cams & more! (SA21)

How to Build Horsepower, Vol. 1 — Building horsepower in any engine. (SA24)

Super '60s Fords — The inside story of the most powerful Fords ever built from 1957-1973. (SA25)

How To Rebuild the Small-Block Chevrolet — How to build a street or racing small-block Chevy. (SA26)

Holley Rebuilding and Modifying — Tuning, modifying, and rebuilding all Holley modular carbs. (SA27)

Chevrolet Big-Block Parts Interchange Manual — Selecting & swapping high-perf. big-block parts. (SA31)

High-Perf Crate Motor Buyer's Guide — Complete guide to all factory & aftermarket high-perf engines. (SA32)

How To Design & Install High Performance Car Stereo — A beginner's guide to high-tech sound systems. (SA45)

How To Build Max Performance Chevy Rat Motors — Hot rodding big-block Chevys. (SA48)

High Performance Honda Builder's Handbook Vol. 1 — How to build & tune high-performance Honda cars and engines. (SA49)

How To Install & Use Nitrous Oxide — How to make max power with nitrous oxide injection. (SA50)

How To Build Horsepower, V.2 — Carbs & intake manifolds. (SA52)

Chevrolet TPI Fuel Injection Swappers Guide — Interchanging & modifying TPI systems. (SA53)

Chevrolet Small-Block Parts Interchange Manual — Selecting & swapping high-perf. small-block parts. (SA55)

High-Performance Ford Engine Parts Interchange — Selecting & swapping big- and small-block Ford parts. (SA56)

How To Build Max Perf Chevy Small-Blocks on a Budget — Would you believe 600 hp for $3000? (SA57)

High-Performance Honda Builder's Handbook Vol. 2 — Suspensions, body mods, brake tech, nitrous. (SA58)

Chrysler Performance Upgrades — Performance improvements on Chrysler muscle cars of the '60s & '70s. (SA60)

Building Ford Short-Track Power, Official Factory Guide to — Written by Ford Racing engineers. (SA63)

How To Build High-Performance Chrysler Engines — Parts interchanges, factory crate motors, cylinder heads, etc. (SA67)

How To Tune and Win With Demon Carburetors — Selecting and tuning for high-perf race, street, & off-road applications. (SA68)

How To Build Max Performance Ford V-8s on a Budget — Dyno-tested engine builds for big- & small-block Fords. (SA69)

Building High-Perf Fox-Body Mustangs on a Budget — Building the complete package. Covers 1979-95 5.0L Mustangs. (SA75)

How To Build Max-Perf Pontiac V8s — Mild perf apps to all-out performance build-ups. (SA78)

How To Build High-Performance Ignition Systems — Complete guide to understanding auto ignition systems. (SA79)

How To Build & Modify GM Pro Touring Street Machines — Classic looks with modern performance. (SA81)

How To Build Max Perf Ford 4.6 Liter Ford Engines — Building & modifying Ford's 2- and 4-valve 4.6/5.4 liter engines. (SA82)

Building & Tuning High-Perf Electronic Fuel Injection — Custom engine management systems for domestics & imports. (SA83)

How To Build Big-Inch Ford Small-Blocks — Add cubic inches without the hassle of switching to a big-block. (SA85)

How To Build High-Perf Chevy LS1/LS6 Engines — Modifying and tuning Gen-III engines for GM cars and trucks. (SA86)

How To Build Big-Inch Chevy Small-Blocks — Get the additional torque & horsepower of a big-block. (SA87)

Sport Compact Turbos & Blowers — Guide to understanding, installing, & using sport compact turbos & superchargers. (SA89)

Honda Engine Swaps — Step-by-step instructions for all major tasks involved in engine swapping. (SA93)

How to Build Supercharged & Turbocharged Small-Block Fords — Everything you need to know about supercharging & turbocharging your small-block Ford. (SA95)

Quarter-Mile Muscle: Detroit Goes to the Drags — Covers the development & success of muscle cars at the drags in all classes in the '60s. (SA98)

High-Performance Dodge Neon Builder's Handbook — Everything you need to know to get maximum performance out of your Dodge Neon. (SA100)

How to Build Ford Restomod Street Machines — Modify your vintage Ford to accelerate, stop, corner & ride like a new high-performance car. (SA101)

How to Rebuild the Small-Block Ford — Covers a small-block Ford rebuild step by step. (SA102)

How to Build Big-Inch Mopar Small Blocks — How to get big-block power out of your Mopar small-block. (SA104)

How to Build High-Performance Chevy Small — Block Cams/Valvetrains — Camshaft & valvetrain function, selection, performance, and design. (SA105)

High-Performance Mustang Builder's Guide 1994-2004 — Build your Mustang for drag racing, road racing, or improved street performance. (SA106)

High-Performance Honda & Acura Buyer's Guide — How to buy the right Honda/Acura to modify for performance. (SA108)

High-Performance Jeep Cherokee XJ Builder's Guide 1984-2001 — Build a useful, Cherokee for mountains, the mud, the desert, the street, and more. (SA109)

Small Block Chevy Performance: 1955-1996 — Covers the latest information on all Gen I and II Chevy small-blocks. (SA110)

High-Performance Ford Mustang Buyer's Guide: 1979 – Present — Guidance on buying the right Mustang to modify for performance. (SA111)

How to Build and Modify Rochester Quadrajet Carburetors — Selecting, rebuilding, and modifying the Quadrajet Carburetors. (SA113)

Building 4.6/5.4L Ford Horsepower on the Dyno — Takes the guesswork out of choosing parts by providing horsepower & torque gains. (SA115)

Rebuilding the Small-Block Chevy: Step-by-Step Videobook — 160-pg book plus 2-hour DVD show you how to build a street or racing small-block Chevy. (SA116)

How to Paint Your Car on a Budget — Everything you need to know to get a great-looking coat of paint and save money. (SA117)

How to Drift: The Art of Oversteer — This comprehensive guide to drifting covers both driving techniques and car setup. (SA118)

High-Performance Jeep Wrangler TJ Builder's Guide 1997-2006 — How to upgrade your Wrangler's suspension, axles, differentials, engine, transfer case, wheels and tires, skid plates, and more. (SA 120)

How to Build Chevy Small-Block Circle-Track Racing Engines — Learn all the insider tricks and secrets to keep you car in front of the pack. (SA121)

High-Performance Chevy Small-Block Cylinder Heads — Learn how to make the most power with this popular modification on your small block Chevy. (SA125)

High Performance Brake Systems — Design, selection, and installation of brake systems for Musclecars, Hot Rods, Imports, Modern Era cars and more. (SA126)

High Performance C5 Corvette Builders Guide — Improve the looks, handling and performance of your Corvette C5. (SA127)

High Performance Diesel Builder's Guide — The definitive guide to getting maximum performance out of your diesel engine. (SA129)

How to Rebuild & Modify Carter/Edelbrock Carbs — The only source for information on rebuilding and tuning these popular carburetors. (SA130)

High Performance New Hemi Builder's Guide — Covers all New Hemi applications. Get the most out of your Hemi! (SA132)

Dyno-Proven GM LS1 Thru LS7 Performance Parts — Reveals the truths and myths of Gen III performance parts through dyno testing. (SA133)

Building Honda K-Series Engine Performance — The first book on the market dedicated exclusively to the Honda K series engine. (SA134)

Engine Management-Advanced Tuning — Take your fuel injection and tuning knowledge to the next level. (SA135)

High-Performance Subaru Builder's Guide — Subarus are the hottest compacts on the street. Make yours even hotter. (SA141)

HISTORIES AND PERSONALITIES

Total Performers: Ford Drag Racing in the 1960s — Covers Ford Motor Company's "Total Performance Years" in 1960s drag racing. (CT407)

NASCAR's Wild Years — Stock-Car technology in the '60s includes the behind-the-scenes battles between factories, rule-makers, track owners, promoters, & racing teams. (CT409)

Quarter-Mile Chaos — Rare & stunning photos of terrifying fires, explosions, and crashes in drag racing's golden age. (CT425)

Fire, Nitro, Rubber, and Smoke: Bob McClurg's Drag Racing Memories — This second title by Bob McClurg focuses on the most fondly remembered era of the sport, the 1960s and 1970s. (CT437)

Funny Car Fever — Celebrated NHRA photographer shares his considerable archive of images of the coolest Funny Cars ever raced. (CT443)

Factory Lightweights: Detroit's Drag Racing Specials of the '60s — Relive the thrilling past of factory produced cars designed to win in Sunday and sell on Monday. (CT444)

Slingshot Spectacular: Front-Engine Dragster Era — Relive the golden age of front engine dragsters in this photo packed trip down memory lane. (CT464)

The Electroline Diaries: A Journey with the Burbank Choppers Car Club — Take a unique look at this popular car club, their cars, and their lifestyle. (CT465)

Gasser Wars – Drag Racing's Street Classes: 1955-1968 — The popular book Gasser Wars is now available in paperback! (CT466)

Super Stock: Drag Racing the Family Sedan — Takes a look at the '60s most popular class of drag racing — factory Super Stock. (CT953)

Ed "Big Daddy" Roth: His Life, Times, Cars and Art — The creator of Rat Fink had a profound influence on hot rodders and popular culture. (CT968)

Gasser Wars – Drag Racing's Street Classes: 1955-1968 — An entertaining look into the most exciting drag racing action of the '50s and '60s. (CT977)

Diggers, Funnies, Gassers & Altereds — An exciting visual history of the Golden Age of drag racing. (CT990)

Indy's Wildest Decade: Innovation and Revolution at the Brickyard — Year-by-year account of Indy's wildest decade, the 1960s. (CT971)

The Garlits Collection: Cars that Made Drag Racing History — Coverage of the most significant cars in Big Daddy's museum. (CT981)

Hot Rod Milestones: America's Coolest Coupes, Roadsters, & Racers — Covers 25 of the most influential, innovative hot rods ever built. (CT980)

Von Dutch: The Art, The Myth, The Legend — Chronicles the life & art of pinstriper Von Dutch. (CT998)

MUSCLECARTECH SERIES

Ford Mustang 1964-1/2 – 1973 — This book gives vintage Mustang enthusiasts the detailed information and illustrations they need to build highly accurate models or restored full-size cars. (SP079)

Chevrolet Camaro: 1967 to 1972 — Provides enthusiasts, modelers, and restorers with 300 color photos showing original details of the popular 1967-1972 Camaros. (SP100)

Chevrolet Corvette 1963-1967 — This book can be used as a restoration guide, modeling handbook, or just as a cool reference for people who like C2 Corvettes. (SP101)

Visit us online at www.cartechbooks.com for more info!

More Information for Your Project ...

REBUILDING THE SMALL-BLOCK CHEVY: STEP-BY-STEP VIDEOBOOK by Larry Atherton & Larry Schreib, This step-by-step Workbench Book & DVD combination shows you how to build a street or racing small-block Chevy in your own garage. The book includes over 600 photos & easy-to-read text that explains every procedure in assembling an engine from crankshaft to carburetor. The 2-hour DVD shows in detail all the procedures that the book describes. Detailed sections show how to disassemble a used engine, inspect for signs of damage, select replacement parts, buy machine work, check critical component fit, and much more! Softbound, 8-1/2 x 11 inches, 144 pages, 650+ b/w photos. *Item #SA116*

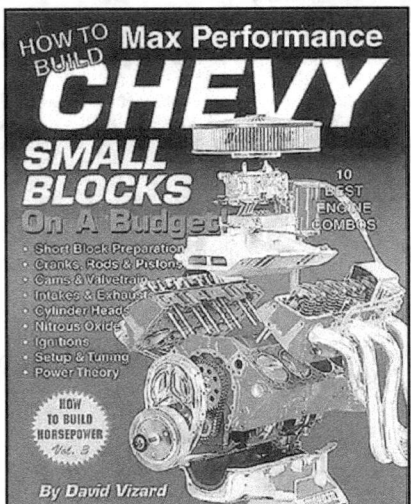

HOW TO BUILD MAX PERFORMANCE CHEVY SMALL BLOCKS ON A BUDGET by David Vizard Highly regarded engine builder and technical writer, David Vizard, turns his attention to the ins and outs of building serious horsepower small-block Chevy engines on a budget — would you believe 600 horsepower for about $3,000? Includes factory part numbers, easy do-it-yourself cylinder head modifications, inexpensive but effective aftermarket parts, etc. Softbound, 8-3/8 x 10-7/8 inches, 144 pages, over 300 b/w photos. *Item #SA57*

HIGH-PERFORMANCE CHEVY SMALL-BLOCK CAMS/ VALVETRAINS by Graham Hansen, This book takes the mystery out of camshaft and valvetrain function, selection, and design. Hansen covers camshaft basics, including a thorough explanation of how a cam operates in conjunction with the rest of the engine and valvetrain. He discusses technical terms like overlap, lobe centerline, duration, lift, and cam profiling. Roller and flat-tappet cams are compared, and the book covers rocker arms, lifters, valves, valvesprings, retainers, guideplates, pushrods, and cam drives, as well as detailed information on how to degree a cam and choose the proper cam for your application. Finally, matching cams to cylinder heads, analyzing port flow, and proving it all through dyno tests round out this informative volume. Softbound, 8-1/2 x 11 inches, 144 pages, approx. 300 b/w photos. *Item #SA105*

HOW TO REBUILD THE SMALL-BLOCK CHEVROLET is a quality, step-by-step Workbench Book that shows you how to build a street or racing small-block Chevy in your own garage. Includes hundreds of photos and easy-to-read text that explain every procedure a professional builder uses to assemble an engine from crankshaft to carburetor. Detailed sections show how to disassemble a used engine, inspect for signs of damage, select replacement parts, buy machine work, check critical component fit, and much more! Performance mods and upgrades are discussed along the way, so the book meets the needs of all enthusiasts, from restorers to hot rodders. A must-have for every small-block Chevy fan. Softbound, 144 pages, 8-1/2 x 11 inches, 650+ b/w photos. *Item #SA26*

HOW TO BUILD BIG-INCH CHEVY SMALL BLOCKS by Graham Hansen, The quest for big cubes doesn't have to lead to a big block anymore. Now you can add cubic inches to your current power plant without having to swap intakes, headers, motor mounts, & other accessories all at once. This book guides you in selecting the best OEM or aftermarket block, crank, rods, & pistons to construct your big-inch short block. Softbound, 8-1/2 x 11 inches, 128 pages, 320 b/w photos. *Item #SA87*

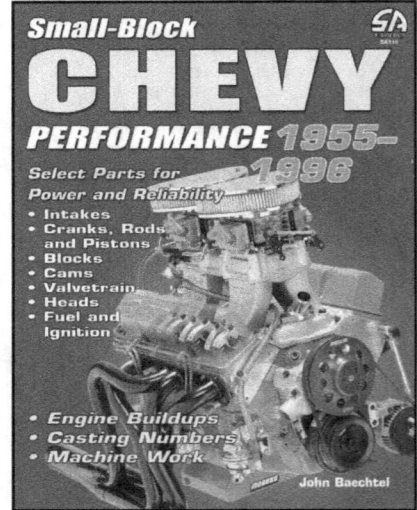

SMALL-BLOCK CHEVY PERFORMANCE 1955-1996 by John Baechtel, The small-block Chevy is widely known as the most popular engine of all time. Produced in staggering numbers and boasting huge aftermarket support, small-blocks are the engine of choice for a large segment of the performance community. Originally published as two separate volumes, this title now covers the latest information on all Gen I and Gen II Chevy small-blocks in one volume. This book continues to be the best power source book for small-block Chevy. The detailed text and photos deliver the best solutions for making your engine perform. Chapters explain techniques for preparing blocks, crankshafts, connecting rods, pistons, cylinder heads, and includes popular ignition, carburetor, camshaft, and valvetrain tips and tricks. Softbound, 8-1/2 x 11 inches, 144 pages, approx. 500 b/w photos. *Item #SA110*

www.cartechbooks.com or 1-800-551-4754

www.ingramcontent.com/pod-product-compliance
Lightning Source LLC
Chambersburg PA
CBHW051412070526
44584CB00023B/3395